VINTAGE VALVE RADIOS
a practical guide for collectors and restorers

VINTAGE VALVE RADIOS
a practical guide for collectors and restorers

TONY THOMPSON BSc., Cert.Ed.

Facing page: Philips 834A, early 1930s

DEDICATION
This book is dedicated to my brother
ALAN THOMPSON

A catalogue record for this book is available from the British Library

Text, photographs and diagrams © R A Thompson 2012

All rights reserved. No part of this publication may be reproduced or transmitted in any form or by any means, electronic or mechanical, including photocopying, recording, or any information storage and retrieval system, without permission in writing from the author.

VRW Publications
18 Coppen Road
Hampton Vale
Peterborough
Cambridgeshire UK
PE7 8JR

ISBN 978-0-9538218-2-2

CONTENTS

VII. Introduction
VIII. Safety notice
9. Chapter 1: Basic theory, direct current, alternating current, voltage, resistance.
13. Chapter 2: Reading schematics, resistors, capacitors, inductors, transformers, tuned circuits, 'Q' factor, Ohms Law.
25. Chapter 3: Introduction to valves, valve base types, half wave rectification, full wave rectification, elements and construction of valves, AF amplifier basics, series heater circuits.
39. Chapter 4: Circuits in principle, signal processing and detection (demodulation), amplification, anode bend and leaky-grid detectors, TRF and superhet comparisons, frequency-changer, mixing principles, inter-valve coupling, power output stages, tone control, negative feedback, loudspeakers.
59. Chapter 5: The typical vintage chassis, six representative receivers with applicable servicing tips.
81. Chapter 6: Choosing the first set – what to accept, what to avoid. How to minimise risks with Internet auctions.
87. Chapter 7: Essential test equipment, tools, materials, safe working practice, vintage/modern capacitor comparison chart, building a safety lamp.
93. Chapter 8: Initial fault-finding methods, cold testing, using an ohmmeter, essential cold checks.
95. Chapter 9: Test equipment, use of multimeters (analogue and digital), signal generator, oscilloscope, building a signal injector/tracer.
99. Chapter 10: Fault-finding using explanatory circuit, testing under power – the dead set, live set but no reception, problems with valves, problems with local oscillator, problems with electrolytic capacitors, problems with resistors, instability, microphony, hum, intermittent faults, general faults, problems with LF transformers, problems with loudspeakers.
109. Chapter 11: Starting restoration, notes and photographs, service data, ethics of restoration, essentials of restoration, mechanical problems, combined electrical/mechanical problems, tuning indicators, component restoration, safety concerns for end user, back covers, emblems, labels.
121. Chapter 12: Restoration procedures, rebuilding capacitors, substituting valves, cleaning and restoring of chassis surfaces, internal woodwork, stripping chassis, respraying chassis.
133. Chapter 13: cabinet restoration and repairs, woodworm, Bakelite cabinets, rescuing a 'far gone' cabinet, repairs to Bakelite cabinets, moulding with Alginate, rebuilding missing cabinet pieces.
147. Chapter 14: Refinishing wooden cabinets by lacquer and French Polish, recovering rexine/vynide cases.

---

155. Appendix
Capacitor value comparator chart, capacitor colour code chart, American capacitors, resistor colour code chart with examples, valve base chart, suggestions for further reading (books and magazines, present and past), sources for components and materials, useful websites.

---

167. Glossary
173. Index

Vintage radio restoration often includes the cabinet. Here, a Cossor 373 circa mid-1930s is pictured during cabinet work (above) and with the work completed

INTRODUCTION

Repairing and restoring vintage valve radio receivers is a fascinating hobby. Developing the skill to locate and rectify faults in such radios is uniquely satisfying, so much so in fact that you may find the hobby becomes an obsession. Luckily, if that happens it can be an obsession that doesn't have to cost the earth. Large quantities of valve receivers left the factories of many different makers in the post-WWII period – from about 1945 to the early 1960s – and the majority of these radios can be obtained for very little outlay. In fact, they will often cost more to restore than to buy. Despite the fact that some receivers built during the decade of the 1930s may, through sheer age, attract a higher price, many can still be purchased at very reasonable cost.

There are a few notable exceptions; the 'round' Ekco series of Bakelite-cased sets, starting in 1934 and finishing post-WWII always come at a premium. These receivers are desirable for two reasons: they are unusual, being fully circular in form when viewed from the front, and the cabinets were designed for Ekco by the brilliant avante-garde architect and designer Wells Coates, famous for his innovative and stylish Deco-influenced designs. Several other famous designers worked in Bakelite for Ekco during the 1930s heyday of the company.

The market for vintage valve radios is as variable as any other antique and collectible market and what is popular one year may be less so another. The best advice to the beginning collector/restorer is to acquire only what appeals and resist undue influence from others (but if starting out, do take note of the recommendations in this book).

From the start of public broadcasting in the early 1920s, valve technology dominated the world of electronics. Valves (vacuum tubes) were produced by the multi-million and developments were rapid.

By the end of the 1930s, superb quality valves were powering the radios that brought home entertainment to the masses. Through the dark days of WWII, the warm, resonant tone of the valve radio lifted spirits and entertained both the forces and the general public alike. The competitor, television, had made a halting start in the late 1930s but it wasn't until well into the 1950s that its popularity began to outstrip that of radio. By the mid 1950s, radio transmissions using frequency-modulation (FM) brought a wider dynamic range and higher quality sound to British audiences as an alternative to the old amplitude-modulation (AM) broadcast systems. By that time, a form of FM had been operating in America for some years. By the early 1960s, valve technology itself finally had a competitor; solid-state electronics had been developed and the transistor and microchip heralded a long, drawn-out end for valves, though they lived on in some high power transmitters and TV receivers and the cathode ray tube of every television and colour television. The CRT was in essence a form of valve that only in recent years has been phased out.

Radios themselves are more than simply antique items for mute display. Properly restored, even today they work amazingly well, surprising listeners brought up on solid state technology. The skill, art and craftsmanship that went into the design and construction of even the most humble radio receiver stands as a tribute to the days when valves ruled the airwaves.

This book has been written in response to very many requests for information and assistance. It is hoped that the reader will be encouraged by the essentially practical treatment of the subject in this, the only modern guide that covers *all* aspects of the subject of domestic valve radio, not just the electronics.

Technical explanations have been kept as simple as possible whilst broadly retaining accuracy and it is felt that anyone with an interest in the subject, regardless of their age or experience, will find much of value within its pages.

Chapters 1 to 4 cover the basics and have been incorporated to guide those without prior knowledge.

There were many technical books published in the days of the valve. Most are excellent but none address the problems of restoration or the kind of faults caused by poor storage, age and mis-use, nor could they be expected to. They are exactly what they were written to be, theoretical treatises or straightforward servicing manuals. Also, though generally well-researched by skilled authors and therefore reliable, there can be a dryness of read quality and the tendency, borne of their published time, to offer rather dense elaboration. Not so here, not that corners have been cut. There are concise explanations but in the interests of practicality the text is intentionally virtually free from maths and jargon. As a result, it is fair to say that inevitably some of the explanatory text, in particular that involving current theory and component and circuit function, is to an extent approximate, with the use of analogy: no apologies are offered for this as radio restoration is an enjoyable and absorbing hobby and this is intended to be an engrossing and rewarding read. If the reader wants to know more, there are many vintage texts to consult plus material freely available on the internet and the aforementioned vintage books are always handy as a reference source, assuming copies can be obtained at a reasonable cost.

The appendix has suggestions for further reading that will assist in that respect. The glossary is worth consulting if you've forgotten what those elusive initials represent or are at a loss to recall the meaning of a technical term.

It is hoped therefore that the interest that led the reader here in the first place can be enhanced by a sound understanding of the basics whilst not requiring, from him or her, a degree in physics or even a high level of existing knowledge. Split into fully illustrated and easily understood sections where component action and interaction is described, the subject builds gradually toward a sound understanding of the basic principles and their application in fault finding and general servicing of valve equipment.

All aspects of component, chassis and cabinet repair and restoration are given coverage.

The information contained here can be used in a variety of ways. You can start at the beginning and read through to the end, especially important if you are an absolute beginner with valve technology. Alternatively, select from the chapter listing to suit your need.

You may prefer to go straight to the pages on servicing and restoring; you should find the information on different models to be useful in this respect, too. Don't forget the appendix and the glossary as these contain invaluable information plus explanations of terminology. Enjoy!

SAFETY NOTICE

All vintage radios should be considered to be inherently unsafe until they can be tested to prove otherwise. You are STRONGLY ADVISED to read and understand the safety information given here (Chapter 5 onward) before ANY set is connected to power or ANY work begins.

CHAPTER 1
BASIC THEORY

CONDUCTORS AND INSULATORS

All matter is made from atoms. Atoms are so small that even the most powerful microscope cannot see them. Grouped together, atoms form molecules from which everything in the universe is made.

Here is a (very) simplified view of the atom. The central nucleus is built up from protons and neutrons, around which spin a varying number of electrons. Protons are said to carry a positive electrical charge, neutrons no charge at all, and electrons a negative charge. Typically, the number of protons in the central core balances the number of electrons and as the protons are positive, there exists an equal and opposite charge to that of the negative electrons. The result, on the average, is zero charge on the atom as a whole because the equal and opposite polarities cancel each other.

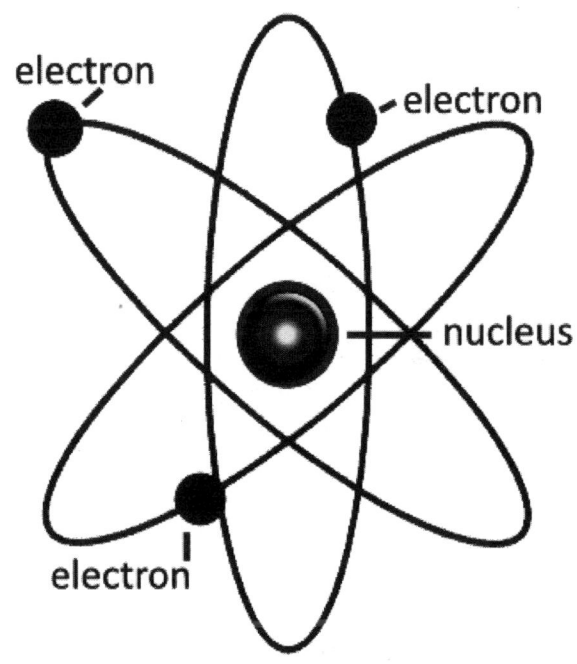

CONVENTIONAL REPRESENTATION OF AN ATOM

The atoms of materials classed as insulators have tightly packed clouds of electrons and there are very few electrons capable of leaving their parent atom – there's nowhere for them to go. In conducting materials such as metals, electrons are more loosely bound to the individual atom, allowing emigration and migration of electrons; those in the outer orbits are free to move at random from one atom to another. When an atom loses an electron to another atom, it becomes positively charged due to the loss of that electron's quantity of negative charge. Atoms so charged are said to be ionised. Because opposite charges attract and like charges repel, another electron will be attracted from a nearby atom. This happens continually with all the atoms of conducting materials. So, although there may be individual atoms with a positive charge, the process is a random one and over a group of atoms there is effectively neither a positive or negative charge. This is a state we call neutral.

Remember that a positive charge (a lack of electrons) will attract electrons. If by some means such a charge is placed on one end of a conducting wire, it will exert an attraction on the electrons surrounding the atoms in the wire.
This lack of electrons is called a difference of electric potential (PD). However, the term Potential Difference is best used to help describe the function of a resistor, which, when a current is flowing through it has a difference of potential – voltage - across it.

Batteries are handy sources of power. Consider what takes place when we touch a short length of copper wire to the positive terminal of a battery.

There will be a movement of electrons toward the attracting positive charge (positive = a lack of negative, remember). Equilibrium is reached when the atoms in the wire that are deficient in electrons – therefore positively charged - exert sufficient back pressure on the electrons. This means that only a momentary shift in electron position has occurred, like the tug-of-war rope being pulled tight, resulting in a strain or static charge but no actual flow of electrons.

You can create static charges by combing your hair with a plastic comb, rubbing a balloon on your clothing, or sometimes even walking on certain kinds of man-made carpet. Even wearing insulated shoes can create static charge, especially on hot, dry days.

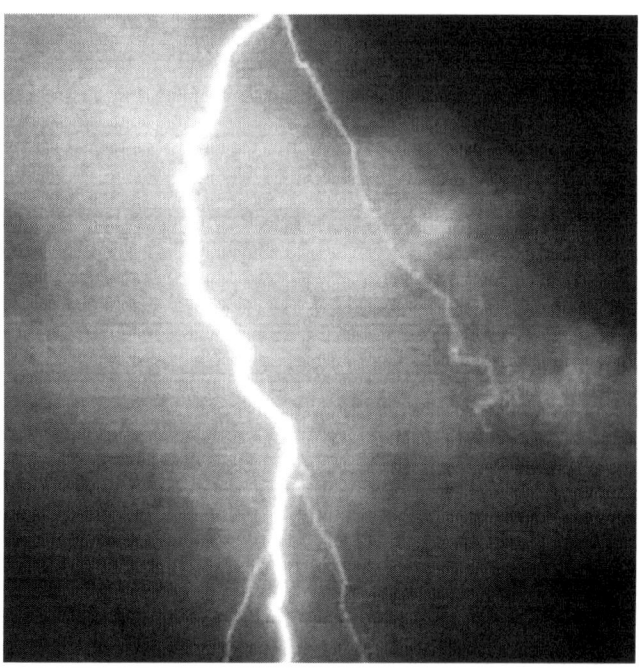

Lightning is an example of static discharge

The effects of these charges are interesting, but their uses, as far as the subject matter of this book is concerned, are limited. To make electricity work for us we need to create the continuous flow of electricity; to create electric current. One way to do this would be to connect the free end of our length of copper wire to the negative terminal of the battery. Because the battery acts in effect rather like a pump, by chemical means constantly creating an imbalance of charge, electrons will now flow in one direction around the circuit toward the positive terminal, with replacement electrons flowing into the circuit from the negative battery terminal. With our length of copper wire forming a complete circuit with our battery, we have the two essentials to create a flow of current – a source of electric potential and a circuit to convert the potential into current.

It is not a sensible thing to do, however, as we have no control over the resultant current. We have turned the tap full on and a heavy current will flow, limited only by the capacity of the battery, i.e. its internal resistance, to supply electrons at its negative terminal to replace those flowing through the wire into the positive terminal, plus the natural resistance of the conducting wire. A small dry battery will rapidly overheat and fail under such uncontrolled conditions. A car battery or wet cell accumulator (low internal resistance, high current capacity) could burn out the conducting wire.

Whenever a conductor, such as our length of copper wire, is connected directly from positive to negative it is said to have created a short circuit, meaning a circuit with effectively no resistance to the flow of current.

Rather than wasting the power of the current in heating up the battery and the wire, we want it to do something useful so we need a way to limit the movement of the electrons.

And, of course, we have one in the form of resistance, which is an electrical property of many substances and materials.

Electrical resistance is actually almost ever-present. Even the best copper wire possesses it, though to a very small degree. Much depends upon the cross-sectional thickness of the wire and the electrical energy passing through it. Generally speaking, the thicker the wire and the lower the electrical pressure in volts, the less effect resistance will have.

Resistance can, therefore, be a problem to overcome but it has important uses, both in radio and in everyday life. We have already met it in the battery and the wire. It was the resistance of the wire that caused them to heat up. This is in effect frictional resistance. No conductor of electricity is perfect (unless you count superconductors cooled to a point close to absolute zero) and there is always *some* resistance, a property that can be used, for example in the electric kettle, cooker, fire, toaster or any appliance that is fitted with a resistive element. It is the resistance of the element, due partly to the kind of metal used and partly to the method of construction (cross section and length of the resistive metal wire), that causes the heating effect.

Edison type filament light bulbs work in a similar fashion only in this case the filament wire inside the bulb is very fine and would, in air, be expected to burn out if a current was passed through it; but the glass bulb is evacuated and has no oxygen in it. Without oxygen, the filament cannot burn even though it will become very hot. It can glow white hot, so hot it gives off light.

What if we want to prevent any current from flowing? That's where insulators come in. Most plastics, dry wood, ceramic and rubber are effective insulators and are used to prevent us getting electric shocks. Thermoplastics of varying kinds form protective flexible 'insulated' coatings around conducting cables.

Fuses are safety devices, designed to fail in the event of excess current flow. There are several types and sizes of glass-encased fuse used in radio, but with vintage valve equipment fuses – if used - are usually about an inch in length. They may be placed in series with the HT (high tension) supply that powers a radio, or in series with the mains input to a radio set. It follows that the rated current of a fuse is important – i.e. the point above which the fuse is intended to fail. The glass contains the molten wire and allows inspection.
Many items in the average home are connected to a 13A AC mains outlet via a plug top fitted with a 13A fuse, despite the fact that few items other than a multi-bar electric fire require such a high current. Vintage valve radios should be fused at about 3A. Any more and a fault within the set could result in damage or even a burn-up. Always fit a fuse appropriate for the purpose.

So far only direct current flow has been described. Direct current (DC) flows in only one direction around a circuit. Which direction? From negative to positive, if you are talking about electron flow. If we arranged a switching system to continuously reverse the polarity of the power, the direction of current flow would continually change, too, and current would flow back and forth around the circuit at the switching rate. In other words, it would alternate. The mains supply is alternating current (AC) for good reason: AC can be stepped up or down in voltage at will, via transformers.

VINTAGE VALVE RADIOS

Although DC mains were supplied to parts of the UK in years gone by, it is much more efficient to distribute very high voltage AC via the national grid, stepping down where convenient to 240 volts, the nominal supply voltage pressure in the UK. The direction change occurs 50 times a second (50 cycles, nowadays called 50 Hz, after Hertz, the German physicist. The mains supply is not switched rapidly in polarity, though. In fact it isn't switched at all. The AC generators that create it cycle smoothly through from a peak in power in one direction, falling through zero voltage/current to rise to a similar but opposite peak. I stated 'smoothly' but that's an ideal and the actual wave shape created may fall some way short of that. It is direct current (DC) that valves need. This leaves designers of mains powered radios with the need to convert the AC power into DC, of course, because amplifying valves cannot function on high voltage AC supplies.

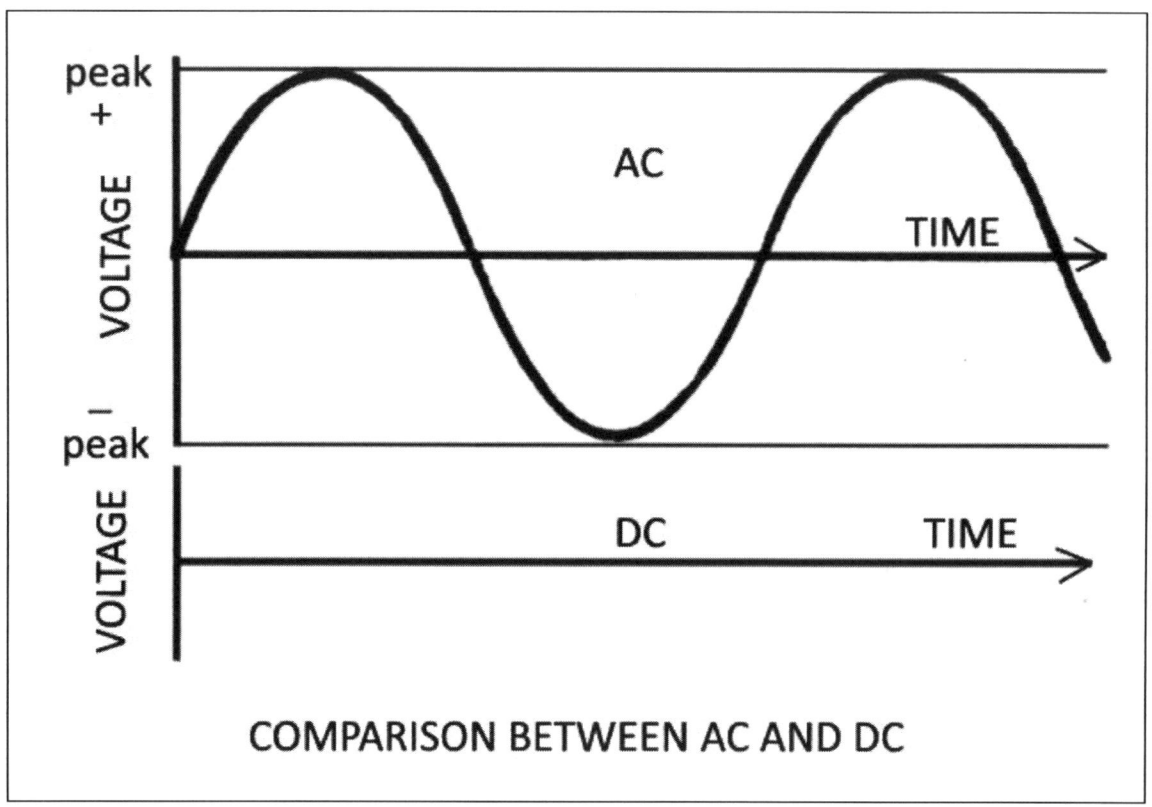

Comparison of AC and DC current flow

Basic facts: An electric current can only flow when a circuit is complete. Switches are devices that break complete circuits. A broken circuit is said to be 'open-circuit'. A circuit with no resistance to current flow is said to be 'short-circuit'. There are two forms of electric current. One is direct (DC), the other is alternating (AC). Valves usually need high DC potentials in order to function.

The last point is significant. Because valves – for the most part – require high or at least relatively high voltage potentials to function, it is essential that the would-be vintage radio restorer works within the safety guidelines given in this document.

CHAPTER 2
THE SCHEMATIC DIAGRAM – RESISTORS – CAPACITORS - INDUCTORS

Resistors and capacitors are sometimes called passive components, which in this context means they do not amplify, rather they limit current and voltage in some manner. Before these are discussed, let's consider the function of schematic diagrams.

Schematics (or theoretical circuits) are collections of component symbols joined up to make circuits and are also known as circuit diagrams or theoretical diagrams. No surprises there, then. The complex appearance of these is a passing effect; with a little effort the reader soon learns to identify both individual components and the methods by which the may be interconnected. No matter how apparently complex, all theoretical circuitry consists of the same relatively few component symbols.

Even so, one look at any schematic diagram and you would be forgiven for thinking that there is enormous complication in the subject. Not so. In vintage radio, the symbols used represent valves, resistors, capacitors and coils. It is how they are arranged, their values and purpose within the circuit that can and does vary from one circuit to another. It is essential that the reader should become familiar with these symbols, remembering the caveat that vintage symbols do not always translate to modern circuitry. Over the years, a process of standardization has occurred and gradually symbols from all countries have become at least partially integrated into a common acceptance of their meaning. This has meant that certain vintage symbols have had to change, a common one being the symbol for a resistor. In modern schematics a resistor is usually represented as a long, narrow rectangle.

The resistor of vintage days is a zigzag (or sawtooth) line. Coils and transformers too may look different: the old way was to represent a winding as exactly that, a winding. Reasonable, you might think but today, many transformer windings are represented by – once again – rectangles.

So it is important to understand the meaning of symbols. But why, you may ask, do we need schematic diagrams? Why not just show the components as they actually are, connected together correctly? That type of drawing is known as a 'point to point wiring diagram' and often appeared in constructor's magazines such as 'Practical Wireless'. These diagrams were certainly helpful, especially to the inexperienced constructor, but once receivers took on greater degrees of complexity, such drawings became impossibly complicated to produce – and probably equally impossible to follow. Think of the theoretical circuit as electronic shorthand. When designing a house, an architect isn't expected to draw every brick. When painting a scene, an artist rarely attempts to draw every discrete blade of grass or ripple of water. The physical reality behind a simply drawn symbol such as the resistor shown above can be very varied, the same symbol applying to a wide range of components, each type with specific function. You could think of it as written music: the notes are there on the page – assuming that the reader has the skill to interpret them - but a note played on a tuba has a very different quality to the same note on a violin.

The RESISTOR

The unit of resistance is the OHM. The symbol for ohm is OMEGA, the little 'horseshoe' Greek letter **(Ω)**.

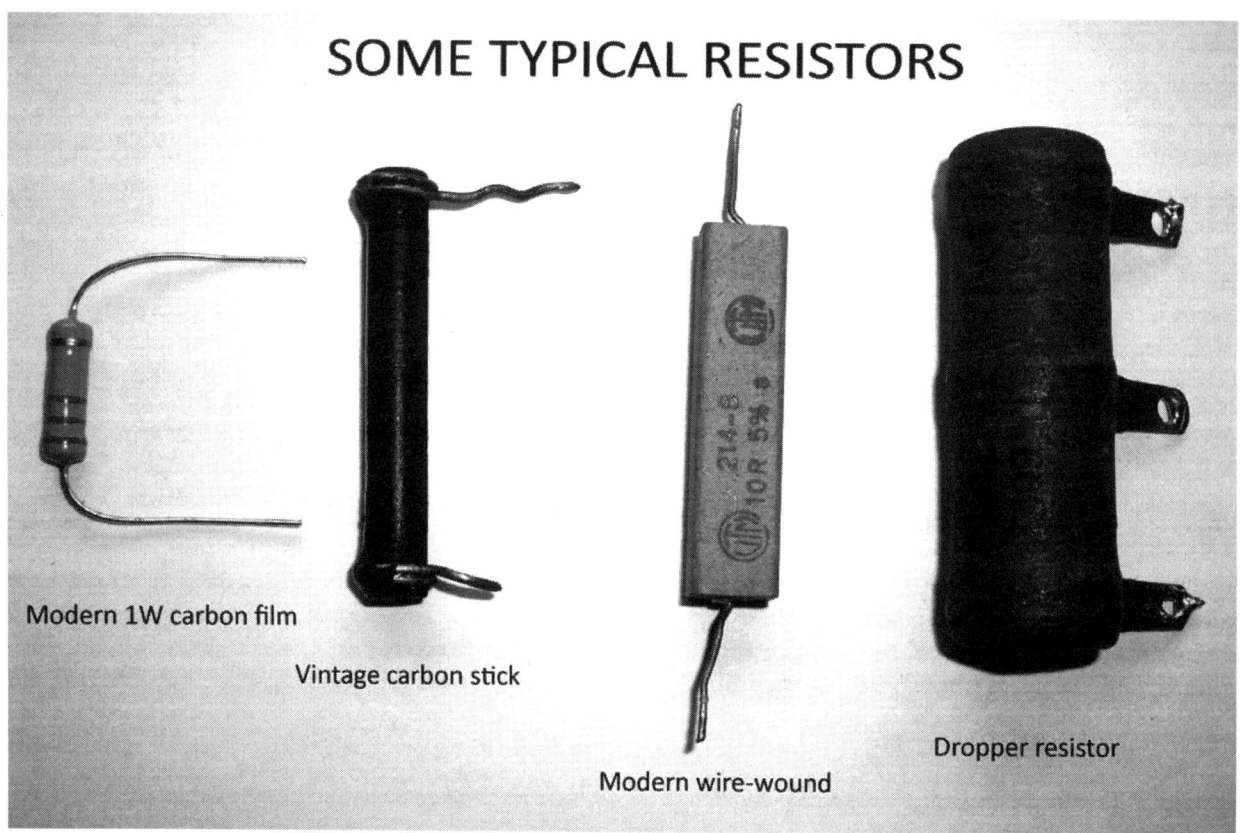

If we want to control the flow of electrons rather than stop them altogether, then insulating materials cannot be used. Instead we employ materials that allow some current to flow, but limit the amount. Such materials are said to possess resistance to electric current flow. Resistors are made from current-limiting materials.

The most common form of resistor encountered in vintage radio is the carbon composition type, in rod (stick) form. Despite being quite large, these types are low-wattage ones, which means they can only handle small currents. There are very large stick types that can handle 3 watts. The Watt is the unit of electrical power **(P)**. All conventional resistors limit current by converting the electricity into heat, which is dispersed by convection (heat rising) into the surrounding air.

Where heavy current flow is likely, for example in the power supply arrangements of an AC/DC valve radio, carbon resistors would overheat due to the excessive power dissipation needed and wire-wound resistors are used instead. These higher wattage resistors are made by wrapping ceramic tubes with resistive wire. They often work at high temperatures, rather in the manner of electric fire elements, though not as hot, of course. Even so they are often hot enough to burn fingers.

Air convection takes the edge off very high temperatures. It may seem wasteful to throw away power in this form, but the resistor is such a simple and reliable device that it is one of the most commonly encountered components in electronics generally and plays an essential part in valve radio.

The picture on the previous page shows the typical appearance of commonly found resistors but as with all electronic components there is variation between makes and types. Carbon composition (stick) resistors from the 1930s use a colour code system known as body, tip, spot. Later carbon composition and high stability resistors use a colour banding system. For information on the colour codes, see the appendix.

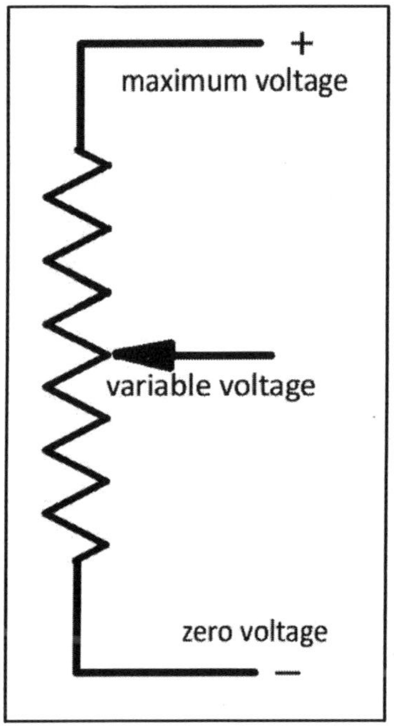

Resistors can be made variable, allowing their value – the amount they resist the flow of current – to be adjusted at will. Variable resistors such as volume and tone controls are actually potentiometers, a term which literally means 'measurement of potential' but in practical terms allows the progressive change of a given value of potential difference.

Potentiometer

If we break the simple circuit we made with the wire and the battery and insert a resistor in series, then a current will flow, the strength of which will then depend upon the potential difference as provided by the source of power, and the amount of resistance in the circuit. If we make the resistor a variable one, we can 'tap off' whatever potential – i.e. voltage - we need, within the rating of the battery, of course.

We now need to get slightly technical. It's not essential that you grasp the basic maths involved in what follows, but it can help later on if you have some idea of the processes that are taking place with resistive circuits. You could miss this section out and return to it later, if you prefer.

Potential difference is measured in voltage **(V)** and the relationship between current and voltage is a simple one. For a circuit with a given resistance, **either** doubling the potential difference (the voltage) **or** halving the resistance will double the current flow.

THE RELATIONSHIP BETWEEN CURRENT AND VOLTAGE

V =	1	2	3	4	5
I =	.1A	.2A	.3A	.4A	.5A
V/I = (Ω)	10 Ω	10 Ω	10 Ω	10 Ω	10 Ω

The symbol (I) is used to represent current. Current is measured in amperes, (usually shortened to amps or simply **A**). We can see that the ratio V over I remains constant. This is because the voltage divided by the current is equal to the resistance as measured in ohms (Ω). In the above chart, the imaginary circuit has a resistance of 10 ohms.

Ohms Law

This is a very neat way to show the relationship between these values. Ohm's Law states that the current through a conductor is directly proportional to the potential difference across it. Our example proves this to be so.

Basic fact: Ohms law only applies to the commonplace resistors made from carbon and from metal alloys, not to special types such as thermistors. See below for non-linear resistors.

So far, we have touched on resistance, current and voltage. The useful thing about Ohms law is that it allows us to calculate the value of any one of these *if* we know the other two. We have already shown that you can obtain the value of resistance in a given circuit by dividing the voltage by the current. If we divide the voltage by the resistance, then we obtain the current: if we multiply the current by the resistance we obtain voltage.

The Ohm's Law triangle

This triangle mnemonic can help you to remember the rules of Ohm's law.

Divide or multiply any two to obtain the third. Cover the value you wish to find and work out the remaining visible figures. Although the values are in volts, ohms and amperes, an ampere is a rather large unit for radio and it is easier to substitute milliamps (mA) for A and kilohms (k) for R. You must substitute both, however.

One milliamp is one thousandth of an Amp. Ten mA equals one hundredth of an Amp and one hundred mA equals one tenth of an Amp.

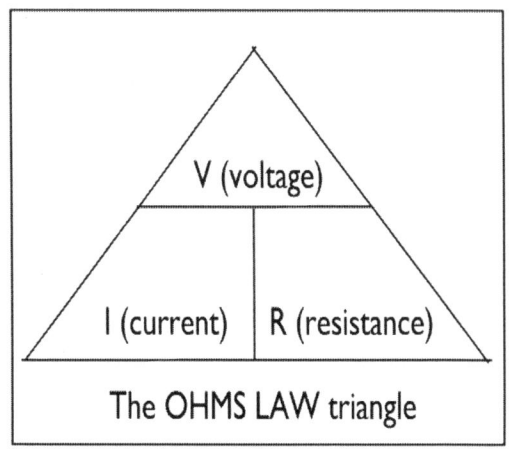

The OHMS LAW triangle

Power

Power is the term used to describe either the rate of production of electrical energy (for example, an electric generator) or the rate of dissipation of electrical energy (for example, a light bulb). The symbol for power is **P**. We use the term watt as the unit of power. It is named after James Watt. Wattage is V X I, useful to calculate the required wattage of a resistor in a given circuit.

Resistors in series

When we connect resistors in series by wiring them end to end, their individual values simply add up and the total resistance becomes the sum of the individual values in the circuit.

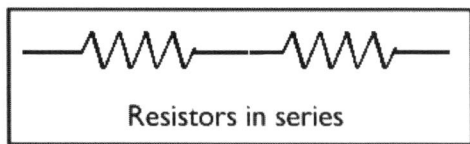

Resistors in series

Why bother? Well, if two are in series, it follows that each will take its share of the power dissipation. Say we wire two identical value 1-watt resistors in series, we will have effectively made a 2-watt resistor whose value is the sum of the two individual resistors: a neat way of preventing premature ageing due to excess heating, as each resistor only handles half of the total power. With two different values, each handles power in proportion to its value ratio.

Another good reason to wire two in series is to expedite a repair or to carry out tests when the exact value of resistor is not to hand.

Resistor range

Resistors come in ranges of so-called preferred values. This prevents the proliferation of values that would give rise to uneconomic manufacture. The designer chooses the nearest preferred value to the mathematical ideal. Usually, this is near enough as valve circuitry rarely needs exact values, especially with the higher resistance ranges.

Another consideration is 'tolerance' which, in simple terms, means the amount a given resistor may deviate above or below from its stated value due to variations during manufacture. Tolerance is stated as a percentage i.e. 10%, 5% etc.

Line Cords are resistive mains leads and will run slightly warm in use. These were fitted to small table radios where the heat from an internal dropper would have been too confined, and certain American-made imports to convert them in as simple a way as possible from 110V to 240V mains. They should never be replaced by standard mains cable or the radio in question will be overrun and its major components could be permanently damaged. Due to age, line cords may be fragile and dangerous to use.

- *Basic facts: Resistors limit the flow of current, dissipating the power as heat.*
- *Resistors cannot drop voltage unless a current is flowing through them.*
- *The values of two or more resistors wired in series – like railway carriages on a track – add together to make a total, which is the sum of the individual values. Example: one 5 Ω and one 10 Ω wired in series = 15 Ω.*

The non-linear resistor

These are components that do not follow ohm's law. A type of non-linear resistor type commonly found in valve radio is the 'thermistor'. These devices, usually rod-shaped in vintage radios, present a high resistance from cold, which drops rapidly as the device warms. They are

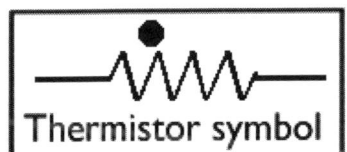
Thermistor symbol

used in the heater circuit to prevent heavy surges of current at switch-on of a radio (cold heaters offer low resistance) and may also occasionally be found doing a similar task where a solid-state HT rectifier diode is powering a set.

Indirectly heated valves, which means almost all valves designed to work from mains supplies, take time to warm up. Because of this, immediately power is applied the HT voltage can rise to a high peak due to the lack of power demand from the still cool valves. Protection to components and valves may be provided by the inclusion of a thermistor to limit voltage surges.

The CAPACITOR

Capacitors (old name, condensers) are made in various sizes and shapes, from a variety of materials. But they all have certain things in common. There is a conducting material used for the plates (or connections) of which there are two except for multiple capacitors, where several capacitors occupy the same can or case - and there is a non-conducting material, an insulator, which is used to keep the two plates electrically separate.

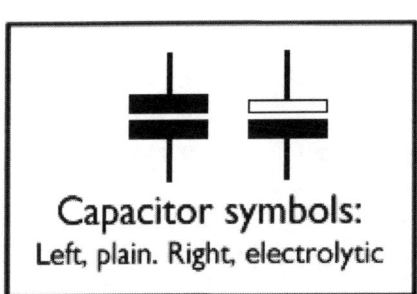
Capacitor symbols:
Left, plain. Right, electrolytic

This insulator is known as the dielectric. It can be paper, plastic film, mica, air or even, with electrolytic types, microscopic gas bubbles.

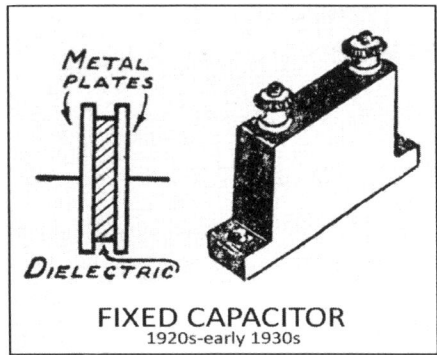

FIXED CAPACITOR
1920s-early 1930s

Capacitors block DC and pass AC, the latter dependent upon the frequency of the alternating signal and the value (electrical size) of the capacitor. They also store electricity and can be charged up, when they hold their charge for brief periods. This capacity to store electricity is used in a number of ways.

In valve radio power supplies, where AC mains electricity is converted into high voltage DC, they can be used in parallel with the supply to store power and give it back as needed, thus smoothing out the slight AC ripples left after rectification. An analogy with water can help here. Imagine that the flow of electric current is an intermittent flow of water and the capacitor is a container with a tap low down on the side.

Tuning capacitors use air as a dielectric and have fixed and moving plates known as vanes

The water may spurt into the top of the container, filling it at regular but jerky intervals. Turn the tap on the side, however, and a steady flow of water occurs. The volume of water contained within the tank has smoothed the flow. Similarly the fluctuating pulses of power (the ripples of AC superimposed upon the DC voltage after rectification) filling a smoothing capacitor in a mains radio power supply are levelled. This is why hum occurs when smoothing and reservoir capacitors dry up and lose their capacity, allowing the ripples that should have been removed to remain and be amplified as a 50Hz or 100Hz note.

Capacitors in series with a supply can effectively pass alternating signals such as the fluctuating voltages that are the electrical equivalents of speech or music, at the same time blocking any fixed DC voltage that the alternating signal may be carried on. This allows valves to be coupled together with relative simplicity.

Basic facts: Capacitors can be charged to hold power temporarily. Capacitors cannot pass fixed (DC) voltages. Capacitors can 'pass' alternating voltages.*
Capacitors designed for reservoir and smoothing tasks are often made in combination – two or three separate capacitors in the same container, usually an aluminium tubular can in all but very old receivers.
*Capacitors do not normally 'pass' any current. Instead, only with AC, 'tidal' electric strain is set up within the capacitor resulting in a constant charge/discharge effect on both sets of capacitor plates. It is

perhaps best to consider that a capacitor passes *changes* of voltage. The value of a capacitor greatly affects its ability to pass or to block alternating signals. Various values of capacitor pass alternating signals at different frequencies.

The greater the capacitance, the lower the alternating frequency it can pass. Values in the order of 0.001µF to 0.1µF are often associated with tone control circuits – audio frequencies - and values in the order of 100pF to 500pF are used in radio frequency tuned circuits together with an inductance (coil, transformer) to select wanted signals and reject unwanted ones.

Typically in valve radio receivers, a 300pF to 500pF (0.0003µF to 0.0005µF) variable capacitor with an air dielectric will be used to allow tuning to the differing frequencies of broadcast stations. Also found in the majority of vintage radios are preset capacitors. These allow final trimming and alignment of tuned circuits which once set at their optimum need no further adjustment. They are usually adjustable by means of a small screw.

Electrolytic capacitors are used whenever very large values of capacitance are required. These use damp paste electrolytes and are usually polarised. They must be connected correctly or they will pass DC, a problem known as leakage. The use of an electrolyte saves physical size. Without this, large µF values would also be physically very large. The technicalities of these types of capacitor need not concern us here. Suffice to say that sub-microscopic gas bubbles act as the dielectric.

Capacitors are measured for their amount of capacity by a unit called the **Farad**, named after Michael Faraday. The Farad is a very large unit, so for vintage radio purposes we mostly work in **Microfarads (µF)** and **Picofarads (pF)**, of which the largest measurement is Microfarad. Most electrolytic capacitors are in microfarad values because large values take up less physical space with electrolytic construction.

Typical values for electrolytic capacitors used in valve circuitry might be 2µF to 100µF. Waxed paper, metal-cased and pitch-coated plain (non-polarised) capacitors usually range from 1µF to 0.001µF. 0.001µF is equivalent to 1000 pF. These ordinary capacitors are found in the audio amplifying stages and as signal bypass devices in automatic volume control systems (AVC). Automatic Gain Control (AGC) is the technically accurate way of describing the same feature. Tiny capacitors mostly used in the tuned circuits of radio receivers can go down to a few pF. These may be flat in style with silvered Mica acting as dielectric and plate, or ceramic in tubular disc or rectangular form.

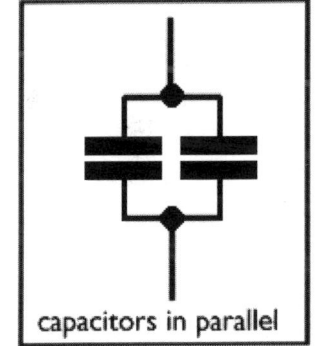
capacitors in parallel

Basic fact: Capacitors in parallel (side by side) add in value. Example: Two one hundred µF capacitors in parallel = 200 µF. Basic fact: Electrolytic capacitors have the great advantage of high capacitance in small physical space.

Capacitors used in valve radio are usually of much higher voltage rating than those used for transistor circuitry. This is because valves are basically voltage driven devices, whereas transistors work in the main as current amplifiers in low-voltage circuitry. As well as their value in decimal fractions of a Farad, capacitors have another important value – their voltage rating. This figure determines the safe maximum working voltage that the component can handle without breaking down. Ignore this at your peril. It is best to err on the safe side when replacing capacitors, and you certainly will be replacing them as they are often the culprit behind the dead, distorted, low volume or crackly set.

The **Volts Working** figure is usually abbreviated to 'V.W'. or simply 'V' when printed on the case of a capacitor and applies most often to DC (Direct Current) circuits.

Some capacitors may be rated by rms voltage for use in alternating current circuits. A further measurement to consider where electrolytic capacitors are used for power supply filtering is the ripple current handling capacity of the capacitor. When AC is rectified by diode action into DC, there remains a proportion of AC due to the fluctuations of voltage across the reservoir capacitor as it charges and discharges in time with the pulses of DC supplied from the rectifier diode.

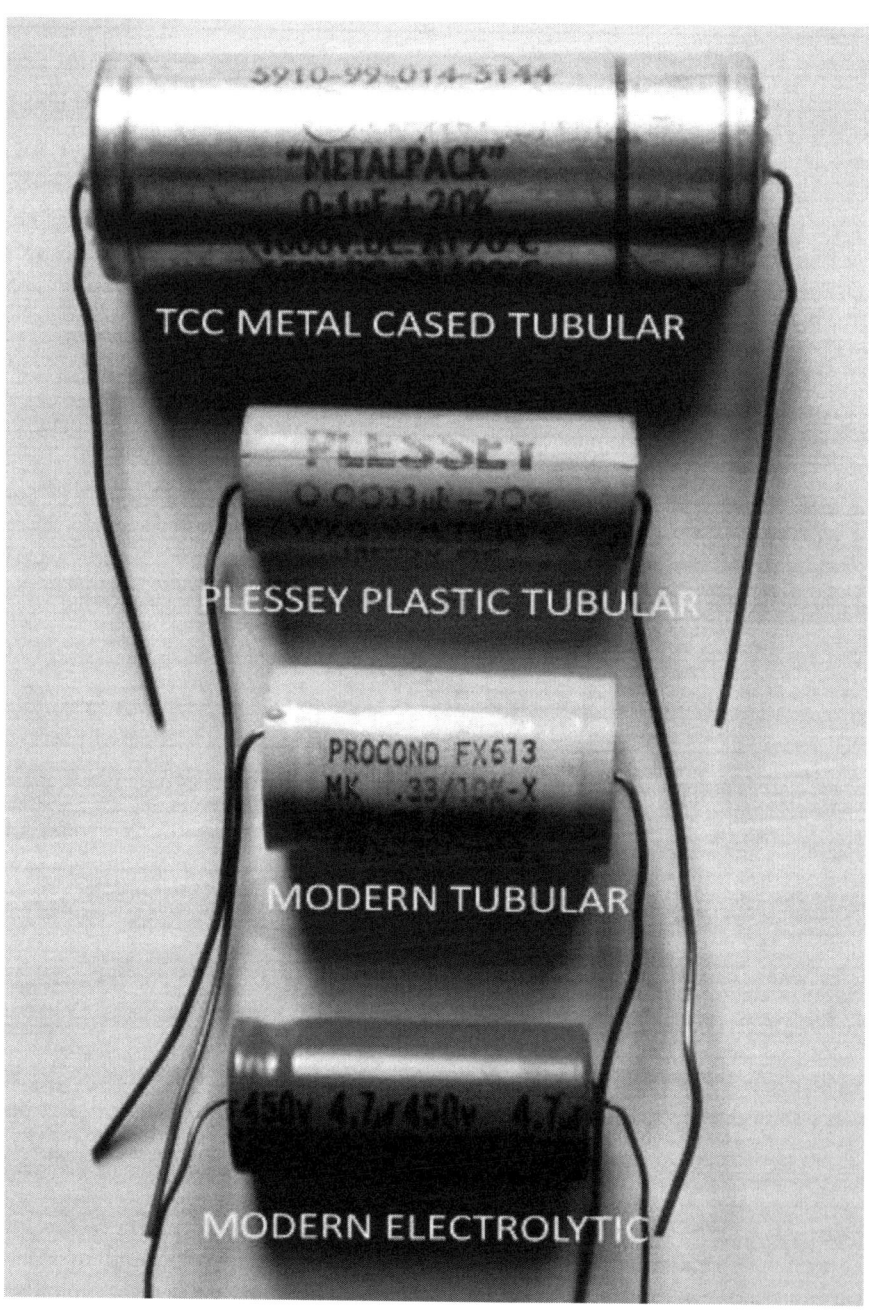

Capacitors come in a multitude of shapes and sizes.
This photograph shows four of the more common tubular types

This AC wave tends to be of a sawtooth form due to the switching action of the diode and the reservoir capacitor must be capable of withstanding this spikiness. Capacitors designed for reservoir use should have a maximum ripple rating printed on the can or sleeve.

The most suitable components for replacement purposes are new types, preferably of a similar style and rating. New old stock components may be thought to be ideal but unfortunately though quite predictably, sources for such spares are becoming rare. A time will inevitably arise when the well will run dry and no old stock types will be left. In particular, high voltage electrolytic capacitors of the can type used for HT smoothing and reservoir purposes are rare and manufacture has almost ceased, so new equivalents are both hard to find and expensive. Also and importantly, age can affect the ESR (Equivalent Series Resistance) of a capacitor, a problem that doesn't always show up when tested but failure in use occurs.

In view of the foregoing, some components are in any case better replaced with new production alternatives. Imagine fitting new old stock waxed paper capacitors in the full knowledge that, being identical to the ones being replaced, they are unreliable in the medium to long term. This alone is a very good reason not to use salvaged or unused old stock capacitors unless you can be very sure of their quality. This is especially so with electrolytic capacitors.

Replacing with modern components can be a little tricky until the restorer becomes familiar with the modern nF values that are now used for capacitor coding.
To simplify this, there is a capacitor (condenser) value comparison chart provided in the appendix.

The INDUCTOR

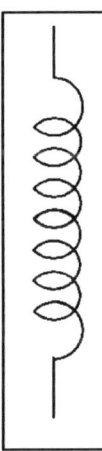

When a direct current flows through a conductor, there is perhaps only a very small resistance to the flow. (Remember that all conductors show some resistance.) The current flow will remain more or less the same regardless of the shape of the conductor. We could, for example, take a length of copper wire and wrap it around a core of some sort, perhaps a cotton bobbin from a sewing machine, or a pencil. This wire **coil** would still pass much the same current as the straight wire did before we wound it into a coil. The basic symbol for an air-cored coil is shown on the right.

Coils offer a low resistance to the flow of a direct current. However, it is very different if we change the direct current for an alternating current. Coils are **inductors**: they possess **inductance**. Inductance means that they are capable when carrying a current of (a) creating a magnetic field and (b) are able to store magnetic energy. Whenever current (whether DC or AC) passes through a conductor, a magnetic field develops around it, at right angles to the flow.

The DC field remains in place for as long as the current is flowing. But as an alternating current varies, so does the field. For example if the current alternates as AC does, the field collapses and reappears in the opposite polarity at every cycle.
This happens with a straight wire of course, but this doesn't usually matter much except for the physical layout of conductors and components within the chassis of a radio, some of which may be affected by the proximity of the changing field.

However in a coil where the windings lie alongside each other, complex interactions takes place resulting in the creation of a magnetic 'brake'. This is the effect we call reactance. It is due to inductive resistance. You may see the term 'back EMF' used when coils such as chokes are described. EMF is an abbreviation for Electro-Motive Force, not a term much used today.

A choke is a coil of wire that has a large inductive reactance to alternating signals, but low resistance to DC. A typical choke is the RF (Radio Frequency, or High Frequency) type, which is often a coil wound upon an air-cored former made of an insulating material. The EMF created when RF signals are applied causes a voltage drop across the coil and therefore RF signal amplification.

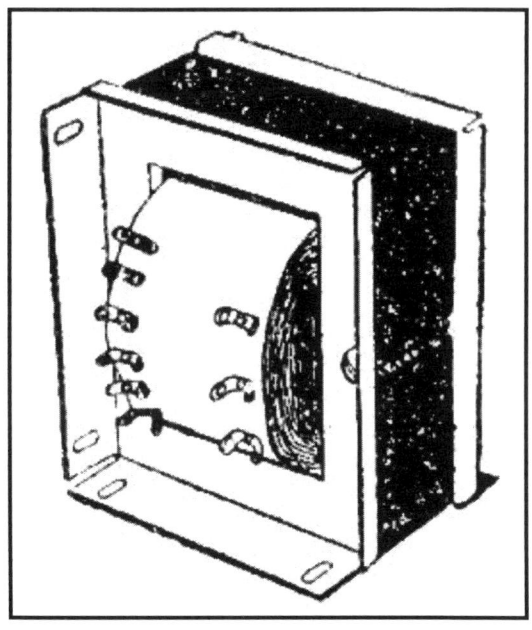

Typical mains transformer

The **transformer** employs the phenomenon of inductance. If a further winding *not connected electrically* to a given coil is wrapped over it or wound upon a common core, which may be soft-iron for power transformers like the mains transformer pictured on the previous page, or air and ferrite cores for radio-frequency transformers (see below), then an alternating current flowing through the first coil will be induced in the second one. The first, current-carrying coil is called the **primary** winding and the second, induced-current coil is called the **secondary.**

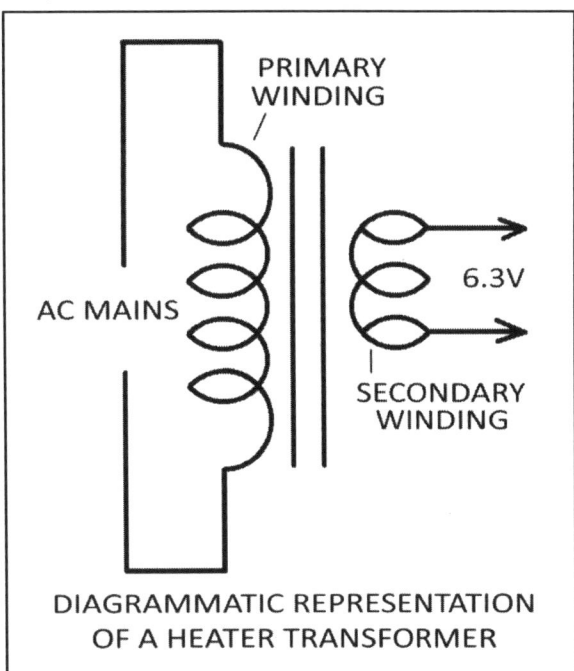

There may be several secondary windings over a single primary, to allow for low voltage supplies to valve heaters and high voltage for the valve anodes, or a single secondary with tapping points along the coil. Mains transformers almost always have a tapped primary which allows them to be set for prevailing mains voltages, perhaps from 200V to 250V.

At radio frequencies, all that may be needed to effect inductive coupling is to place the coils near each other, usually by winding them on a common insulating tube. This is how the IF transformers in valve radios function. To tune such coils, fixed or adjustable capacitors or metallic iron dust (ferrite) cores are used to make sharp points of resonance. Tuning coils are often air-cored in the older radio.

At the point of resonance of such a circuit, peak current flows for only a minimum input. This makes the circuit, in effect, into a frequency-selective amplifier which may be adjusted (tuned) either by changing the value of the parallel capacitor (changing the setting of the variable tuning capacitor) or by altering the position of the metallic core relative to its coil.

HF transformers are widely used. Usually called tuning coils, they use coils wound to suit radio frequency transmission bands, for example long wave or medium wave. The transformer action is used to couple and amplify the tuned signal. Careful design allows coverage of a complete waveband by a single winding, tuning being achieved by the use of a variable capacitor (tuning capacitor). Two or more RF 'front-end' tuning coils with inductive or capacitive coupling are called **band pass** circuits and improve selectivity without noticeable loss of sensitivity whilst passing (amplifying) a band of frequencies. The ideal curve has a flat top (the pass band) with steep side rejection (the stop band). The use of band-pass tuning requires an extra tuning gang and many TRF designs of the 1930s will be found to have three-gang tuning capacitors.

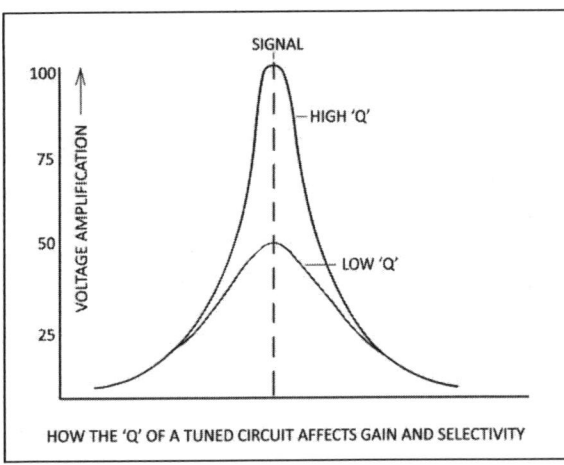
HOW THE 'Q' OF A TUNED CIRCUIT AFFECTS GAIN AND SELECTIVITY

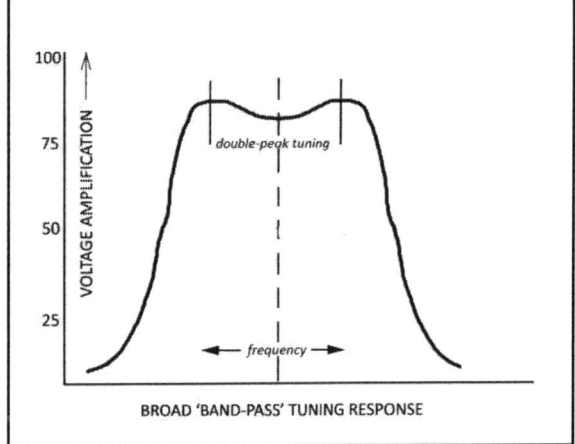
BROAD 'BAND-PASS' TUNING RESPONSE

'Q' factor

This is a term used to represent the ratio of the reactance of a given tuned circuit coil to its resistance. The greater the resistance to lower the 'Q'. An ideal tuned circuit would have no resistance but in practice this is unattainable. A high Q coil is capable of high selectivity because it can be peaked quite sharply by either careful positioning of a tuning slug within the coil core or adjustment of a parallel trimming capacitor.

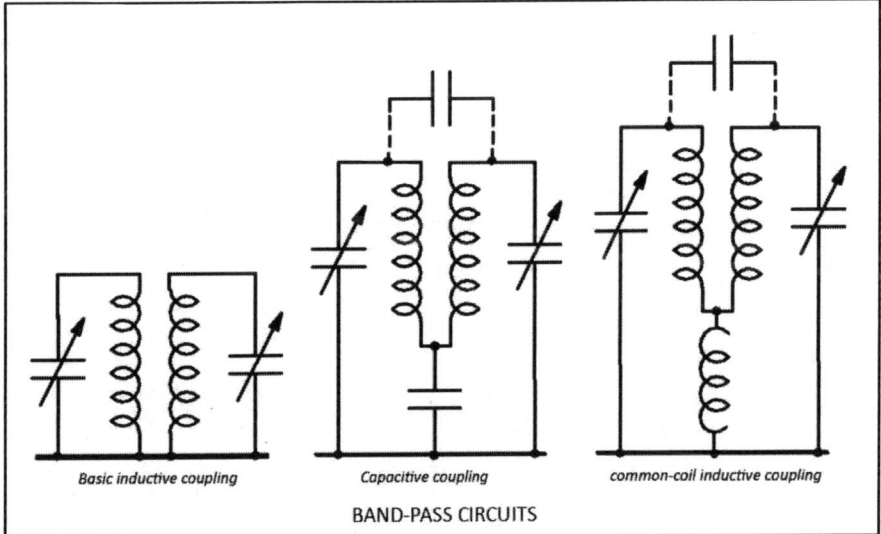
BAND-PASS CIRCUITS

Wound components in power supplies

At the much lower frequencies –and much greater power requirements – of mains power supplies, air is inadequate as a core material. Here, the use of a soft iron core, built up from thin laminations which are insulated from each other to limit losses due to excess heating of the iron, helps concentrate the magnetic flux.

The **LF Choke** is a single winding on laminated core and is used to help to filter ripple current after rectification of AC mains power as it offers low resistance to DC but a higher resistance to the AC ripple left after rectification from AC to DC by the diode. LF chokes look like output transformers but have only two connection terminals. The field coil in energized loudspeakers generally doubles as a choke.

The **Mains Transformer** only works with AC mains – remember, all transformers only work with alternating currents. Transformer action means that current flowing through the primary coil will induce a current to flow in the secondary coil even though there is no fixed (i.e. wired) electrical connection between the two. Changing the comparative number of the turns on the windings allows the voltages to be stepped up or down. The difference between the number of primary and secondary turns is called the **turns ratio.** It can also isolate radios from the mains, which tends to make them safer to work on.

The **Audio Output Transformer** is used to convert the voltage changes present at the anode of the sound output valve into a form suitable for the loudspeaker to handle. The primary winding becomes the anode load. These transformers often look like a smaller version of a mains transformer. There is a class of mains transformer that is called a heater transformer because they produce power only for the valve heaters: the HT is derived directly from the mains. These look like audio output transformers. Diagram on page 22. *See* glossary: impedance.

Tuning coils from an early 1930s TRF. Note the paper labels to aid subsequent identification

CHAPTER 3
INTRODUCTION TO VALVES

Before discussing the valve diode, let's take a look at the solid-state and metal-oxide types of diode, the symbol for which is shown here.

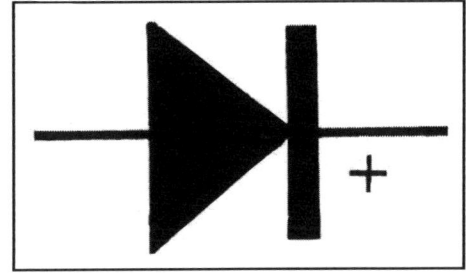

Solid-state devices have their origins in another very early invention, the cat's whisker or crystal diode, as used in crystal radio receivers from the early 1920s. The arrow on the symbol is the anode and the line is the cathode, the latter sometimes being marked positive or input.

The symbol is the same for all non thermionic (in other words, non valve) solid state diode devices, including the metal oxide rectifiers found in some sets. Current can flow in only one direction through the diode. Electrons flow from the cathode to the anode. This creates the current flow and is a basic property of all diodes.

Remember, current will flow in only one direction. Whenever the anode is positive with respect to the cathode or filament, the diode will conduct and current will flow from the cathode through any complete circuit back to the anode. Therefore in terms of electron flow, the cathode is input. In other words, electrons flow into the diode through the cathode connection. Often, in circuitry the 'plus' symbol is placed at the cathode of a diode.

This may seem puzzling, but it is easier if you remember that the arrow shape of the anode represents conventional current flow (which is positive) whereas electron flow, being the opposite of positive, is in the opposite direction. This is because the terms positive and negative were a means of describing the flow of electricity around a circuit, before a complete understanding of electron flow emerged.

Tiny, glass encapsulated diodes are called SIGNAL DIODES and are used for the DETECTION (also known as rectification or more commonly demodulation) of radio frequency signals. These are found in some radios, especially the early transistor radios where discrete transistors were used rather than microchips. The crystal diodes, as used in crystal sets of the 1920s, worked on exactly similar principles as point-contact solid state diodes and early transistor junctions. The symbol for these types of diode is therefore the same as the one for solid state types and also metal-oxide rectifiers, described below.

Many older valve radios use air cooled metal oxide rectifiers. These have large fins for efficient heat convection. A variation sometimes found is the contact cooled version where mounting directly to the metal chassis removes the need for cooling fins because the chassis acts as a heat sink. Where these devices are found to have failed, replacement by modern rectifier diodes is possible.
For power supplies in mains radios, diodes are combined with inductors in the form of chokes and/or transformers, and capacitors.

Basic facts: diodes and rectifiers
A diode is so called because it has two elements (connections, electrodes).
All diodes can pass an electric current in only one direction – from cathode to anode.
The arrow part of the diode symbol denotes 'conventional' current flow.
Metal rectifiers work by the contact of dissimilar metal oxides. The fins are there to dissipate heat.
Contact cooled rectifiers lose their heat through contact with a metal chassis.

Valve bases
4 and 5-pin based valves were common in the 1920s and 1930s. 7-pin bases came out in the early 1930s. Some valves were available in either base form, necessitating a base side connection for an output pentode in a 5-pin version. Side contact types were introduced in the earlier 1930s but were relatively short-lived, being superseded in the later 1930s by International Octal (American Octal) valves. For a time, there were a number of valves that were electrically identical on offer with either an IO or a side contact base, for example the side-contact based EBL1 detector/output valve is identical to the octal based EBL31. International Octal valves were very successful and were used throughout the wartime period and well after until they were replaced with the miniature bases such as the B8A and the all-glass B9A. Octal valves were favoured for home construction in the post-war years, especially where the simpler type of equipment designed for the improver was concerned, as the large 8-pin valve base with its central locating spigot made pin identification and wiring an easy task - and there were large quantities of war-surplus valves offered at reasonable prices.

The DIODE VALVE

Depending upon the type and intended function of the valve, there may be a number of other electrodes incorporated, to create the TRIODE, the TETRODE, the PENTODE and many other types. Before we describe these valves we'll take a look at the most basic precursor of all thermionic valves, the DIODE.

The diode valve (valve in UK, vacuum tube or simply tube in US) consists of an evacuated bulb, often tubular in shape and almost always glass, containing a metal anode (plate in US) and a cathode or filament which is thermionic. This means that it is coated with material that, when heated, produces a plentiful supply of electrons. This process is called Thermionic Emission. The diode valve, then, has an anode (plate in America) which is a metal plate, surrounding a cathode (or filament in a directly heated receiver). These electrodes are held within a vacuum, usually a glass casing. Probably the first type of thermionic diode was the vacuum tube attributed to Fleming.

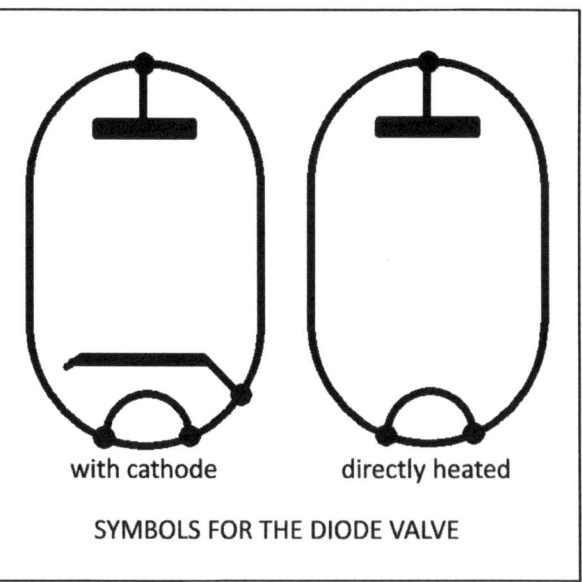

with cathode   directly heated

SYMBOLS FOR THE DIODE VALVE

Commonly used as rectifiers in 1930s receivers, early rectifier diodes were directly heated – no cathode. Later rectifier diodes were fitted with separate cathodes. This change had two advantages: 1, the valve warmed up at about the same rate as the other valves in a set, limiting the initially high voltage of the cathode-less type, and 2, the heater could be placed in series with the heaters of the other valves, i.e. in a heater chain. This method was used with AC/DC receivers and some AC only ones.

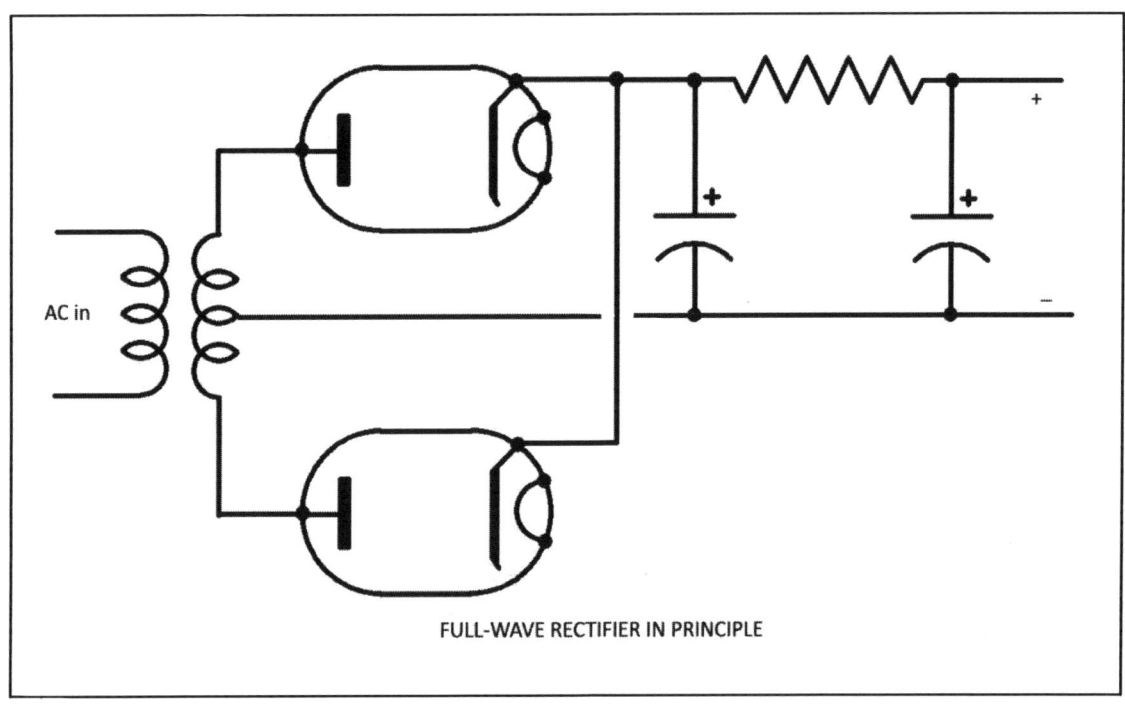

FULL-WAVE RECTIFIER IN PRINCIPLE

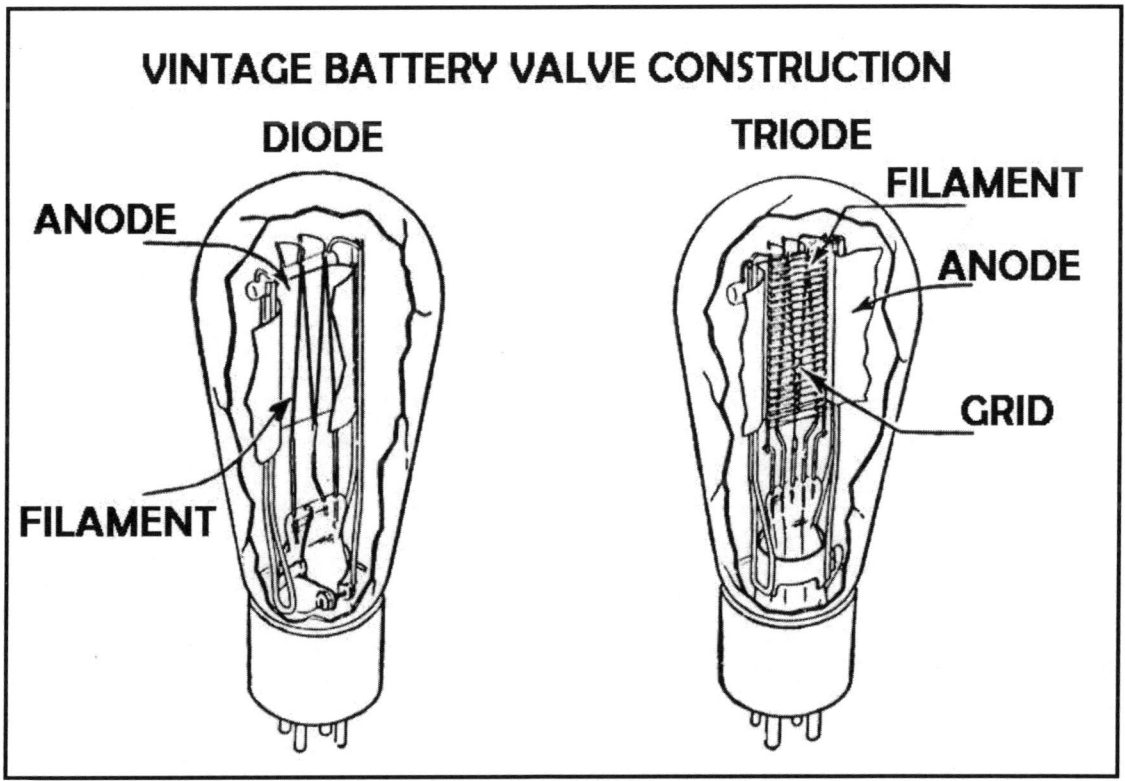

VINTAGE BATTERY VALVE CONSTRUCTION

Valves were so named due to the similarity of the device to a mechanical one way valve because they allowed an electric current to flow one way only, similar to the way the crystal diode or metal rectifier functions, though the mechanism used is a different one.

In the diagram (p. 27), two separate rectifier diodes are used together with a mains transformer with a centre-tapped secondary to create a full-wave rectification system. Each diode conducts alternately, on every half-cycle of the AC mains. The output at the filaments supplies 100Hz pulses of DC into the reservoir capacitor which acts as a short-term store. The smoothing choke and the smoothing capacitor combine to filter out remaining AC ripple to produce a level DC. In practice the two diodes would be combined in a single valve and in lower-cost sets the choke would be replaced by a resistor (see pp.36 and 37).

Let's consider how the valve works in a little more detail.
If a current is allowed to flow through the filament of a valve, the heating of the filament releases electrons which form a cloud called the space charge in the vacuum around the filament.
When the anode is connected to a high positive voltage source, the electrons are attracted to the anode, creating a current flow (flow of electrons) between the filament and the anode.

Valves with a cathode require a warm-up time because the cathode has to reach operating temperature. The cathode is heated by the heater winding, a filament of wire which is encased within the cathode. Valve types without cathodes (i.e. directly heated) almost instantly conduct when power is switched on, because there is no cathode to heat up, which would cause a time delay. Such valves are found in battery operated radios and sometimes as output valves in very early mains receivers, also as rectifiers.

The diode cannot amplify, but its unidirectional action makes it useful for power rectification (AC into DC), for signal detection – demodulation – and Automatic Volume Control (AVC, known now as Automatic Gain Control – AGC).

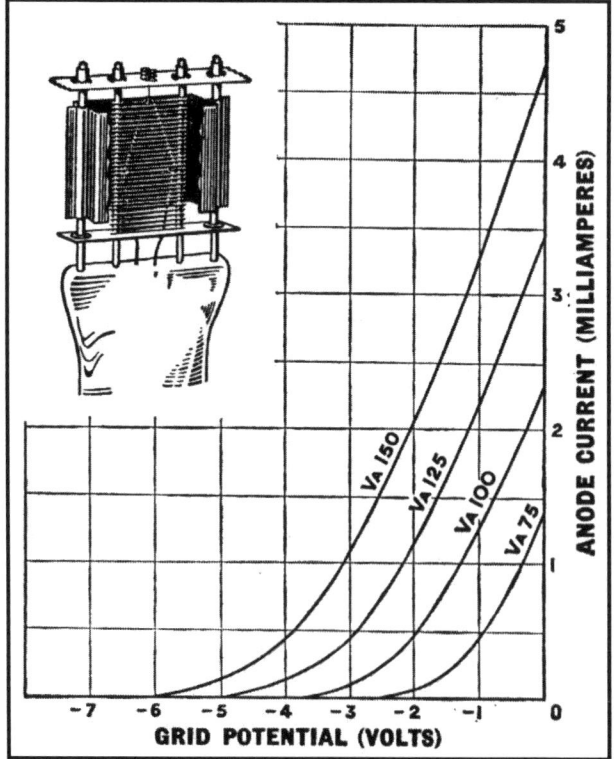

The functions of demodulation and AGC voltage derivation are usually carried out by diode anodes incorporated into other valves, creating multiple valves within a single envelope, though many early radios did use separate diode valves for the purpose.

The TRIODE VALVE

The TRIODE valve has a spiral of metal wire called a GRID. The grid surrounds the filament (in a directly heated valve) or the cathode (in an indirectly heated valve) and is in turn surrounded by the metal cylinder of the anode. This places the grid between the source of electrons – the cathode – and the collector of electrons, the anode.

The grid is a fine, open winding of wire and it has virtually no effect upon the current between cathode or filament and anode, so electric current flows unhindered through its wires. Until, that is, a negative voltage is supplied to the grid connection. As this potential rises negatively the electrons leaving the cathode are increasingly repelled causing the flow of current through the valve to reduce until finally it stops. This is called the 'cut off' point.

The explanation for this effect is as follows: Electrons released from the cathode due to thermionic emission exist in a cloud in the space surrounding the cathode. This you will recall is known as the space charge. When they are attracted to a positive potential on the anode, they will create a current flow.

Because the grid is placed between the cathode and anode, a negative potential on the grid will repulse them. If the valve construction is such that the grid is close to the cathode, even a modest negative potential will have a marked effect upon current flow, causing some or all repulsed electrons to stay within or return to the electron cloud around the cathode or filament. The graph on the previous page shows a 'family' of traces with changing anode and grid voltage. The higher the anode voltage, the greater is the current through the valve, thereby increasing valve amplification.

The triode valve was the earliest thermionic amplifying device. Thermionic is in principle the term given to any device where a surface is heated to give off electrons. In practice, however, the term is usually restricted to the action of vacuum tubes – valves.

Basic Triode Amplifier Circuits

In the simple circuit shown here an AF signal of small voltage range is applied to the grid as an input. The changing potential of the signal modulates the flow of electrons passing from the cathode through the grid wires (represented by the broken horizontal line) to the anode. This results in a varying current passing through the anode load resistor Ra. Due to the action of the load resistor, the continuous changes in this current produce a voltage at the anode which varies in sympathy with the grid signal. The grid signal may change in the order of a few volts but the resultant voltage changes across the anode resistor will be far greater. This enlarging process is called amplification.

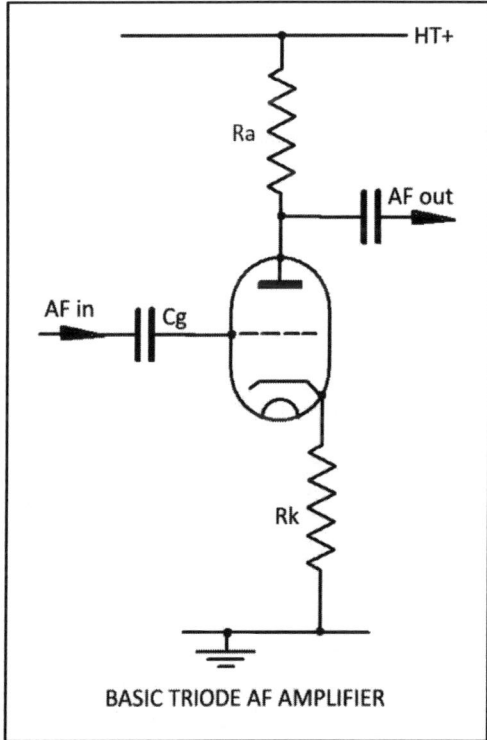

BASIC TRIODE AF AMPLIFIER

The choice of value of anode load resistor is important. Too large a value and the anode will 'bottom out', preventing the valve from passing sufficient current to amplify the peaks of the grid AF signal. This will result in severe signal distortion. Too small a value will cause insufficient voltage swing at the anode. The result of this will be too low a level of amplification. The grid, like all grids, needs to be biased slightly negative with respect to the cathode. A low voltage battery could have been used to provide the negative potential (grid bias), the level of which again is critical for correct operation of the valve but in this circuit, the cathode resistor Rk is passing current and is therefore positive at the cathode with respect to ground, so there is a small voltage drop across it. (See below) Control grids must always be negative with respect to the cathode or the life of the valve will be greatly limited.

The cathode resistor bias method is known as auto bias and is usual in mains powered receivers but not in all early battery receivers, where a special tapped GB battery may be employed. The valve shown in the diagram below is a pentode, which means that it has five active electrodes. You will recall that the grid needs to be negative with respect to the cathode. This can be accomplished by making the cathode positive with respect to the grid.

This is how it works. The current passing through the valve must also pass through the cathode resistor. If you think of the fully conducting valve as a low-value resistor (which when fully conducting in effect it is), then if you ignore it's resistive effect and assume it is a short-circuit you can then see that we have in effect two resistors in series – the cathode resistor R2 and the anode resistor R4, making a potential divider. (Refer back to resistors if you are not sure). A positive voltage is present at the junction of the two resistors (i.e. the anode), the level of which is determined by the *comparative* value of each resistor. The actual values must be chosen to suit the current capabilities of the valve.

As the valve only needs a low level of bias voltage, the cathode resistor is invariably only a few hundred ohms or so compared to the much higher typical values of the anode load resistor.

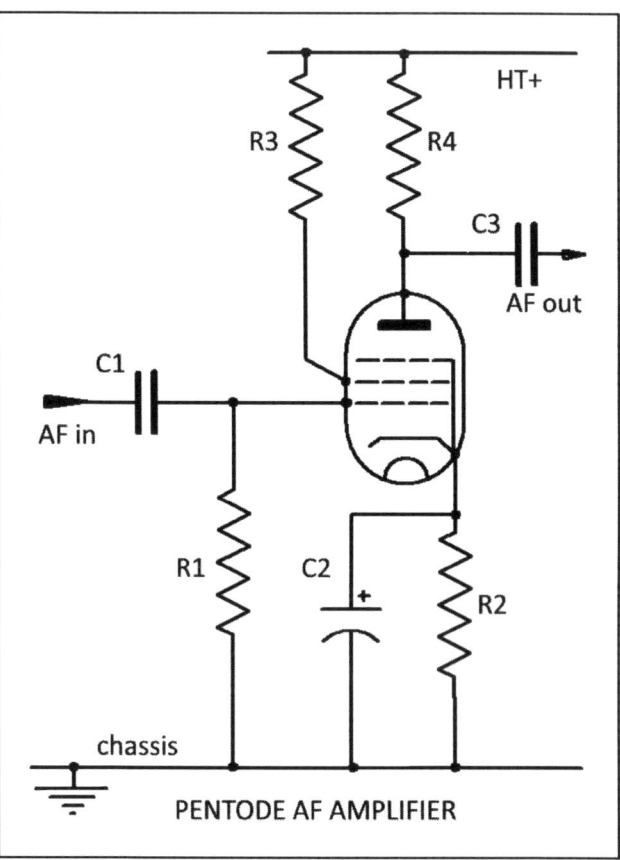

PENTODE AF AMPLIFIER

You will note the presence of a capacitor, C2, connected across the cathode resistor. This is, in AF amplifier circuits, usually an electrolytic type, often 10 – 25 microFarads. It is needed because the current through the valve is not steady, but fluctuating as it follows the grid signal. Without the capacitor, the cathode voltage produced across the cathode resistor would also fluctuate in time with (follow) the grid signal, causing a loss of amplification. This effect is one of the forms of negative feedback and it can be a good thing, minimising distortion and keeping circuits 'stable' and free from unwanted oscillation, but in correctly designed circuits, the capacitor is best left in place.

If you are wondering why the pentode and other valves have more grids than the triode or why, for that matter, pentodes are needed at all, the reason is that the triode suffers from inter-electrode capacitance. Because the electrodes within the valve envelope – grid, cathode, anode – are conductors and because they are separated by a vacuum which acts for much of the time as an insulating medium (dielectric), it is as though the triode valve has built in capacitors. The effect of these virtual 'capacitors' is less of a problem when the valve is used at low frequencies as an AF amplifier but as the frequency of the amplified signal rises, they act more and more as by-pass components and effectively place a limit on the signal frequency range that can be amplified. This phenomenon is known as the Miller effect, named after the American physicist J. M. Miller, who discovered it.

Basic facts. Directly heated valves do not have cathodes. Their filament supplies the electrons for conduction within the valve.

Directly heated diodes are found as HT rectifiers in some early mains receivers.

Directly heated valves are found in battery sets that use DC for filament supplies.

Some early sets used directly heated output valves (no cathode) and supplied the filaments of these with AC. Hum caused by this was minimised by the use of a centre-tapped transformer winding, allowing cancellation of the hum. This was assisted by the use of a 'hum bucking' adjustable resistor across the winding.

Indirectly heated valves have a cathode between the filament – now called a heater – and the control grid. These valves are designed to work using AC heater supplies.

The heater heats up the cathode until it begins to emit electrons to form a so-called 'space charge' – a cloud of free electrons in the space between cathode and anode (the warm-up period experienced with indirectly heated valves).

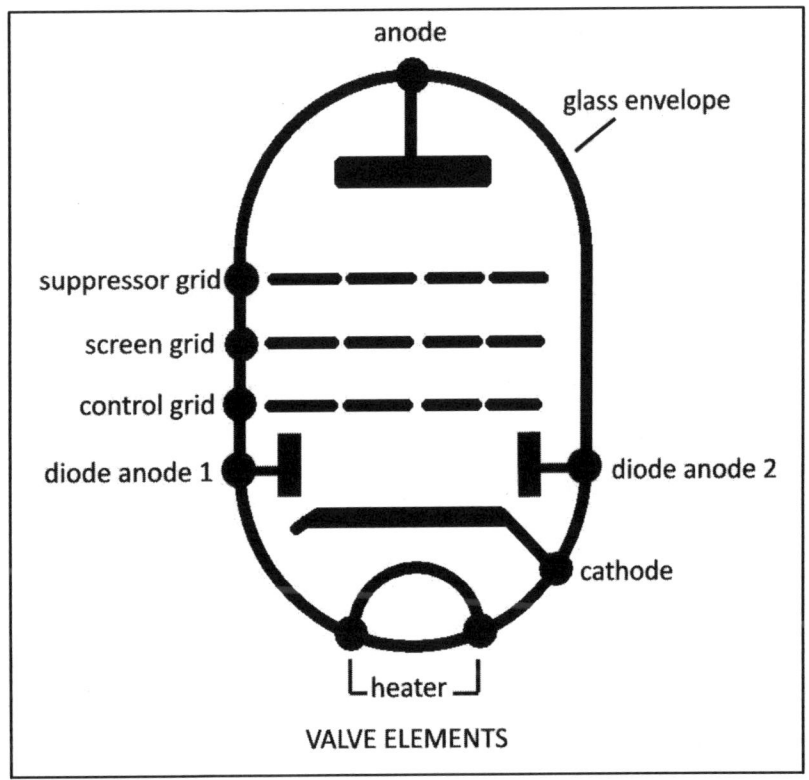

Valves come in a wide range of types, often double or triple valves in one envelope. A common multiple valve, a double-diode-pentode, is shown here

The TETRODE VALVE

It is possible to overcome the problems of the triode to some extent by elaborate external circuitry, but the addition of a screen grid creates, in effect, two separate and electrically isolated capacitors, allowing greater gain and better stability.

Tetrode means four-element valve. Four active elements, that is; two grids, one cathode (or filament) and one anode. This valve, then, has one more grid than the triode. The additional grid is called the screen and is fitted *between* the control grid and the anode. This additional grid is designed to overcome certain deficiencies present in the triode. As detailed above, internal capacitance within the triode limits the gain of the valve, especially at radio frequencies, due to the Miller effect. This places a limit on the range of frequencies that can be amplified by a triode and also causes instability – oscillation – at high levels of gain. It's worth noting here that the reason many valves designed for use at radio frequencies have top caps for either control grid or anode connection is to minimise the capacitance between the internal connections of these two electrodes.

Alternatively, the screen can be made long enough to screen even the base wire connections within the valve envelope.

A very common use for the tetrode is as an AF output valve. Here is shown a typical (simplified) single-ended output stage circuit using a 6V6 beam tetrode valve. This is a famous octal-based output valve and uses beam forming plates between the screen and the anode to concentrate the electron beam. Tetrodes were developed to bypass patents held by Philips on pentode (see below) valves but in certain respects, tetrodes are the equal of and possibly superior to pentodes.

The term single-ended (class A) refers to the fact that only one valve is used for the stage. Push-pull output (class AB or class B) stages use two valves.

Single and double output stages
Class A: the valve is set up to work under conditions of minimum harmonic distortion. This is brought about by the biasing circuitry. Normally, the control grid should be negative with respect to the cathode (or filament). When the grid is at zero volts, maximum gain occurs. When it is at a certain negative potential, amplification ceases and the valve is said to be **cut off**. This can be plotted as a curve, showing grid voltage against anode current.

SINGLE-ENDED TETRODE AF OUTPUT STAGE showing typical component values

Under class 'A' conditions, the circuit is set up in such a way as to bias the grid at the centre point of this curve. This arrangement is used as a standard for single-valve output stages. It is important that control grids should never be allowed to run much into positive voltage or the grid will act as an anode (grid current) with a potentially disastrous outcome for the valve and possibly associated components.

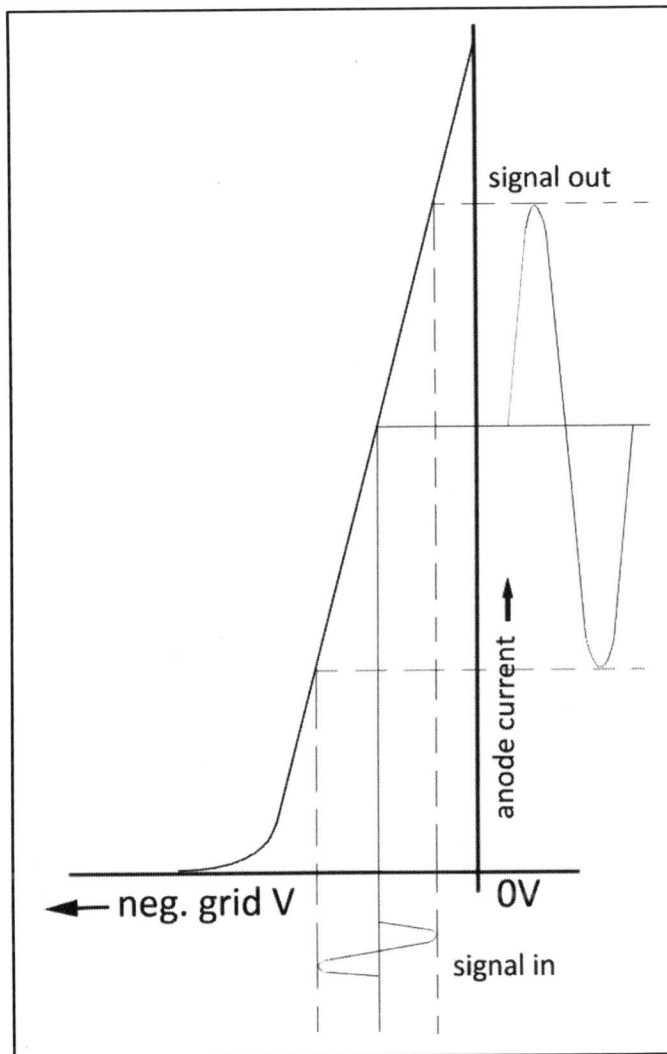

The bias points of class 'A' valves are set so as to centre the input signal – shown at the bottom of the diagram – with the straight portion of the valve's curve. The dotted lines represent the signal swing. It will be seen that a much larger input signal will cause amplification across the non-linear part of the valve curve (at the bottom of the curve) and the valve will reach its maximum (bottom out) at the top of the curve, once the maximum anode current is approached. Severe distortion is the result of overdriving or incorrect setting of the bias voltage on the grid.

Class 'A' curve

Class AB circuitry is set to move the bias point toward the negative end of the slope. This introduces considerable distortion, as does class B operation, where the bias point is fixed as the cut-off point. A moment's thought will show that under class B conditions, only the positive-going half-cycles of AF signal will be amplified – hence the severe audio distortion. Class AB is not quite as bad, but still severely distorted as the negative half-cycles are severely crushed.

It follows that neither class B or class AB are suitable for use with a single valve output stage. Instead, they are used with two valves, each supplied by a valve circuit called a phase splitter. This circuit supplies one of the valves with the positive-going AF half cycles and the other with an inverted version of the negative-going AF half cycles. The inversion process converts negative to positive, allowing each valve to fully amplify its own half of the signal.

The point at which one valve takes over from the other is called the crossover point and unless bias points and component values are chosen with care, this can result in distortion. Class AB provides close to four times, and class B provides in excess of four times, the power output of a single ended circuit.

Although some quality radio receivers use such push pull circuitry, it is found more commonly in Hi-Fi amplifiers and quality radiograms. There is quite a lot more involved in these output stages and it is well worth seeking further information for those interested.

The PENTODE VALVE

Although the tetrode has the advantages stated, it also has a 'kink' in its gain if the screen voltage rises to a point approaching that of the anode. This is caused by the phenomenon of secondary emission, which occurs when electrons bounce off the anode and are collected by the positive potential on the screen. This in turn means that great care has to be exercised by the designer to ensure that at all times the anode potential is substantially higher than that of the screen grid.

This fact limits the usefulness of the valve and superior results can be obtained by the addition of a third grid, making the valve a pentode, or five – element valve. This third grid is called the suppressor grid and it may be internally or externally connected to the cathode and is therefore at or about zero potential. Placed between the screen and the anode, it prevents secondary electrons by slight repulsion whilst still allowing the rapidly moving primary electrons access to the anode.

It might seem from the foregoing that the pentode was at all times superior to the tetrode but things are not quite so straightforward. It should be remembered that during the heyday of the valve continuous development occurred, especially during the period 1930-1938. A 'kinkless' tetrode was developed by increasing the physical distance between the screen and the anode. This minimised secondary emission and allowed the tetrode to work almost as efficiently as the pentode in some circumstances.

Another variant is the beam tetrode. This works by the use of beam-forming plates that focus the flow of electrons onto the anode. A very popular example of this type of tetrode is the 6V6. Beam tetrodes are often found in power output stages where their gain can rival that of the power output pentode. The pentode valve can be found operating as an AF or IF amplifier and AF output.

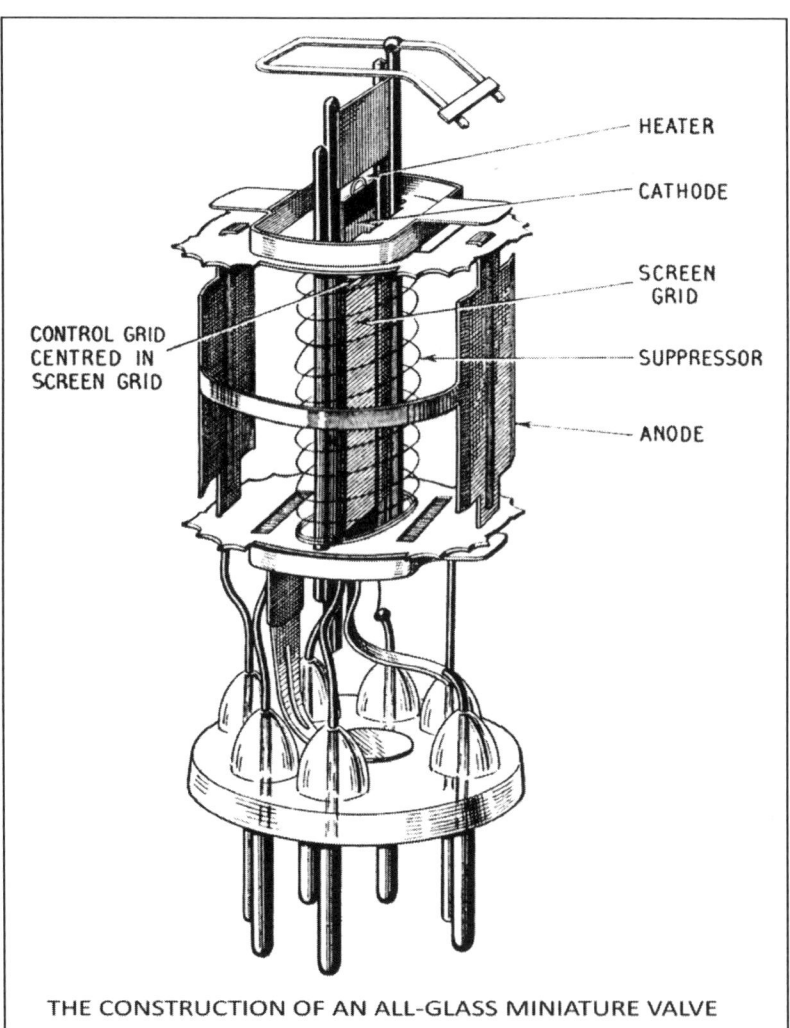

THE CONSTRUCTION OF AN ALL-GLASS MINIATURE VALVE

When miniature all-glass valves were developed, a problem that had to be solved before successful production was how to ensure a permanently air-tight seal around the valve pins. It was known that that heat transfer down the pin would break the seal, allowing in air and destroying the valve. The answer was a clever combination of glass (Pyrex) and special pin construction using multi-alloys.

MORE ON RECTIFIER VALVE CIRCUITS

The purpose of any diode is rectification – the conversion of an alternating current into a direct current, but the term is reserved for high voltage circuitry. The terms 'detection' or 'demodulation' are generally applied to signal-voltage diodes.

The valve rectifier is to be found in the majority of vintage radios, probably because it was more efficient than the alternative copper oxide and similar solid-state rectifying devices then available. The receiving valves of all radios work from DC and sets designed to work from AC mains supplies always have a means of converting the AC into DC.

Rectifying valves may be half or full wave, i.e. with one or two anodes, and either indirectly heated (with a cathode) or directly heated (with a filament). In full-wave sets, an isolating mains transformer is usually fitted with a separate heater supply for the rectifier. In half-wave AC/DC sets where no transformer can be used, the rectifier – which must be indirectly heated i.e. possess a cathode - is supplied from the same tapping point as the receiving valves, forming a series chain. There are numerous variations on the basic principle but in the end they all perform much the same task. We will now examine some standard rectification circuits.

Half-wave rectifier

This is perhaps the simplest form of rectification and consists of a single diode rectifier which only conducts on the forward (positive-going) cycle of the applied AC wave. It can therefore only pass half of each alternating cycle whenever the anode is positive with respect to the cathode. The negative half-cycle simply cuts the valve off and that half is effectively lost.

Each positive half-cycle therefore produces a pulse of voltage across the reservoir capacitor C1. The pulse is at the frequency of the AC mains: in Britain this is 50Hz.

Two problems exist with this system. One, though it is economical in terms of components, and basically very simple in design, it is unfortunately wasteful of power, and two, due to the pronounced 50 Hz ripple caused by the pulsing nature of the rectification, it is inherently difficult to smooth adequately.

Half-wave rectification, optional for AC only receivers, is standard for AC/DC receivers as DC will simply pass straight through the valve. There are 'live chassis' sets that use series heaters and half-wave rectifiers but with heaters supplied via transformers or HT by autotransformers, making them AC only.

Note the separate cathode in the diagram on page 36, which isolates the heater from the rectified HT. Many rectifier valves designed for use in AC only receivers have one end of their cathode connected to the heater, making them unsuitable for use in series heater chains. Notice too that the rectifier heater (V5) is placed at the top of the heater chain, where the least potential difference limits heater-cathode strain on the valve. With the diagram shown here, the power for the valve heaters is supplied from a tapping on the single secondary winding and the valve heaters are wired in series.

As stated previously, it is more usual for a separate low-voltage winding to be used, with the valve heaters in parallel.

Rectifier valves allow only current in one direction but that current is far from steady as the polarity of the mains supply changes (alternates) fifty times every second (50Hz), hence the term Alternating Current (AC), and the rectified output from the valve anode follows this, producing pulses of power with gaps where the negative-going half cycles were before rectification. This means that the *average* voltage output is far lower that the 'mean' mains input so, even though the current flow is unidirectional due to rectification, these rapid pulses of voltage and current cycle from zero to peak and back to zero then stay at zero until the next cycle rises. As this happens 50 times per second it is obvious that the rectified output requires further processing before a sufficiently smooth DC supply can be obtained at the high voltages usually required for valve operation.

What is needed is some way of filling in the gaps where the 'lost' negative half-cycles were. This is achieved by the use of the reservoir capacitor C2, which charges up at the peak of the positive-going pulse and releases power during the gaps. We now have a higher voltage but still with considerable AC ripple superimposed upon it so further filtering, using a resistor (R1) and a second capacitor C1, called a smoothing capacitor, smoothes and removes all but a slight residual ripple which manifests itself as audible hum from the loudspeaker. The resistor-capacitor combination is known as a 'time constant' circuit.

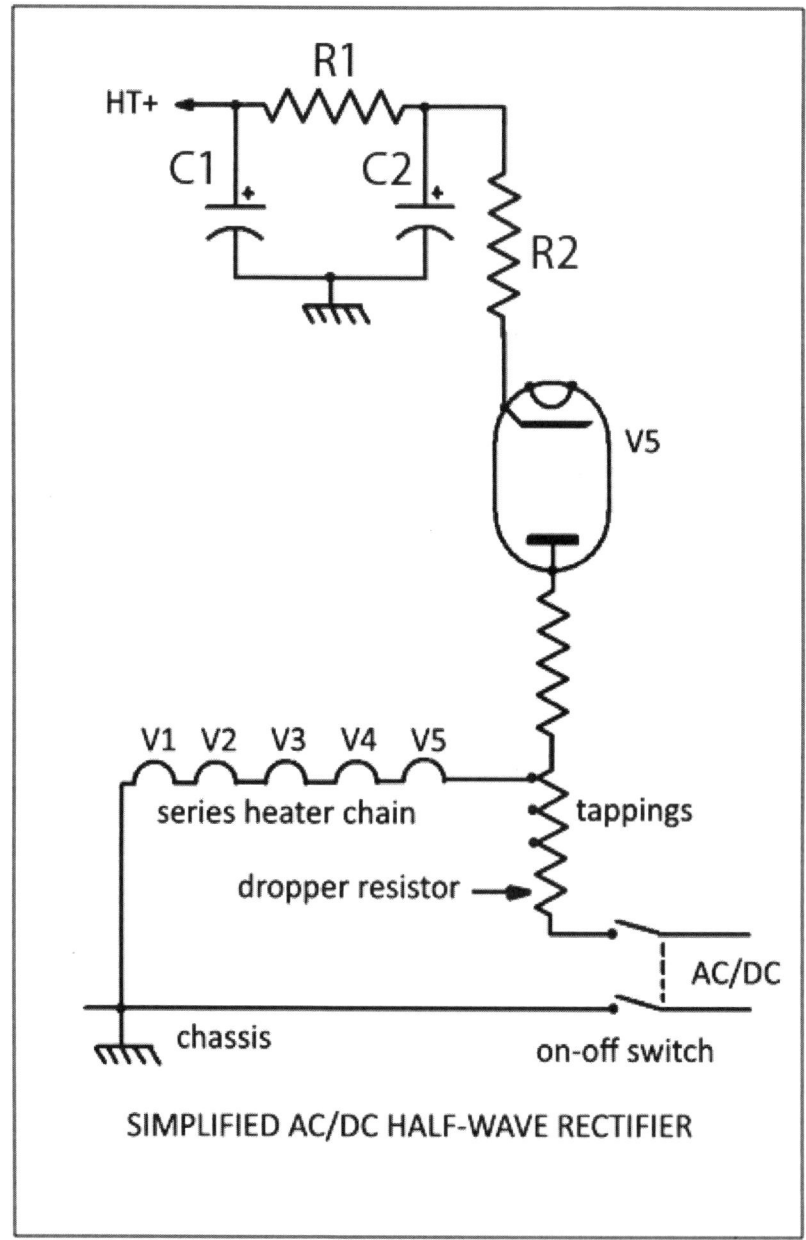

SIMPLIFIED AC/DC HALF-WAVE RECTIFIER

A rather more efficient – but bulkier and costlier - alternative to a resistor for smoothing is a choke.

The choke is an inductance, which offers high resistance to AC but low resistance to DC. Despite this, for reasons of economy and space a high-wattage resistor is often used instead. The resistor (R1 in the diagram) works in much the same way as a choke but is rather wasteful of power

The mains dropper is a large wire-wound component. The tapping points on the dropper resistor allow the selection of differing mains voltages. Resistor R2 in the circuit on page 36 is a series limiter to protect the rectifier valve by increasing rectifier impedance.

Full-wave rectifier

Here we have two diode valves or, in practice one valve 'envelope' containing two diode anodes and a common cathode (V5 in the diagram on p. 36) this time fed by a tapped transformer. Because transformers need alternating current, this circuit can only work on AC supplies. Due to the zero-volts centre-tap on the transformer the anode potentials of each valve alternate at 100Hz, resulting in energy being delivered to the load at twice the rate of the half wave rectifier circuit. No 'lost' half-waves of power with this circuit. A resistor is again shown taking the place of a choke or a loudspeaker field winding but in practice any one of these alternatives may be found.

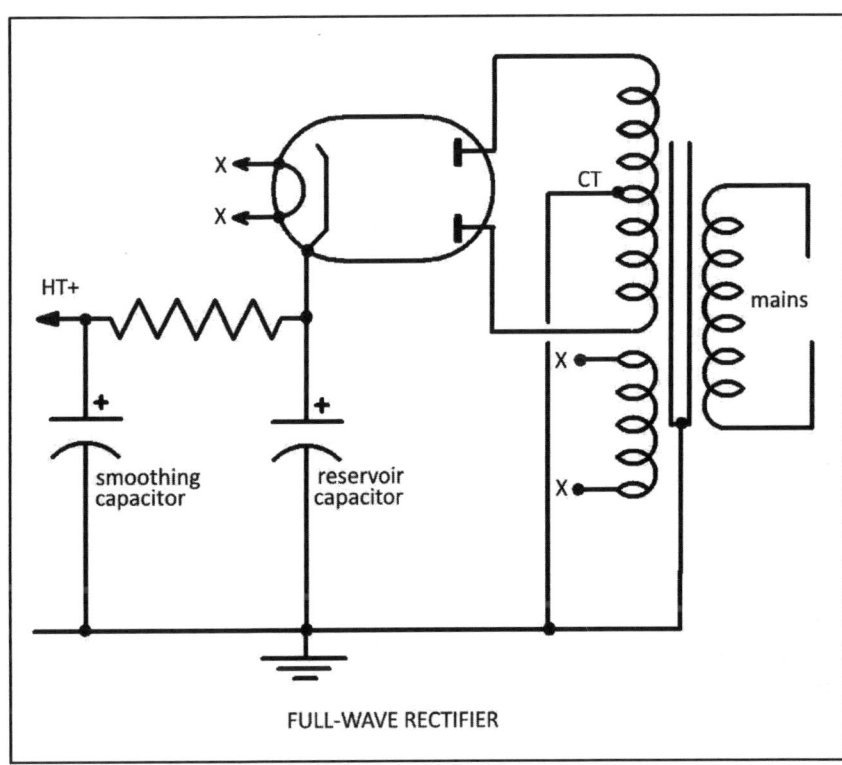

FULL-WAVE RECTIFIER

Also, each diode carries only half the total current. 100Hz is easier to filter and smooth, resulting in less hum which is of a higher frequency, making a more efficient circuit, in fact, than the simpler half-wave type.

Another important advantage lies in the ability of the transformer to step up the voltage from the mean mains level. To work at their optimum, valves designed for AC operation can sometimes require high HT potentials of 300V or more.

Metal rectifiers in radio receivers

In theory, there is nothing to stop metal oxide rectifiers being used instead of valve types, and in fact some manufacturers – Pye and Ekco for example - used them quite often in the early 1930s. They make an economic substitute for a valve rectifier as there is no requirement for heater supplies but being metal, rather resistive and operating at high voltages, the devices did generate heat and required some means of cooling. The diodes took two general forms; there was the contact cooled type which was bolted to the metalwork of the chassis and used the metal as a means of 'sinking' the heat by distributing it to the chassis' large surface area.

VINTAGE VALVE RADIOS

These are often found in small so called 'universal' sets, some of which were designed to be semi-portable form and operable from either battery or mains power.

The other form is the finned variety of rectifier, where large metal fins are attached to the central core of the device and act as air-cooling 'radiator' heat sinks. It is important with these rectifiers to ensure that free air can circulate around them and to mount them so the fins are vertical (heat rises). Not all manufacturers took these precautions to heart, however.

POWER SUPPLIES: GENERAL POINTS

AC only receivers are sets defined as being able to operate ONLY from an AC mains source. AC mains are standard throughout Britain today but in the earlier days of radio there still existed large areas served by DC mains – and others where no mains of any type was available. This led to the need for sets that would work from DC only or from both AC and DC, plus battery operated types. DC only sets were in the minority and were produced during the late 1920s and very early 1930s. The AC/DC receiver was far more prevalent as it was less expensive to manufacture than those for AC only due to the use of a dropper resistor rather than a transformer.

The dropper resistor lowered the voltage to a level suitable for the valve heaters, which were all of the same current consumption and wired in series (though their heater voltages can differ considerably). Yet another alternative – though for AC only – is to use an autotransformer, which is a single coil winding with a tapping at the heater voltage point. This is not a true transformer. There is no protection against shock as it does not isolate the chassis from the 'raw' mains.

The back view of two wartime civilian receivers, showing the newly-made back panel Of 4mm MDF and label (right) compared with an original (left)

CHAPTER 4
CIRCUITS IN PRINCIPLE

Amplitude modulation is the transmission system for all British receivers made prior to 1954. In very simple terms, an AM radio transmitter consists of a high power sine-wave AC generator producing continuous waves at the pre-determined transmission frequency. An aerial circuit connected to the output of this generator causes the emission of radio waves into the air (or space). Superimposed upon and modulating the amplitude (height) of this so-called 'carrier' wave is the low-frequency audio signal.

The task of a receiver, whether of the superheterodyne (superhet) or Tuned Radio Frequency (TRF) type, is to, select, amplify and separate the audio signal from the carrier. In the most basic form, selection is achieved by using a tuned circuit consisting of a coil and a variable capacitor to select (tune into) the required transmission frequency whilst rejecting all others.

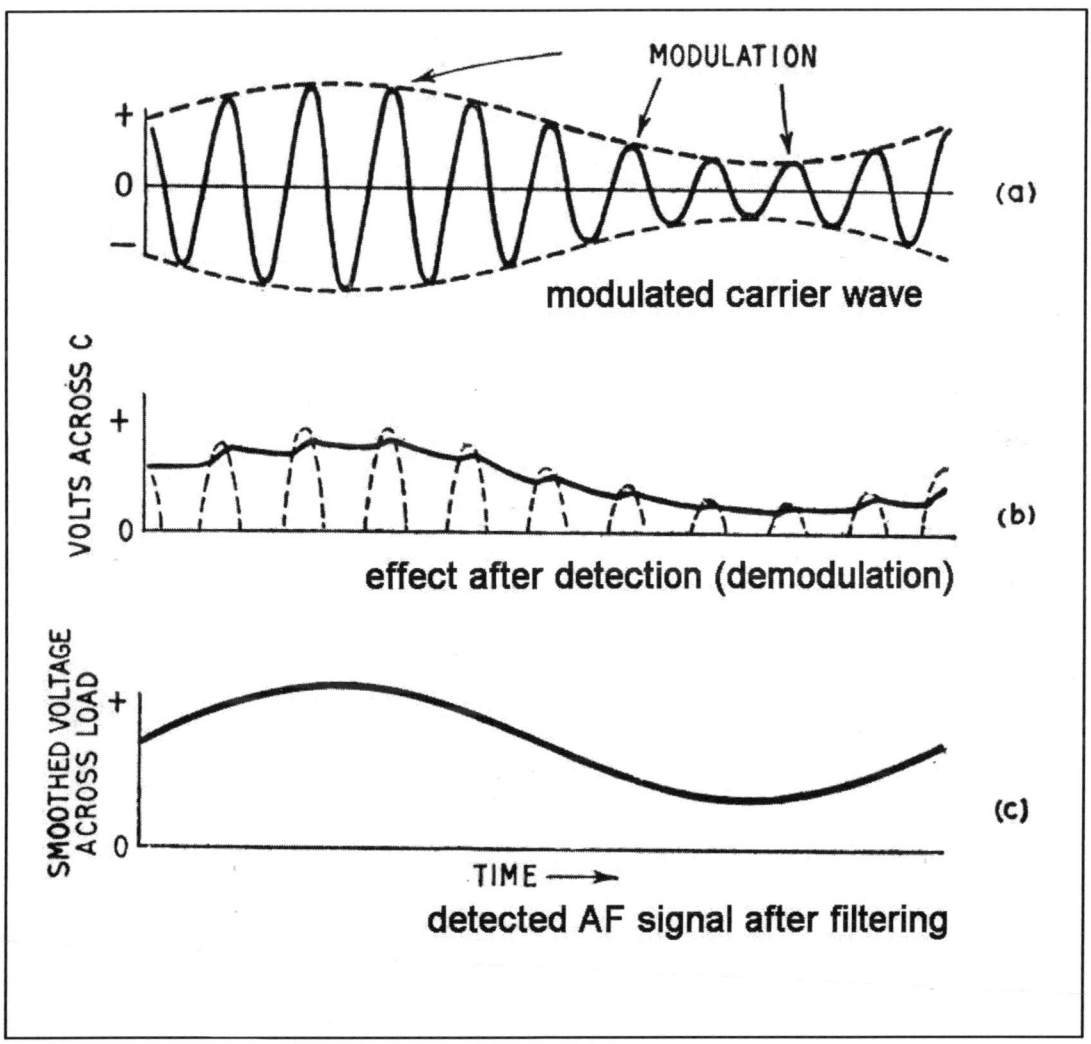

VINTAGE VALVE RADIOS

To achieve this, tuning coils have parallel capacitors to form tuned circuits. Capacitive reactance falls as the frequency rises. Inductive reactance rises as the frequency rises. The falling reactance of the capacitor meets the rising reactance of the inductor at a frequency determined by the values of both. This coincident point is highly resistive and the circuit resonates, boosting any transmitted signal at that frequency. In practice two or more tuned circuits are necessary to obtain sufficient sensitivity.

A signal such as the modulated carrier wave shown in (a) in the diagram on p.39 could be seen using an oscilloscope monitoring the RF section of a receiver tuned in to a transmission on long, medium or short waves.

The purpose of amplification

The signals as received by the aerial are extremely small and amplification is needed before the process of detection can be carried out efficiently. The crystal sets of old had no amplification and simply detected the tiny aerial signals, which is why they needed a highly efficient aerial and earth system. After detection by crystal, valve amplification could be used to boost the signal to loudspeaker level. No crystal set could operate a loudspeaker unaided and because they had a single tuned circuit (with variations) they were woefully unselective, allowing several stations to be received at the same time. This major drawback led to their demise in the UK in the later 1920s when new BBC transmitters drowned out some of the other stations for many crystal set listeners.

This led to an enforced obsolescence for crystal receivers. In any case, as radio 'came of age', the rapid improvements in valve design and manufacture began to create ever greater interest and more and more people bought valve radios. Valves could amplify and this allowed the use of two or more tuned circuits, providing a great improvement in sensitivity and selectivity compared to the crystal receiver.

Tuned Radio Frequency (TRF) sets used two or three tuned circuits, each of which was fully adjustable over the band required; medium, long or short wave. Each tuned circuit required a variable capacitor and early sets had something of the appearance of a scientific instrument rather than a household entertainment device. To avoid the need for two or three separate knobs – and to simplify the operation of the radio – 'ganged' capacitors were designed. These were two or three (or even more, occasionally) variable capacitors operated by a single spindle. This in turn led to extra 'trimming' components to compensate for variations in components and wiring and to allow the alignment of the tuned circuits for optimum results. These components are usually in the form of compression-variable capacitors, known in fact as trimmers, or occasionally a fixed small-value capacitor.

Superhet sets converted the received signal to a fixed Intermediate Frequency (I.F.) and it was this fixed frequency that was amplified, making the sets more sensitive and stable compared with a TRF. More on this topic over the following pages.

Detection of signal

In order to hear the original audio-frequency sound, the low-frequency sound variations that modulate the high frequency (RF) carrier wave require demodulating, or detecting. This is a process of rectification which converts the alternating wave into a unidirectional form by removing one-half of the carrier wave, and also separates the audio variations from the carrier. This can be seen at (b) on p. 39 and again at (c) where filtering components have removed the remnants of the original RF carrier wave to leave a clean positive-going audio signal: a voltage level that varies with the audio content.

Because of the Miller effect and other limitations with the triode design, the triode valve is less than ideal for use in the RF sections of a radio receiver and other more complex valves are often used for better results. In fact, if triodes are used as RF amplifiers, the stage gain must be kept relatively low and careful design employed to prevent the tendency the triode has of becoming unstable - bursting into oscillation.

Nevertheless, many early designs of home-built TRF radios used the triode as a combined RF amplifier and detector. The main forms employed were Leaky Grid detection, Anode Bend detection and Power Grid detection.

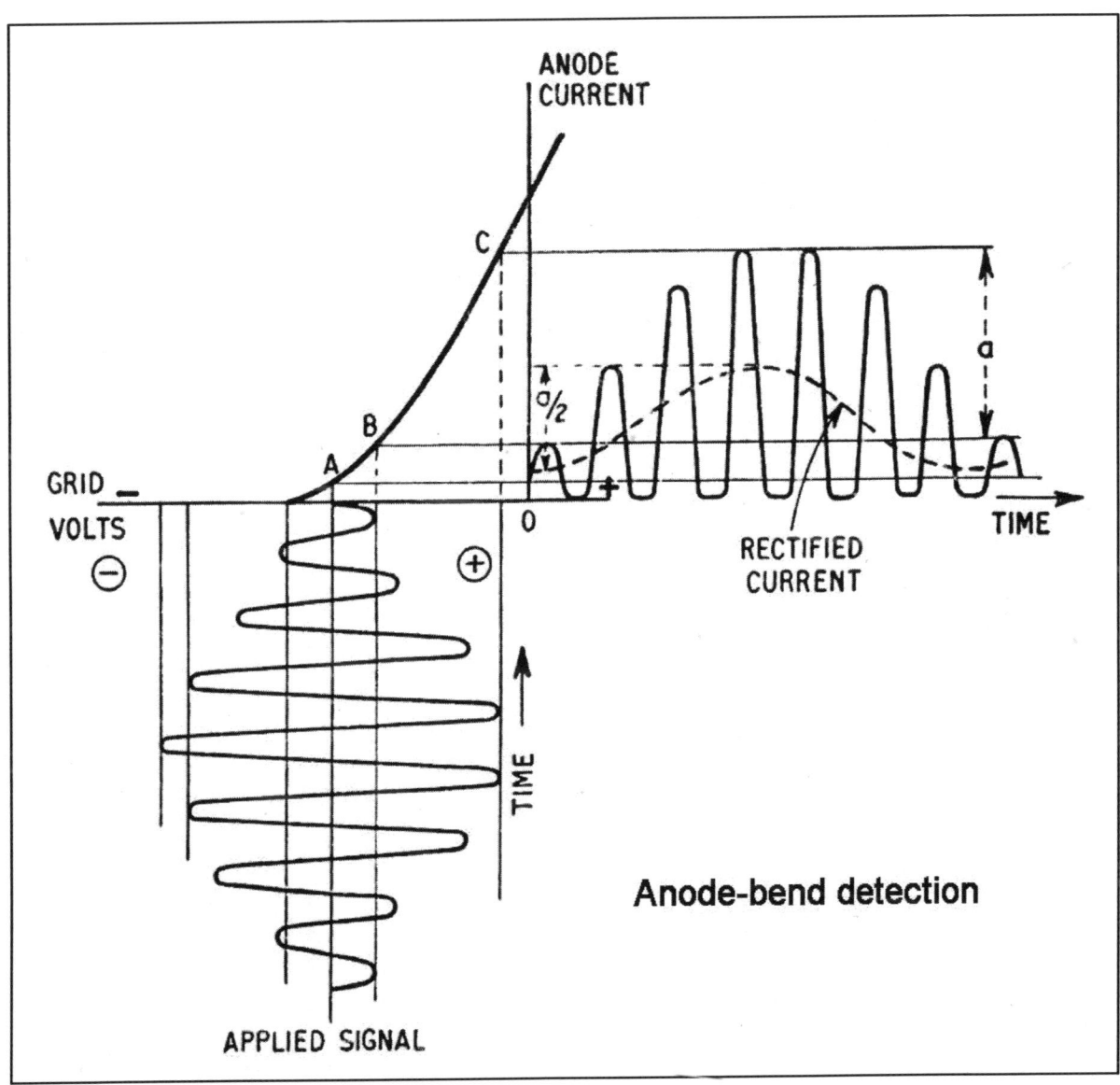

Anode-bend detection

Anode bend detection works by selecting the values of the circuit components that set the grid bias negative potential so as to bring the central point of the applied signal to a position such as 'A' in the diagram on p. 41. Provided the input signal is strong, positive-going cycles are amplified normally, but negative-going signals are 'crushed' out of existence.

The main drawback to anode-bend detection is the need for a large input signal to prevent unacceptable levels of distortion. In practice the circuit is obviously better than detection by diode alone as amplification is also provided, which no diode can provide. Anode-bend detectors must have negative grid bias in order to function. This is usually provided in mains sets by a cathode resistor with a bypass capacitor. Otherwise similar in appearance to a leaky-grid detector, the component values differ and the grid coupling capacitor may not be present. The circuit is sometimes found in early superhets.

The leaky grid detector offers greater sensitivity and was used extensively in the TRF days. It is shown in the diagram below. The capacitor C1 and the grid leak resistor form a time-constant circuit. The time-constant is the length of time a capacitor needs in order to charge up to approximately two thirds of its maximum value when a steady voltage is applied to a series resistor/capacitor network. Capacitors charge and discharge exponentially and in theory takes an infinite time to become either fully charged or fully discharged.

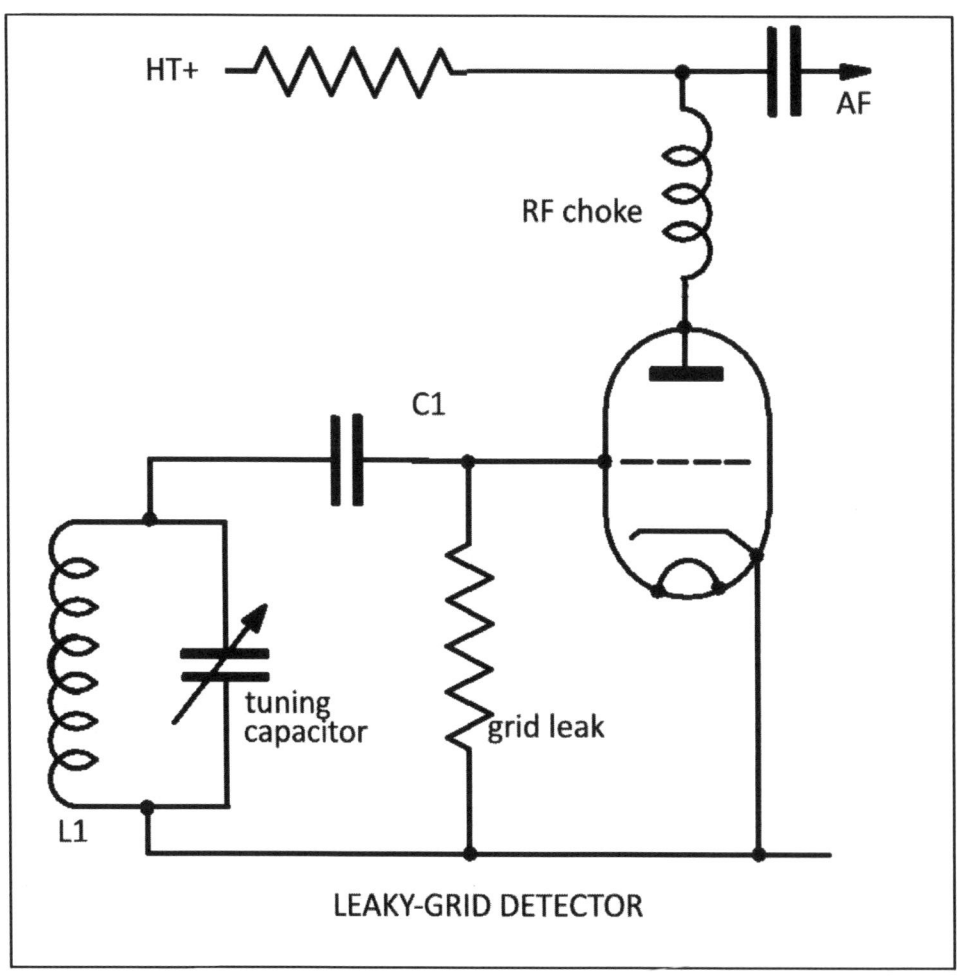

LEAKY-GRID DETECTOR

Bearing that in mind, consider the leaky grid circuit shown. Assuming C1 to be discharged and therefore offering a low resistance. The incoming signal tries to charge C1 to develop a potential difference across the grid leak resistor. This potential difference would, of course, be the same as the incoming alternating signal except that on the positive-going half cycle of signal the valve grid switches the valve into harder conduction, thereby removing the positive potential.

The grid positive causes electron flow – opposites attract, remember - to occur through the grid leak, which charges the plate of C1 that is connected to the grid, or more simply put, charges C1.

At the end of the positive-going half cycle C1 remains charged negatively so that the grid remains negatively charged also. When the negative half-cycle arrives, the grid becomes still more negative. At this time the electron flow to the grid stops, allowing C1 to discharge through the grid leak. This rate of discharge is determined by the time constant of grid leak and C1 and must be, in practice, very small. In fact, the value of C1 must be small enough to become fully charged on each positive signal cycle, smaller than the period of one half cycle of signal.

Neither must the time constant be of a value that would cause excessive distortion of the shape of the grid signal envelope, though some distortion is inevitable - typical values of C1 being in the order of 150pF, and the grid leak in the order of 1MΩ.

The amplified and by now unidirectional signal current appears at the anode as a modulated current envelope filled by tuned RF oscillations. This is then passed through a filter, often an RF choke, which removes the RF and leaves a clean envelope of audio-frequency signal. There may also be a small value bypass capacitor at the 'hot' end of the choke. In some very old sets, reaction circuits were employed to increase sensitivity and these would tap off the RF at the anode and feed it back positively to the grid via a coil loosely coupled to the tuning coils. The coupling could be physically varied or a variable capacitor could be used to set the critical level of feedback, which for greatest sensitivity was just before the circuit went unstable and burst into oscillation.

Although the foregoing detector designs used triode valve as examples, the same principle applies to pentode valves. Another variant used for detection, Power Grid Detection, was used with indirectly heated AC mains valves. The values for both the grid leak resistor and the capacitor had rather smaller values and the detector valve operated with a very high anode voltage. These modifications provided a relatively distortion – free signal rectification (detection) process.

In commercial TRF designs, RF amplification is used to boost the received signal before detection. Typically, a pentode valve was employed for the purpose, due to the pentode's superior performance when working at high frequencies. A special form of pentode was developed called the Vari-mu (vari-μ or VM). With this valve, varied spacing of the turns of the grid spiral wire allowed gain control by varying the grid bias level, using a potentiometer. This method of volume control was used in some TRF designs, but the Vari-mu valve came into its own when used in superhet circuits (see later) when, due to the greater sensitivity of the superhet design, the need for automatic gain control became pressing.

Sometimes a sloping arrowed line is drawn through the pentode symbol to identify the vari-mu characteristic.

DRAWBACKS TO TRF RECEIVERS

With any TRF circuit there is the problem of getting the tuned circuits to track (keep in step) over the wide range of received frequencies – and essentially all the tuned circuits must all be fully variable over the reception bands, as the TRF amplifies the received signal at its original frequency, perhaps over two or more stages. Another is poor selectivity, where two or more stations may be heard at once. Unless physical design is carried out with care, there is a tendency for circuits in either TRFs or superhets to become unstable and burst into oscillation when high gain is aimed for (the TRF is more susceptible to this problem), yet high gain is essential for good reception.

Reaction considerably improves TRF performance, but this can require a certain knack on the part of the operator, especially when striving to receive some distant or weak station that is at the very edge of the set's sensitivity. Some sets had a manually-operated concentric variable trimming capacitor built in to the main gang capacitor to minimise the component count.

For these reasons, the TRF design, commonplace in the 1920s was by the early to mid 1930s generally rejected in favour of the superior performance of the superheterodyne circuit, though some makers, Philips for example, continued to offer both types for a few years. In truth, the performance of a well-designed TRF can be comparable to a superhet.

THE SUPERHETERODYNE PRINCIPLE

Problems inherent in the TRF are therefore largely overcome by the use of the superheterodyne principle. Superhet receivers employ a method of reception called 'beat reception' where the received radio-frequency signals are combined with the signal generated by an oscillator in the receiver. This is called the local oscillator and is often part of a combined valve that does the two tasks, namely generating the local frequency and mixing it with the incoming signal.

The complete stage is called the Frequency-Changer, the reason being that the oscillating and signal-mixing process results in a beat frequency, well away from the original radio-frequency signals and so not subject to interference by them. We call this beat frequency the intermediate frequency, or IF and it is this frequency that is amplified before being demodulated for AF amplification.

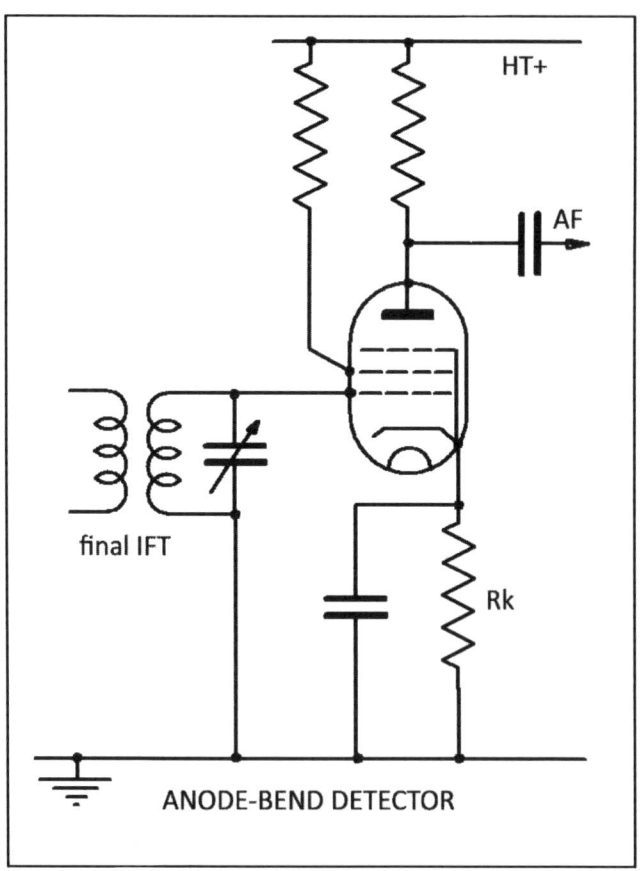

Early superhet designs sometimes used anode-bend detection and a typical arrangement is shown here

The point about this is that the IF remains as a fixed frequency and because it is fixed it does not require variable tuning no matter what radio signal frequency is being received; so the IF circuits are fixed tuned and less of a problem to design and can offer greater and more stable gain, resulting, when well designed, in a more sensitive and powerful receiver.

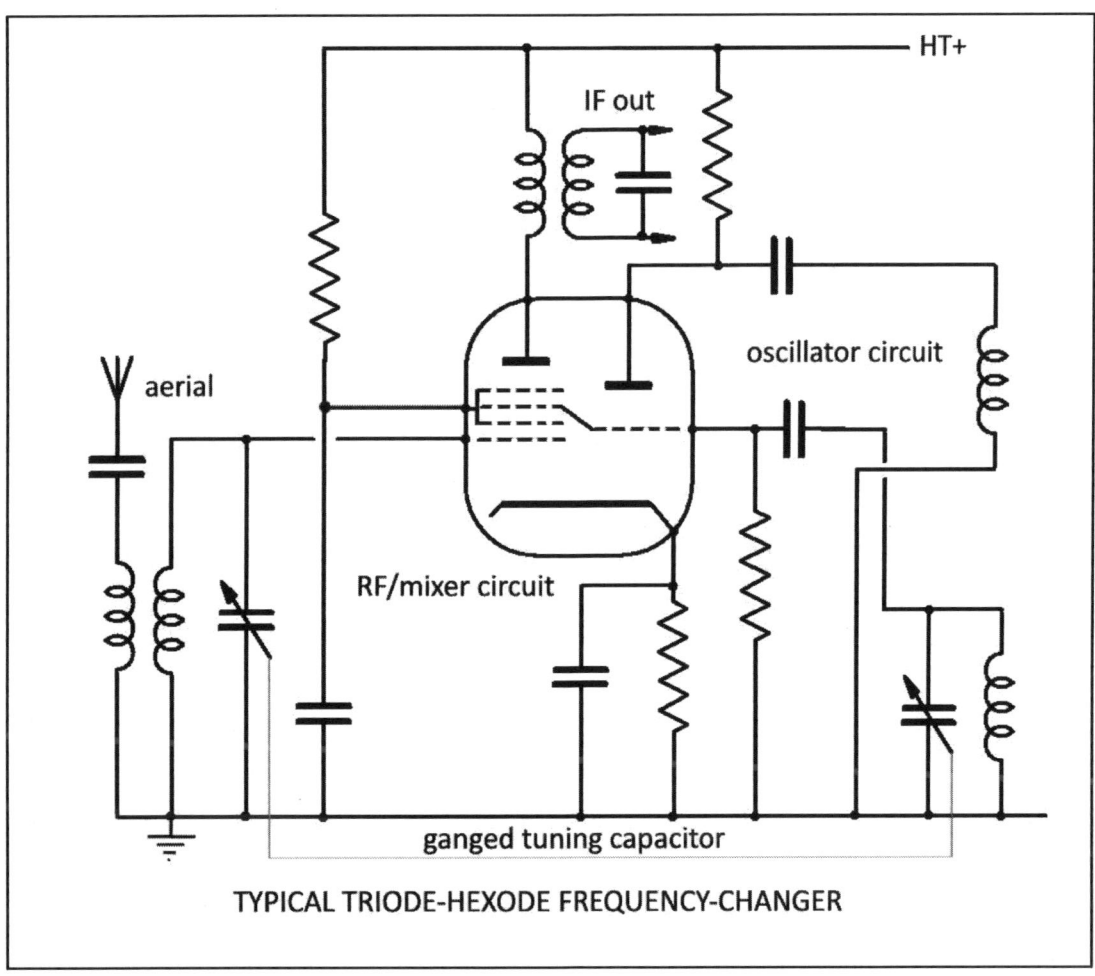

TYPICAL TRIODE-HEXODE FREQUENCY-CHANGER

How the triode-hexode frequency-changer works
There are several types of frequency-changing circuit. Above is a very common circuit using a triode-hexode valve (a hexode has six elements). The first thing to note is the use of a HEXODE as a tuned RF (HF) stage, where the signal is tuned in a conventional manner (like the TRF) and into the control grid of the so-called mixer section (the hexode) of the frequency-changer valve. Meanwhile, the triode oscillator section of the valve is generating oscillations at a frequency spaced apart from the received radio signal by an amount equal to the IF frequency required. This is created by positive feedback from triode anode to triode grid, via the coils. This oscillatory signal is internally injected into the hexode grid system.
As the HF section of the tuning gang is adjusted, the oscillator section moves by the same amount as the two are ganged to a single spindle. This keeps the IF frequency, which is the difference between the received RF and the oscillator frequency, in step - irrespective of the actual frequency of the radio signal. This form of signal mixing is known as multiplicative and is best explained visually: see chart overleaf.

Instead of a signal varying at radio frequency appearing across the HF amplifier anode load as it would in a TRF design, the signal mixing process creates a signal *fixed at the IF frequency,* which appears across the mixer anode load.

This anode load is an inductive one, being the primary of the first IF transformer (IFT). This IF signal is modulated by the programme content being received. IF transformers are designed to provide high gain, and this is possible because maintaining stability with high gain is much easier when working to a single fixed frequency. The transformers are very efficient once accurately set, commonly by adjustment of cores within the windings, a process known as alignment.

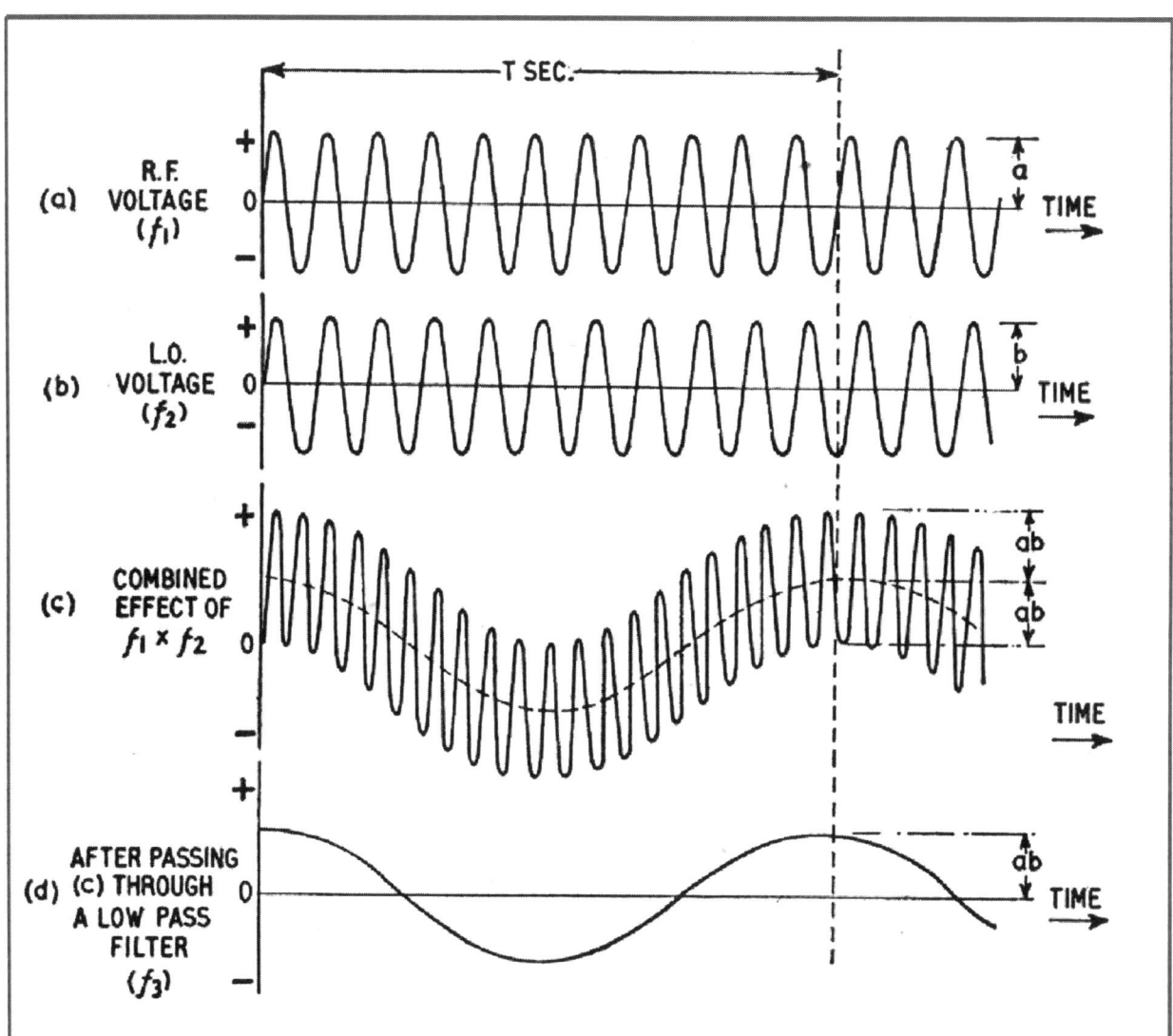

Combining two signals to make a third: the principle of the frequency changer. RF signal mixes with the local oscillator signal to make a third, marked 'c' which is then 'cleaned' by filtering of the high frequency signal to produce 'd', the Intermediate Frequency

With earlier receivers and also with battery superhets, a single pentagrid valve is commonly used as a frequency changer, with a grid acting as the local oscillator anode.

Typically two IF stages follow the frequency changer, one being the changer itself, with an IF amplifier valve (often a pentode) following the frequency-changer stage. Then a demodulator (detector) stage filters off the now unwanted IF content of the signal, leaving the audio information to be amplified by the AF output stage or stages which supplies the loudspeaker. Yes, it is rather more complicated than the TRF but the improvement in ease of use and sensitivity of the superhet could not be denied and it quickly established a lead over the TRF.

BASIC SUPERHET AGC AND DETECTOR CIRCUITS

The detection process for TRF receivers has been covered earlier and the process for superhets is much the same except that diodes are used instead of amplifying valves. In practice, to save separate diodes, recovery of the audio component from the amplified IF signal is usually done by the employment of a valve with one or two diode extra anodes. These are often given codes with 'DD' as in, for example, HL41DD. One diode (D1) is used to detect – demodulate – the signal whilst the triode section of the valve itself (not shown here) usually forms the

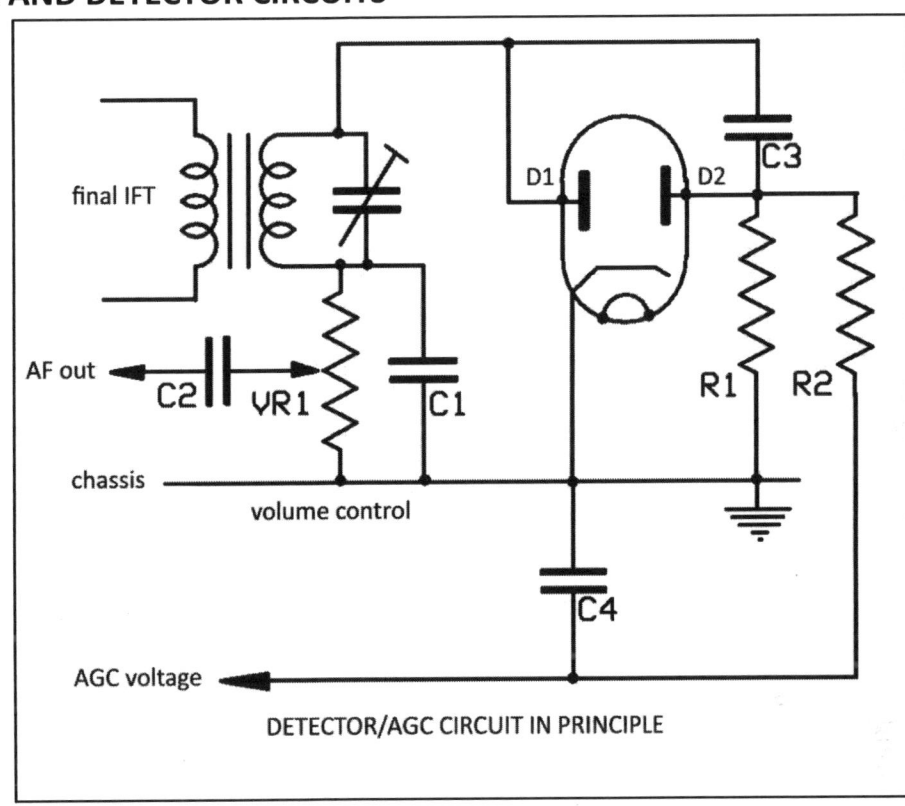

DETECTOR/AGC CIRCUIT IN PRINCIPLE

first audio amplification stage. The diode load resistor is the volume control, bypassed with a small value capacitor (C1) to filter off residual IF signal. C2 is the AF coupling capacitor. The same diode or the spare diode (D2) can be used to develop a DC voltage which varies in sympathy with the signal strength. This voltage may be used as a variable bias to control the gain of any or all vari-mu valves used in the RF stages. It is known as automatic gain control (AGC). In the vintage era this was referred to as automatic volume control (AVC), though AGC is strictly speaking a more accurate title for the process. C3 couples a portion of the IF signal to D2 and its load resistance R1. The negative potential at D2 is filtered and smoothed by C4/R3 to create the AGC voltage.

BASIC AF AMPLIFICATION AND OUTPUT STAGES

This is about the way audio frequency signals are handled in valve radio technology: in other words, signals after demodulation (detection). The processing requires small signals from the detector to be increased sufficiently to drive the loudspeaker or loudspeaker system at adequate volume (anything from 100 milliwatts in a portable set to 5 watts or higher in a typical valve receiver).

It is also essential that manual control of this amplification is available - volume control and optionally, tone control.

INTER-VALVE COUPLING METHODS

Audio Frequency (AF) stage valves may be connected in series to multiply the gain sufficiently to drive a loudspeaker. Simply, this means that the audio signal from the detector stage is linked to the grid of an amplifying valve, usually via a variable resistor which acts as a volume control. The important point to note about inter-stage AF coupling is that whilst the signal itself must be coupled, no DC component must be allowed to pass. For this reason, coupling is normally via a capacitor.

Referring to the left of the two R-C stage diagrams (R-C coupling 1):
R1 is the anode load for a valve of the double-diode triode type. One of the diodes would be the detector, the other diode commonly being used for AVC (AGC).
Assume that an amplified AF signal appears at the anode of the triode. The signal is developed across the resistor R1 and coupled to the control grid of the pentode output valve via C1. This capacitor is usually in the order of 0.01 microfarad, often a paper dielectric and the very often leaky, causing a positive DC voltage to appear on the pentode control grid. This is not a desirable situation as it is likely to result in the early demise of the valve and damage to peripheral components, so the capacitor is a candidate for replacement during restoration of any vintage radio. As well as controlling volume, VR1 acts as an earth (chassis) return, essential to prevent a DC potential from developing on the grid. C2 and R2 are the cathode bypass and load respectively. The load provides a positive potential on the cathode, biasing the valve by making the grid effectively negative. C2 acts as a reservoir, preventing the cathode voltage from 'following' the audio at the grid as the valve amplifies. Without it, the cathode potential will vary along with the signal so the removal of this capacitor will produce negative feedback, reducing the gain but also reducing the amount of audio distortion created by the stage.

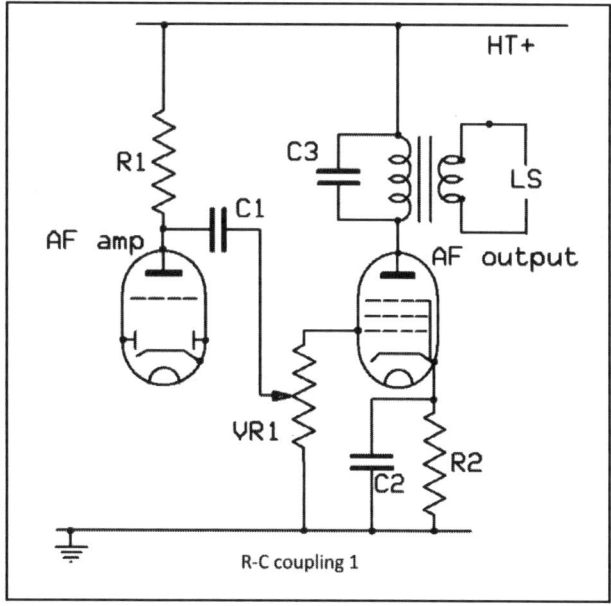

R-C coupling 1

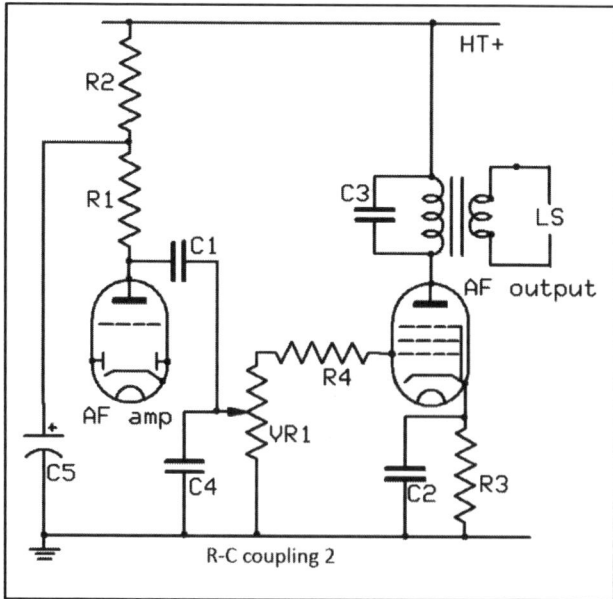

R-C coupling 2

C3 is a fixed-value tone corrector, bypassing a proportion of the higher audio frequencies to chassis (earth). These are fitted to improve the toppy response of the pentode - at least, that is the claim made for their existence. Usually they are to be found wired across the primary of the output transformer. They are another candidate for early replacement as a shorted tone correction capacitor will severely overrun the output valve.

Referring now to the right-hand part of the diagram (R-C coupling 2):
The double diode triode is employed again. The output stage still has the fixed tone corrector C3. This circuit uses more components and is a refinement on the simple one described above. Note that the anode load of the AF amplifier now consists of a split load – R1,2. R2 and C5 are a decoupling circuit designed to prevent AF signal current from appearing on the HT+ supply line where it might feed back and affect the circuits of other valves in the set, causing instability. C5 therefore acts as a reservoir for the HT+ supply to the detector/AF amplifier valve and eliminates AF signals at the junction of R1,R2.

C4 is an additional bypass capacitor to remove any IF signal that may have reached the anode of the AF pentode. Its value is chosen so as to remove the high frequency IF currents without impacting the low frequency AF currents and will usually be in the order of 100-500 pF. Also additional is the resistor R4. This is known as a grid stopper and is there to help maintain stability with the highly efficient pentode output valve. Such resistors have a very small value and therefore a negligible effect on AF signals. They are usually to be found wired very closely to the valve holder. The same general circuit

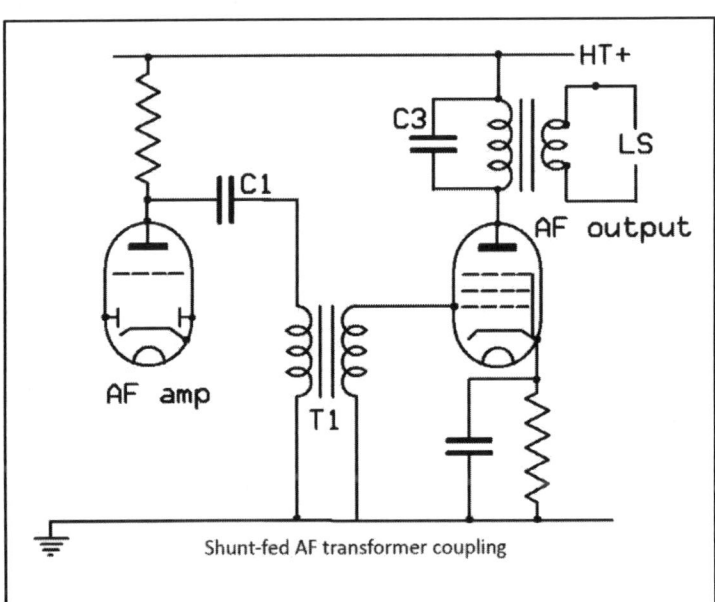

Shunt-fed AF transformer coupling

arrangement is used with tetrodes, too.
TRF receivers may be found to use an AF coupling transformer either in place of or as well as a coupling capacitor. Transformers may provide a step-up in gain, typically 1:3 or 1:5, a worthwhile gain especially for battery receivers, though the use of transformers can, unless they are very well designed, result in distortion of the audio due to the changing inductance over the audio frequency spectrum. However this was not a problem with TRF sets utilising cone loudspeakers as these reproducers were themselves of indifferent quality, especially lacking in bass, which is why they were usually very large in size, typically 12" diameter cones, an attempt to improve the lower note capability. The advantage of a cone loudspeaker was its greater sensitivity, requiring only a modest power input for full volume reproduction. Series-fed transformer coupling has the primary of the transformer in series with the anode of the AF amplifier. This means that the primary replaces the anode load resistor and so passes the full current taken by the valve. The alternative is the shunt-fed type. Transformers for shunt-fed circuits (as shown above) are often very small as they are not required to act as the valve anode load. C1 couples the signal but isolates DC.
The foregoing circuit descriptions apply to single-ended output stages.

POWER OUTPUT STAGES

Output stages in conventional valve radio fall into one of several categories:

Class A is where current equal to the complete AF signal flows through a given output valve. This is by far the most common. Typical stages have been discussed above. Other output stages less commonly found in vintage valve radios are listed below.

Class AB is where a given valve may be cut-off for part of the input signal. (This is where another valve takes over as in push-pull)

Class B is where each amplifying valve carries current for only half of the signal input. There are special class B double valves designed for early battery circuits (QPP valves, see below).

Each category has its advantages and disadvantages, either in terms of initial cost, power consumption, complexity of circuit or requirement for specialised components or valves.

The idea of push pull is that two valves are better than one if you want serious power delivery, hence their use in Hi-Fi amplifiers. Transformer coupling is considered later but the use of a valve phase splitter is often found. In the push pull circuit the two valves must work 180 degrees out of phase with each other and to do this the input signal has to be split into two opposing signals. There are a number of variations of the push-pull circuit; below is shown a quite common one.

R-C coupled push-pull using a phase-splitter

Assume a signal from an earlier AF amplifying stage has reached the grid of the triode phase splitter via C1. R2 and R4 are of equal value and so the current through the valve is divided equally between them (ignoring the presence of the low value R3, there to bias the cathode). C2 and C3 are outputs from the valve: each going to one or other of the output valve control grids.

Note the presence of R5 and R6 disposed across the two outputs with a centre-tapping to ground. Also grounded are the cathodes of the output pair via the

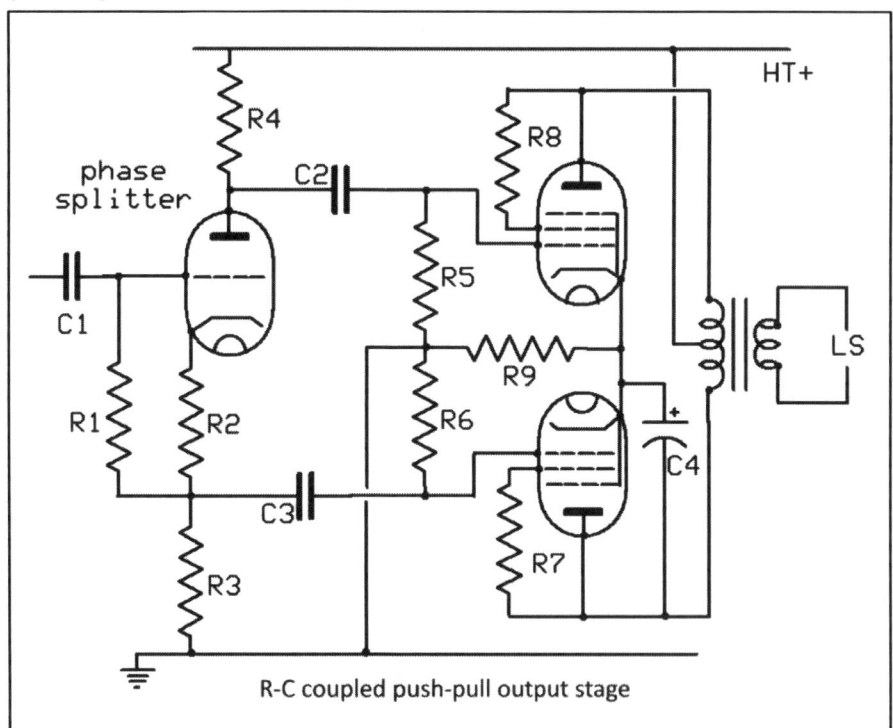

R-C coupled push-pull output stage

common bias load R9. C4 is the common bypass capacitor for both cathodes. The gain of the phase splitting stage is unity (no gain or loss), hence the need for an earlier AF amplifying stage. The outputs at cathode and anode of the phase splitter are of course sensibly equal but of opposite phase to each other.

A little thought shows why this is: Imagine a positive-going (growing less negative) signal at the grid of the phase splitter. The valve conducts harder as the signal goes less negative, resulting in a decrease of voltage at the anode but an increase in exact proportion at the cathode.

The output transformer has a centre-tapped primary driven from each end by the output valves acting in unison exactly out of phase - one pushes as the other pulls - and is an important element in maintaining good quality audio. In the diagram the screen grids are shown as connected via R7 and R8 to their respective anodes. Alternatively they may be connected to HT+ or to tappings on the output transformer primary.

R9 will be a high-wattage component of a low value, in the region of 100Ω to 400Ω. Separate cathode resistors may be used. Screen grid resistors will be low in value, of a similar order but not as high a wattage rating.

Transformer-coupled push-pull stage

The use of a centre-tapped secondary on an inter-valve coupling transformer obviates the need for a valve phase splitter and makes for simplicity though has quality limitations.

The stage is shown here as an outline circuit and in practice more components are likely to be found; but only the essentials are shown here. The left hand triode is a conventional AF amplifier and signals appear on its anode, the primary of the transformer acting as the anode load. The split secondary feeds antiphase signals to each of the output valve grids, the cathode bias arrangements being common to both valves.

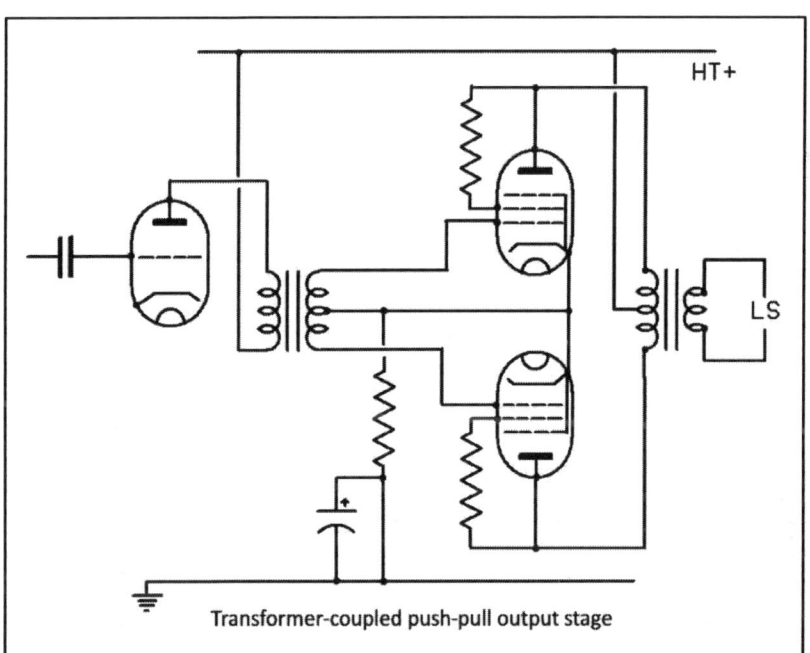
Transformer-coupled push-pull output stage

QPP output stage

Most pre WWII battery radio receivers used the minimum of valves - three or four - in the conventional way. Battery sets were always a problem because of their current consumption. Batteries - especially HT batteries -were expensive (and remained so up to their demise around 1973) and so ways were sought to improve gain and performance without increasing the drain on those precious batteries.

One early method devised was to use a special combined valve; the circuit overleaf is that of a double pentode but double triodes were also used and the circuit for these differs little in principle from the pentode one about to be described.

'Standard' push-pull stages use two output valves. As the gain of one valve falls, the gain of the other rises.

With this battery system however, things are arranged slightly differently with the aim of minimising standing current. To achieve this, the two sections of the double pentode are over-biased in such a way as to allow only a small anode current through each valve under no-signal conditions, with a greater current when a strong signal is present. In a single ended output stage severe audio distortion would result from this over-bias condition but each valve makes up for the other, resulting in acceptable sound quality.

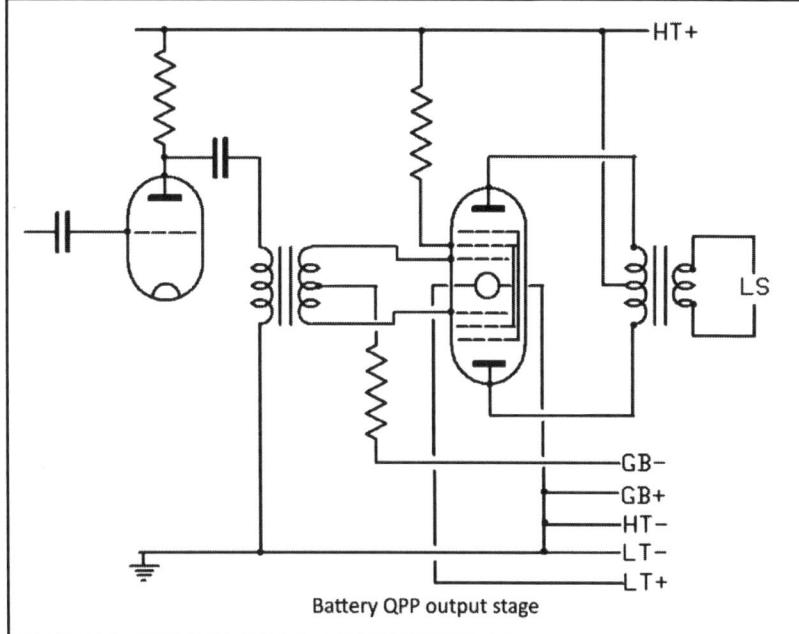

Battery QPP output stage

This type of circuit arrangement is known as Quiescent Push-Pull or QPP for short. A QPP stage requires twice the input voltage that a standard push-pull arrangement requires for a given output level which is why the more sensitive pentodes are used rather than triodes. Although at peak levels of signal the power consumption is much as a normal push-pull stage, at low signal levels the anode current falls. The result is a worthwhile saving of battery power over a period.

Note that for clarity, this QPP outline circuit has been drawn to show the use of a grid bias battery. In practical circuits there may be an auto-bias arrangement used, obviating the need for a separate bias battery.

TONE CONTROL

Tone control as used in most vintage radios is a relatively simple affair, often consisting of little more than a top cut circuit. Although minimal in cost for the manufacturer to offer as an extra, tone controls were a good selling point. The function of these is straightforward. Some typical examples are shown on p. 53. For (a) and (b) there is a variable resistor 'R' (the manual tone control itself) of around 10kΩ and a series capacitor 'C' of around 0.05µF. For (c) and (d) the values are in the order of 500kΩ and 0.005µF.

The reactance of the capacitor - resistor combination forms a variable time-constant, progressively bypassing the higher frequency audio to ground in the case of (a), (c) and (d) and to the HT+ line in (b). Although the arrangements shown at (a) and (b) was common enough, the failure of capacitor 'C' allows HT voltage to pass through 'R'. A leaky but not shorted capacitor will cause the control to become very noisy in operation. (d) is a variation of (c) with the advantage of progressive top cut, increasing as the volume is reduced, creating a bass boost at lower volume levels in compensation for the human hearing curve which is less sensitive to bass frequencies at low volume settings.

This is the equivalent of what today might be termed a loudness control. The volume control will be seen to be a special tapped type. These are almost impossible to obtain should a replacement is needed but a little time spent understanding the function of the circuit can pay dividends in that an alternative but almost as effective method may be substituted that does not call for a special potentiometer.

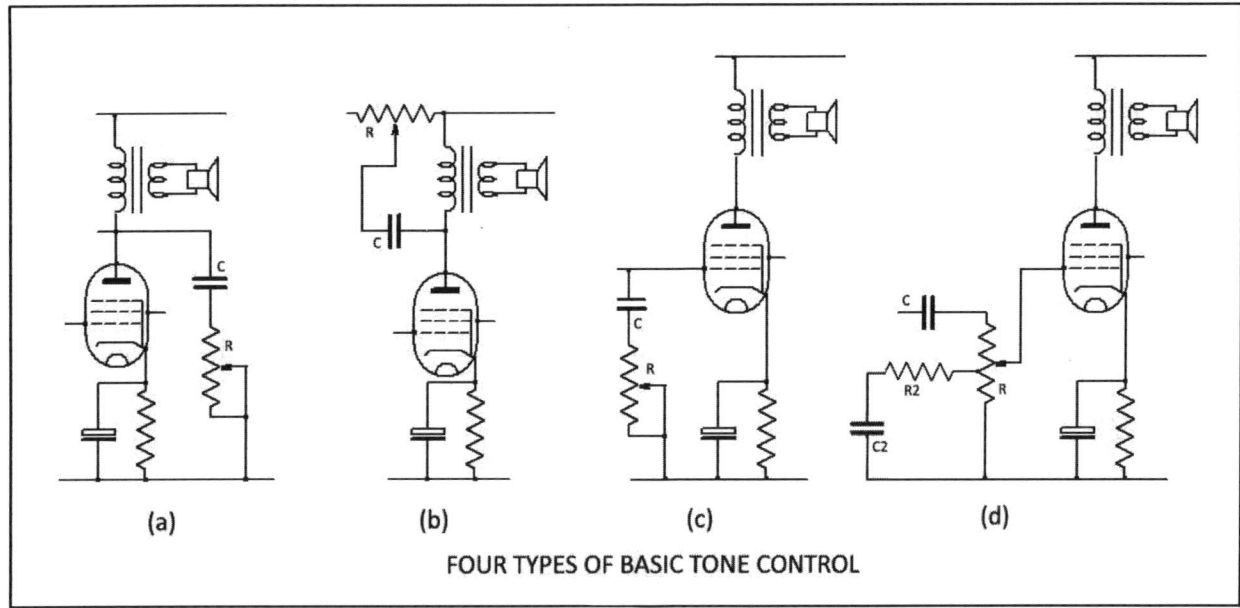

FOUR TYPES OF BASIC TONE CONTROL

A dead short in the capacitor 'C' in all but (c) will cause the control to overheat and burn out.
The configuration of (c) is better in that no DC voltage can reach the tone control components – unless an AF coupling capacitor fails.

NEGATIVE FEEDBACK

Negative feedback is a method used to improve the frequency response of a given circuit and also to reduce harmonic distortion. Stability may also be improved. The principle behind the process is to take a proportion of the signal from the output and feed it back in opposite phase to the input, thereby causing a reduction in the input as opposite phases cancel each other out.

Obviously, feed one hundred percent back and the result would be zero output - a

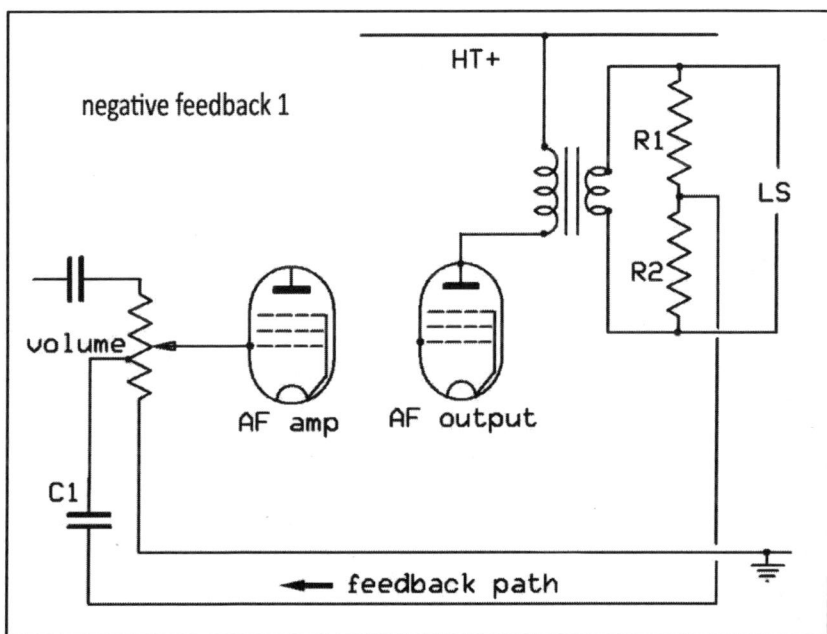

pointless exercise. In practice only a small percentage is fed back.
In the diagram 'negative feedback 1', the feedback is taken from the potential divider R1,R2 which is across the secondary of the output transformer. The use of a tapped volume control converts it into a loudness control. C1 is frequency conscious, allowing more of the higher frequencies to be fed back to the tapping on the special volume control, forming a tone compensation circuit (the lower the volume, the greater the reduction of the higher audio frequencies, therefore apparently - the greater the bass boost).

In the diagram 'negative feedback 2', R1 and C1 form a series connection to chassis from one side of the secondary of the output transformer. The voltage developed across C1 is fed back to the junction R2,3. R2 is the standard cathode bias resistor and C2 is its bypass capacitor. R3 will have a low value in the order of a few tens of ohms.

The result of this circuit is to feed back all audio frequencies, resulting in a fixed feedback amount.

Full audio frequency range negative feedback has considerable value in reducing distortion and improving output stage performance at the cost of slight loss of overall stage gain.

Component values are quite critical for optimum performance. It should be noted that the correct side of the output transformer secondary winding must be chosen or the result would be positive feedback and severe instability.

LOUDSPEAKERS

The earliest loudspeakers were little more than a telephone (headphone) earpiece positioned horizontally, with an exponential horn attached. These horns amplified the sound in much the same way as the horn in an acoustic gramophone amplified the vibrations produced by the needle on a diaphragm, but hi-fi it certainly was not. The main limitation was the poor audio frequency coverage, especially lacking in bass response because of the necessarily limited cone size.

'Tinny' was one of the words often used to describe this sound. Very large exponential horns were however used in cinemas, their size ensuring good bass response.

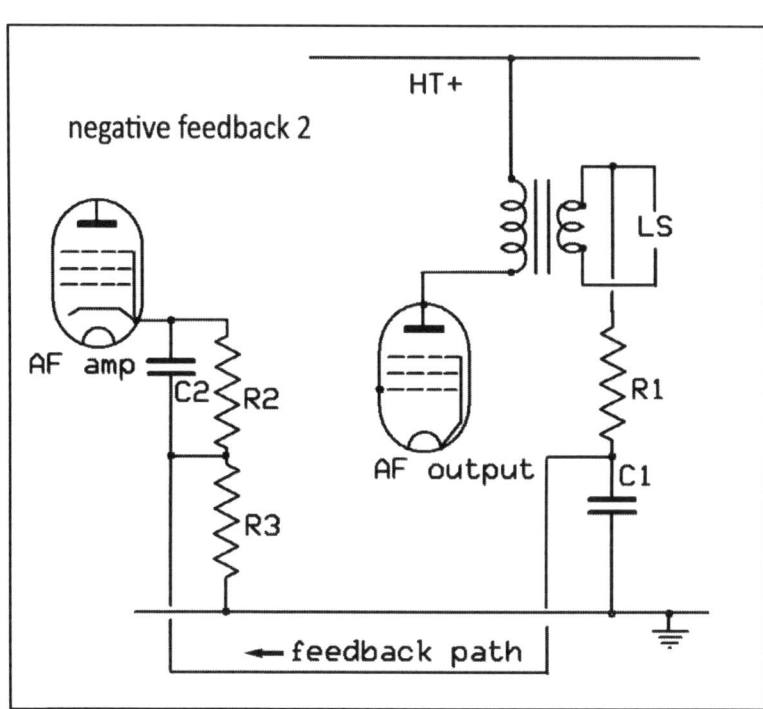

Cone loudspeakers

As radio development gathered pace, it became imperative that a better solution was found. The first cone type loudspeakers were of the moving iron form, where a stiff paper cone was flexibly supported around its maximum circumference and its apex attached to a strip of iron – an armature - by means of an adjustable bolt. Fixed at one end but free at the other, the armature was placed close to the core of a small electromagnet, the winding of which was often fed directly from the output valve anode. Current variations through the winding varied the field strength and therefore the magnetic pull on the armature, so vibrating the cone to produce sound.

Invariably fitted with large cones of 10" to 12", these loudspeakers were sensitive and suited the modest outputs typical of the simple TRF designs of the late twenties/early thirties.

Design weaknesses in this cone form or reproducer limited the bass response due to the uneven nature of the pull on the cone – the cone rod actually moves through a slight but significant arc and excessive movement caused by low audio frequencies tended to cause the armature to contact the magnetic pole piece, creating mechanical chatter. Increasing the spacing between the armature and the pole piece prevented this but at the expense of sensitivity to the weaker signals. Manual adjustment was usually provided by a knurled knob on the connecting rod to set for best sensitivity whilst avoiding contact rattles.

Some improvement was gained with the balanced armature type where the armature slots between a split magnetic winding. This arrangement gave rather better control over the movement of the cone and allowed for a wider spacing of the gap between pole pieces and armature, but being less sensitive was suitable only for sets with a relatively high output power.

Few sets were other than low-cost economy models were fitted with cone-type units after 1930. The moving-coil loudspeaker supplanted them, once adequate output valves had been developed.

Moving coil loudspeakers
The moving coil loudspeaker overcame the limitations of the cone type and has become the standard loudspeaker that everyone is familiar with. The basic design was so good that it has changed little since its introduction in the late 1920s.

A permanent magnet is used in PM loudspeakers. The speech coil is a very finely wound coil of copper on a stiff paper tube, free on its inner end and with the outer end connected to the loudspeaker cone. A centring device of some kind, known as a 'spider', is often used to keep the speech coil correctly placed within the magnetic gap and from rubbing on the pole piece or the magnet walls. Audio signal is fed to the speech coil from the secondary of the output transformer. Because of electromagnetic field interaction, the fluctuating current through the coil causes it to move in relation to the fixed magnetic field from the magnet and pole piece. The greater the current through the speech coil, the more displacement and the greater the movement and this causes the cone, which is suspended at its outer periphery by a flexible mounting, to move in or out in time with the audio signal, producing sound.

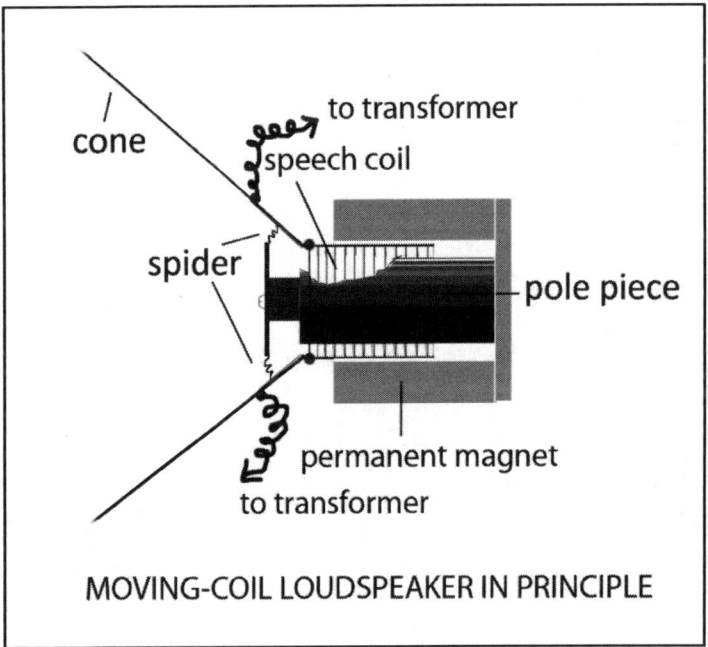

MOVING-COIL LOUDSPEAKER IN PRINCIPLE

Although not as sensitive as the older cone dynamic units, the moving coil system is superior in frequency range and general reproductive quality. The diagrams show the principle but the loudspeaker frame has been omitted for clarity. Both permanent magnet and energised loudspeakers work in a similar way.

This diagram shows a typical energized loudspeaker, where the necessary magnetism is obtained by passing a current through the field winding. Many mains receivers used such an energized loudspeaker, doubling the winding – known as the field winding – as a smoothing choke. Such windings are necessarily wound with thousands of turns of very fine wire and are a weak link, often found to be open-circuit in vintage receivers. Although the field can be rewound, an alternative is to replace the faulty loudspeaker with a permanent magnet unit of the same cone size. A smoothing choke can be used to take the place of the field smoothing. Much depends upon the degree of authenticity the restorer is prepared to sacrifice.

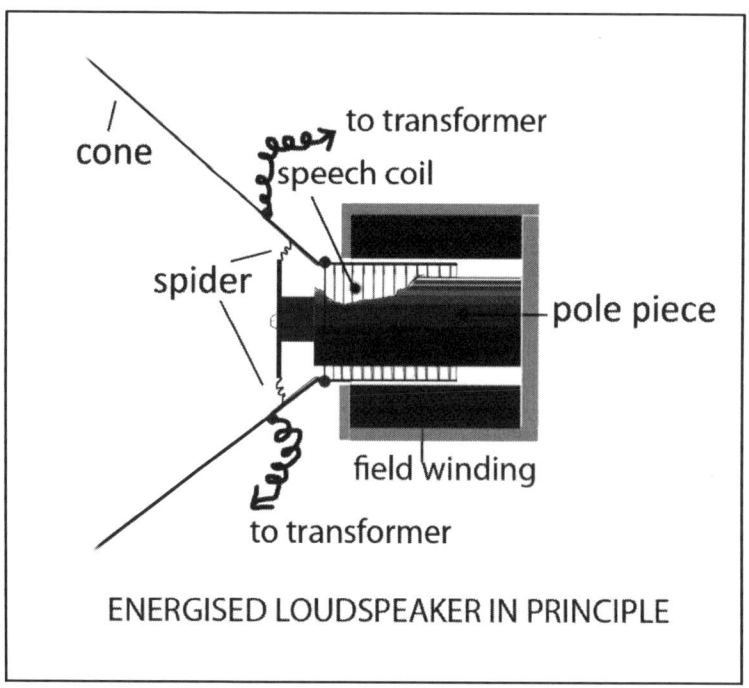

ENERGISED LOUDSPEAKER IN PRINCIPLE

RESTORING A MOVING-COIL LOUDSPEAKER

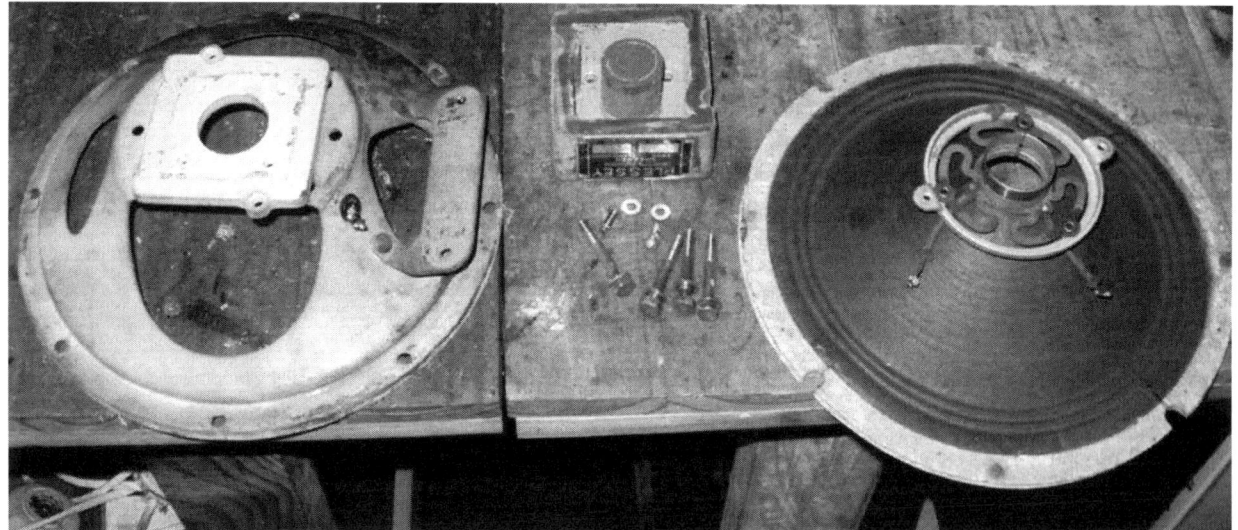

First the magnet then the cone is removed – very carefully – by separating the thick card compression ring from the frame. The rusted pole piece can then be cleaned without risk of damage to the speech coil. The coil can be seen above right, with the circular bracket that helps keep the coil central but allows free movement along the coil axis.

The cleaned and resprayed steel loudspeaker chassis ready for reassembly.

The ultra-flexible speech coil connecting leads from the cone must now be unsoldered from the transformer or tag strip end, not from the cone. This should allow the cone and speech coil to be lifted clear (any centring spider arrangement that screws into the pole-piece must also be removed). The magnet assembly should be dismantled – not an easy job, as the permanent magnets are incredibly strong and resist being separated – and then the rust from the pole-piece can be cleaned away using a strip of fine abrasive paper. A vacuum cleaner will remove the detritus.

The loudspeaker chassis should be cleaned and refinished as desired. When reassembling the magnet, three narrow strips of card can be placed symmetrically around the pole piece to create the even gap for the speech coil. Without the card there will be a strong tendency for the pole piece to go off-centre.
The cone may be glued in place around its periphery with any suitable adhesive; I prefer Copydex latex adhesive for this task. After the connections are re-soldered and the centring spider refitted, the unit is ready for use.

Trade adverts from the post-war era

CHAPTER 5
THE TYPICAL VINTAGE CHASSIS

The chassis is the electronic heart of the radio, all the works of the set. It consists of a supporting structure, the chassis proper, which in turn carries all the components of the circuitry plus the mechanical items such as valve-holders, screens and, often, the scale assembly and its cord drive system, though the glass or acrylic dial plate itself may be mounted within the cabinet shell along with the loudspeaker. Occasionally, with miniature 'mantel shelf' radios, the loudspeaker is mounted on the chassis too, but for best results, loudspeakers are usually firmly fixed to a 'baffle' board of wood or very thick fibreboard within the cabinet. Let's take a look inside a typical receiver. Below is the first of two annotated photographs. This one shows the top view of an average 'budget' priced 1940s set.

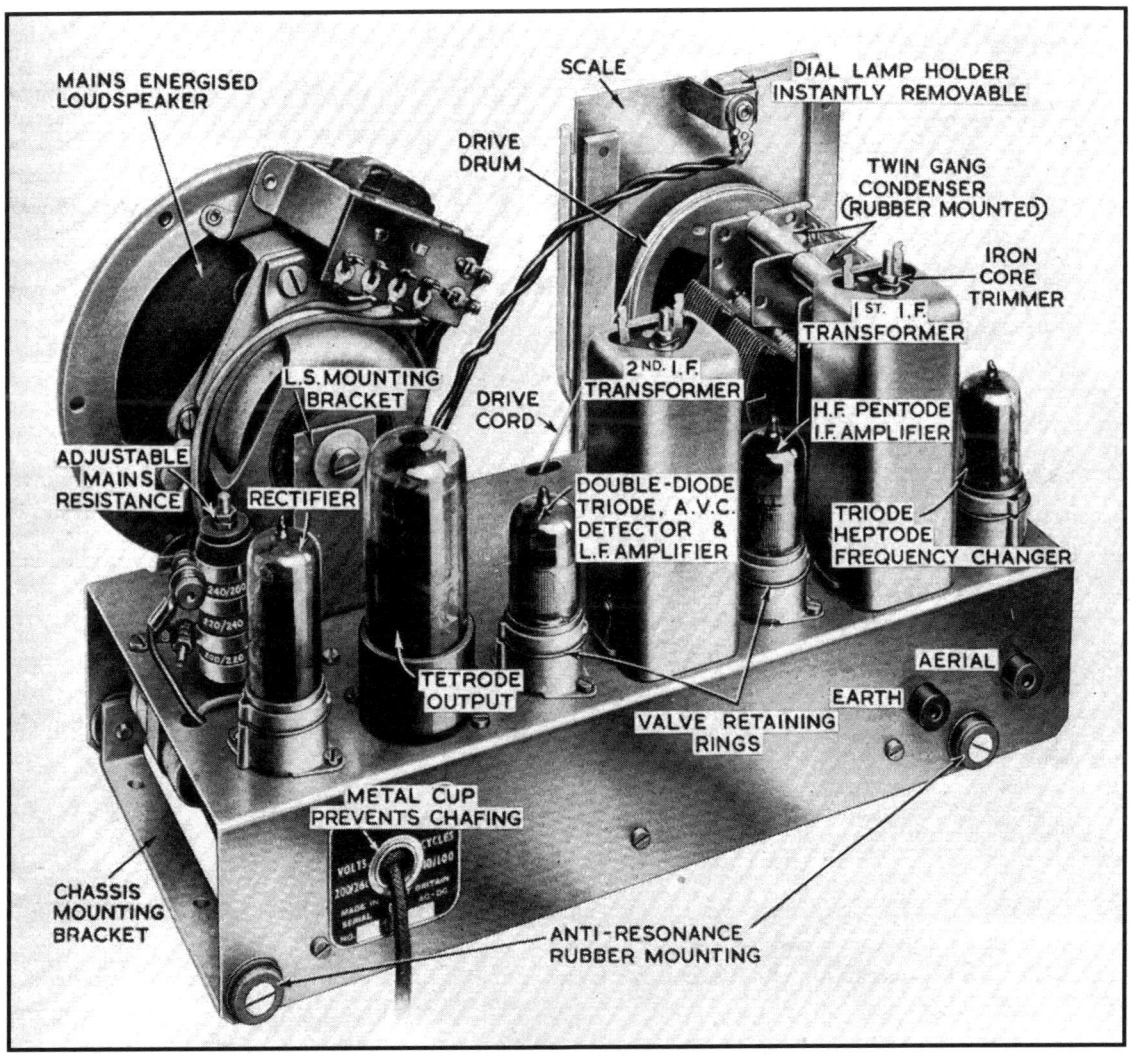

(Note that the two views are not of the same chassis but are chosen as they offer a clear view of the components).

Above the deck
The receiver can be seen to be an AC/DC set as there is no mains transformer but instead a dropper resistor, labelled 'adjustable mains resistance'. 'Adjustable' usually means that there are several tapping points along the length of the ceramic-cored wire-wound component, allowing input voltage to be set to suit the voltage level of the local mains. Such dropper resistors generate heat and can cause long-term damage to cabinet tops and back covers. Some makers fit heat shields in an attempt to alleviate this problem. It follows that droppers are wasteful of energy and, as they are connected directly to the mains supply, they pose a risk of shock for the unwary.

The chassis itself is of metal, usually steel, either painted or plated. Transformer cans are often formed from light alloy. At a glance it is immediately obvious that much engineering work went into the production of the chassis. Note the tuning drive drum and cord arrangement as these are often the cause of trouble in vintage sets. Though some are trickier than others, fortunately the drums are usually not impossibly difficult to restring and it helps if you have service data to hand.

With this particular set there is a mixture of valve base type and size: the tetrode output is an octal based valve but the remainder of the valves are of the smaller B8A 'lockfit' type. You can speculate on why this is, and why valves of the same base type and size were not fitted. The reason isn't immediately obvious, although it could simply have been that the set makers had an agreement to purchase only the valves of a specific maker – and that maker's range did not include a suitable selection of valves using a common base. It could also have been for economy (the octal output valve being perhaps lower in cost than a similar lockfit type) or it may simply have been that the makers already held large stocks of octal output valves. Post WWII set designers often had limited choice and used what was to hand.

Then again, perhaps the heater voltage of the octal valve was more suited to the needs of this set, bearing in mind that the series heater chain has to disperse quite a high voltage in an AC/DC set if the wire-wound dropper isn't going to be excessively large – and become excessively hot in use, perhaps limiting its life.
As this receiver dates from the 1940s post war period, perhaps valve shortages caused the adoption of the octal valve. Whatever the reason, variations of this nature can be found in many vintage sets. It is possible to come across evidence of 'rebranding' of valves, sometimes from surplus MOD numbering.

Although service data is highly desirable for the successful restoration of receivers, many modifications perhaps to eliminate troublesome problems or to employ a different valve range may have occurred over the production period of a radio and deviations from the service data are common. Such variations are prevalent in sets manufactured before 1934.

Below the deck
The second of the two pictures (see p. 61) shows the view beneath the chassis of a fairly typical late 1940s high-quality receiver. This chassis is probably AC only, with a double-wound transformer out of sight on the top of the chassis, and might have been fitted into table receivers and also radiograms, perhaps with minor changes. It boasts three-waveband coverage (long, medium and short), tone control and a tuning indicator.

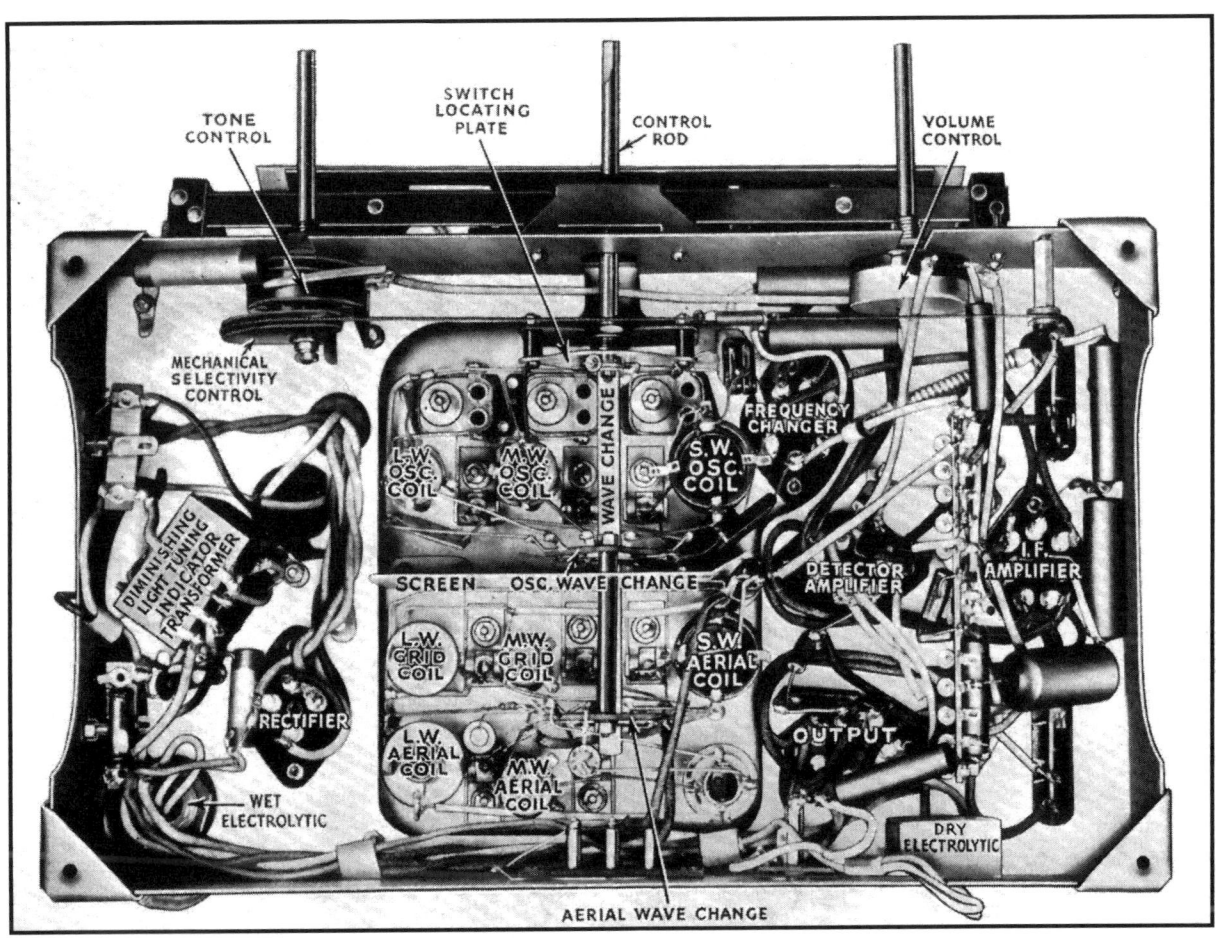

The wave-change switching is well separated and mechanically screened between the oscillator and the RF sections: the central shaft for the switch extending deep into the chassis to achieve this. The intention was to prevent possible instability due to feedback between the circuits. The switch locating plate works by a captive, sprung-loaded ball-bearing settling into detents as the plate is rotated. Note the use of both wet and dry electrolytic capacitors. The wet types were quite common at the time but due to the acid electrolyte leaking, they are usually in a corroded state and are prime candidates for immediate replacement, perhaps by refilling (see later for techniques).

Along with these luxury models, there were countless numbers of compact sets produced. Most were quite basic in specification, usually with medium and long wave coverage only and often, unlike this superhet, without benefit of tone control, tuning indicator or short-wave coverage. Cabinets were often Bakelite, but veneered wooden cabinets were offered 'for the more discriminating purchaser' at a higher price.
 To repeat: if there's one thing that stands out in these images it is the build quality, even with the budget set. These chassis were examples of engineering and metalworking the like of which, at least in domestic electronic equipment, we are extremely unlikely to ever see again.

The effort that went into the design and assembly of these chassis would make them impossibly expensive to produce and it is one of the features of vintage radios that make them so fascinating. The chassis were designed with servicing in mind; unlike much of today's electronic product, it was intended that they should be maintained and repaired if needed from time to time. Receivers were viewed as a long-term investment by purchasers.

If we now look at a Bush DAC90A (above), a well known and popular economy receiver from the very early 1950s, we can see evidence of similar engineering values, though somewhat scaled down from the 1930s level. The chassis is formed from Aluminium alloy instead of steel.

From left to right: the circular wire-wound frame aerial is actually an enlarged tuning coil. Immediately next to it is the twin-gang tuning capacitor. The first valve is the Frequency changer. The Ist IF transformer (note the side core adjusters) sits between the frequency changer and the 1st IF amplifier valve. Next is the 2nd IF transformer, then the detector/AF amplifier valve, the output valve, and lastly the rectifier valve. The loudspeaker is placed centrally and the scale cord can be seen angling across it to operate the scale pointer mounted at the top of the cabinet.

Note the adapted mains lead input; this set was originally fitted with a two-pin 'male' plug which was replaced for safety. The chassis is secured into the cabinet by means of the two lugs, one either side of the rear chassis rail.

SIX REPRESENTATIVE RECEIVERS

Although there is a very wide range of receiver circuitry design, the majority of sets will fit fairly well into one of six categories. With that in mind, the circuit functions of six typical receivers, each representing a category, will now be discussed in detail. The sets and categories are:

Battery TRF: Cossor 373
AC Superhet: Cossor 494
AC/DC Superhet: Bush DAC90A
Mains and battery: Ultra 'Coronation Twin'
All-dry battery: Vidor CN414 portable
VHF/FM: Bush VHF80

Remember that most of the comments apply in general to that type of receiver; for example, the statements regarding the Vidor CN414 hold true for most other battery-only all-dry portables of whatever make. Note too that TRF receivers can be mains powered in exactly the same way that superhets can, be it mains or battery, AC or AC/DC.

COSSOR 373

The battery-powered 373 was one of Cossor's 'Super Ferrodyne' TRF series, so titled because of the inclusion of iron cores for some of the coil windings, a bold superlative in view of the relatively minor nature of the modification which was possibly their designer's answer to Philips' 'Superinductance' range of TRF receivers. It was produced around the early to mid 1930s, a time when it was fairly common practice for makers to mix and match cabinets and innards, knobs and dials, surely the better to facilitate mass production with minimum financial outlay.

It was common practice to have two or more HT+ lines and the 373 has a single main HT+ plus a lower 45V HT+ line specifically as a screen feed for the RF amplifier valve. HT batteries were made with tappings for a range of voltages, accessed via sockets. Also there are two grid bias tappings (The 9V batteries for grid bias were provided with a range of tapping sockets) at a time when auto-bias was standard for mains receivers, perhaps another indication that the 373 was designed on a cost-paring basis.

C1 isolates the aerial input from the primary of TC1, the aerial tuning coil. Top-end coupling to the secondary is by C2. Tuned by C14, one gang of the twin tuning capacitor, signals reach the control grid of RF amplifier V1, the gain of which is controlled by R2 by varying the setting of the grid bias to the variable-μ valve. Amplified RF in the anode circuit of V1 is developed across the detector tuning coil TC2 and tuned by the tuning capacitor detector gang C13. V2, R5, C7 and R6 form a leaky grid detector. Variable capacitor C6 is the reaction control, a conventional solid-dielectric component. AF signals are developed across R10 and pass to the control grid of the output valve V3 via C10, T1 choke-capacity coupling with C9 filtering RF. Pentode tone correction is by R12, C12. The loudspeaker is an 8" PM type. C11 decouples the 120V HT+ line. V1 screen grid has a separate supply requirement of 45V+, decoupled by C4. A small MES bulb rated at 3V, 0.15A is mounted on the rear chassis rail and is in series with the HT negative lead, acting as a fuse. All in all, a commendably simple and economic circuit offering a maximum result from almost a minimum of components. By the time this radio was manufactured the TRF design was distinctly dated, having been overtaken by the more sensitive circuitry of the superhet. The latter however was more complex with a larger component count and manufacturing costs were therefore higher.

The TRF remained popular with some makers and also with the more conservative – or perhaps less knowledgeable and/or less wealthy – section of the UK buying market and despite the dated design the TRF did have a few things going for it: the simple circuitry aided reliability, factory assembly was less complex, less setting up was needed after manufacture, service or repair and, certainly in the case battery sets like this one employing a single-ended output, running costs were relatively modest as HT current consumption was only a few milliamps and batteries lasted well as a result. LT was of course supplied by the usual rechargeable 2V wet cell.

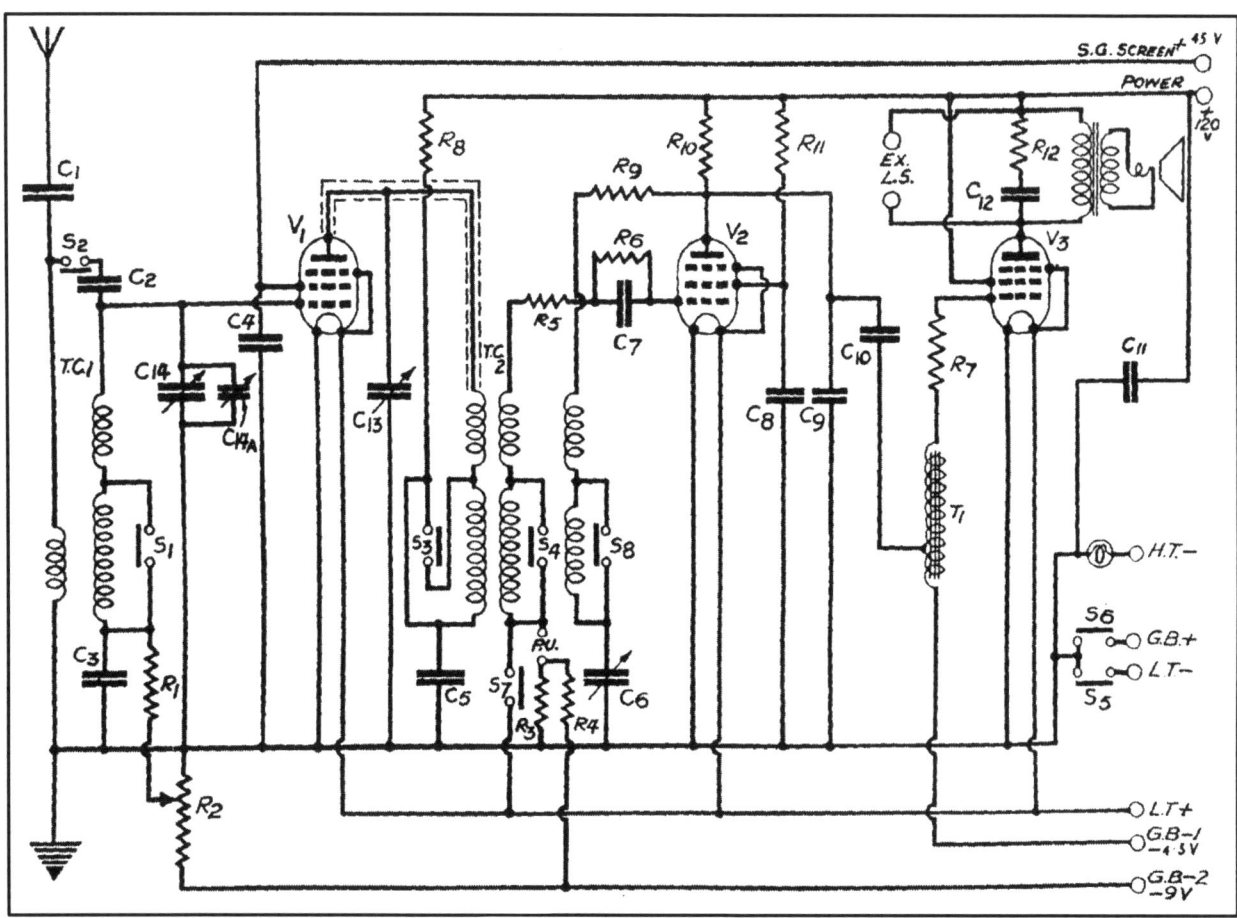

Reaction improves the sensitivity level. Not all TRF receivers use reaction and many were technically rather more complex.

There was something of a contest between TRF and superhet taking place earlier in the 1930s. Philips was one maker who believed in the qualities that the TRF design bestowed – low distortion being an important one. To make a TRF work in a manner comparable to the performance of the average superhet meant very careful mechanical design of the RF stages, especially with screening and in the design of the tuning coils. Eventually and inevitably the superhet won out.

This relegated TRF designs to be used when cost rather than sensitivity or build quality was the main consideration, which brings us neatly back to the set in question; With only 3 valves, just two wavebands, no manual tone control and no auto grid bias, this was an economy model.

Cossor 373 battery TRF

WHAT TO WATCH FOR
If you buy such a set with a view to electronic restoration, remember that you will need to provide power supplies in the form of HT and grid bias batteries, and a 2-volt supply for the valve filaments (dry batteries simply won't be capable of providing the current needed).

Any capacitor connected between HT+ and chassis will be working hard. C11 (2µF block capacitor, replace with electrolytic rated well above HT+) would be the first capacitor to change. Close on its heels as candidates for replacement are C8 and C10 (each 0.1µF), for much the same reason – and a leaky C10 can damage the output valve.

The presence of the C11 might puzzle you, but it is there to cushion inevitable fluctuations in HT voltage as signal variations make transient demands upon the battery; in other words, it really is acting as a reservoir. The insulation on the flexible wiring used for battery connections may be found to be in a dangerous state and if so should be replaced. Switches and controls that are noisy in action may be quietened by careful use of switch cleaning lubricant (not WD40, as this may attack certain materials). The loudspeaker speech coil gap may be rusted due to poor storage but sometimes these units can be dismantled and cleaned.

Among the resistors that might be well out of specified range, the grid leak resistor R6 is an already high 2MΩ and such high values often drift higher with age. Similarly R1 should be listed for careful checking. Finally, all resistors and any waxed paper capacitors should be checked for correct working, although the few components used in sets such as this makes for easy replacement. The rule should be: if in doubt, exchange – but one at a time.

The underside of the Cossor 373 chassis after restoration

The underside view shows just how simple the receiver is. Many TRF sets lend themselves to a relatively straightforward process of 'back to bare metal' stripdown and rebuild. An exception would be the Philips Superinductance series, built in a tank-like and complex manner that does not lend itself to straightforward dismantling. Back to the Cossor, the large 2µF capacitor C11 – the black tubular one mounted on the rear runner of the chassis – was emptied and rebuilt by fitting an appropriate component (an electrolytic capacitor as 2µF paper capacitors are no longer common) into the casing. By this means, visual originality was retained. The controls are, from the top left: solid-dielectric variable capacitor (reaction control), variable resistor (potentiometer, volume control) and wave-change switch.

COSSOR 494

This was the first set to use Cossor's Bakelite 'stepped' cabinet design. The cabinet houses a 4-valve plus valve rectifier 3 waveband superhet. Developments followed, with AC/DC chassis as well as AC only. Model 501 looks very similar to the 494 and does use the same basic cabinet moulding, though the colour of the Bakelite may be rather garish, more leopard-skin than Walnut but the thing to look for is the scale/grille surround. On the 494 this, together with the vertical divider bar between the scale and the grille, is moulded in one with the cabinet and may be painted cream, though this surface paint is liable to wear and might have been removed by previous owners, leaving the surround the same colour as the cabinet proper.

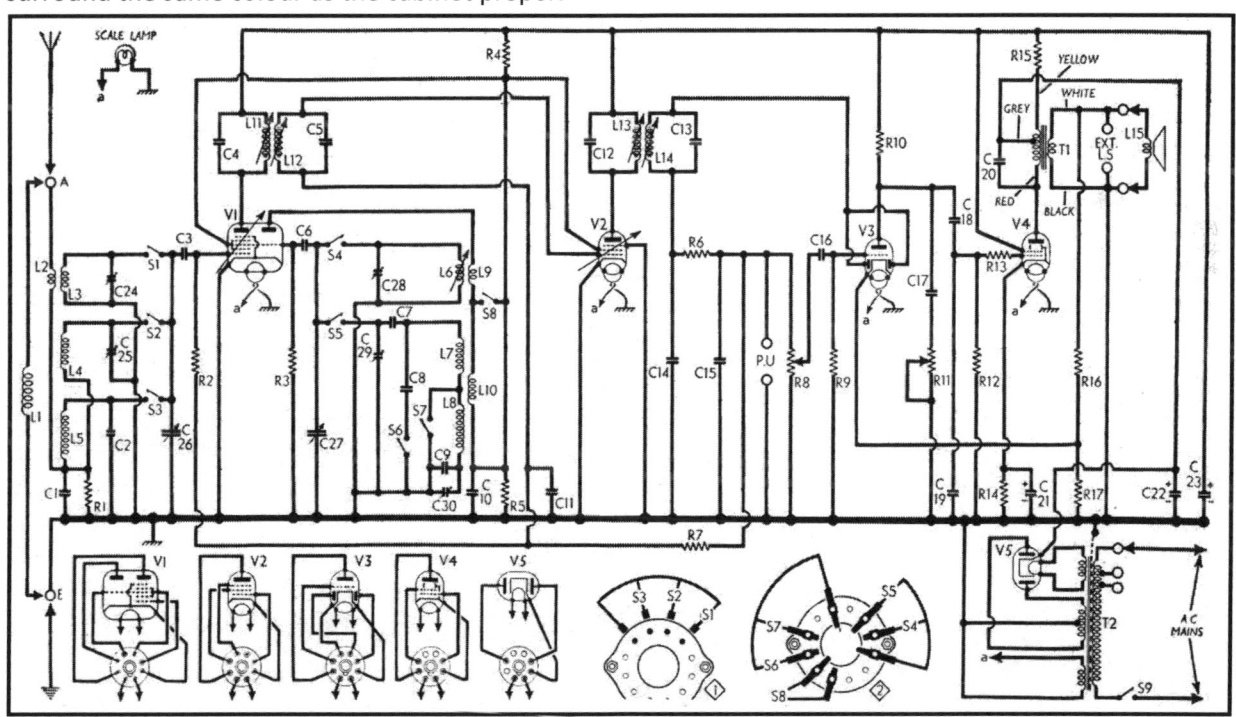

Cossor 494 circuit diagram

On the 501, Cossor chose to modify the cabinet moulding by removing the escutcheon from the one-piece compression moulds, adding it afterwards as a thermoplastic clip-in feature of contrasting colour. The divider bar was added as a pressed metal strip.

Although this modification was perhaps used to prevent damage to the vulnerable paint it always looks less neat than the 494 and more often than not it is warped out of shape, cracked, broken or completely missing, spoiling what is otherwise quite an acceptable set. Look then for genuine 494s.

The circuitry is conventional. A rather crude frame aerial, identified by L1 in the diagram, is mounted on the inside back cover and is quite adequate for local station reception. There is no RF amplifying stage; the signal is tuned by C26 (part of the twin-gang unit of C26/7) and appears at the control grid of the heptode section of V1. The triode section is the local oscillator for this very typical superhet design. The valve has internal coupling and the product of the mixed signals appears across L11, IFT1 primary. Inductive coupling produces the signal across L12, IFT1 secondary. Both coil windings are slug-tuned and mounted on a common former. The slugs allow the tuning response to be peaked at 465 kHz.

The signal is then fed to V2 control grid and amplified to appear across IFT2 windings. Note that the secondary winding of IFT2 is connected directly to the diodes of V3, a double-diode triode. The diodes are connected in parallel because in this particular circuit a single diode is used for both signal detection (demodulation) and AGC. The AF signal is taken from the other end of the secondary, L14. C14 and C15 remove remaining RF from the demodulated signal which is then passed via volume control R8 and coupling capacitor C16 to the triode AF amplifier grid.

The pick-up sockets across the volume control allowed the use of a record-playing deck without an amplifier of its own, quite common in the 1940s and early 1950s. The amplified audio is developed across R10, the anode load resistor, and coupled to V4 control grid via C18 and R13. This latter resistor is a 'stopper'. Such resistors are commonly found physically close to grid inputs as their function is to stop parasitic oscillation – instability. They may be mounted on or inside the top cap connections to certain valves, but in this case the resistor is below chassis, close to the valve-holder grid pin.

The fully amplified signal appears across the output transformer T1 primary winding. The transformer steps the impedance down to suit the low impedance of the loudspeaker. Note the additional hum-reducing tapping on the primary. The rectified and smoothed HT supply is fed through a part of the winding, which forms part of a residual mains hum cancellation system. Tone control is by negative feedback from T1 secondary, via resistive divider R16/17. This is full audio spectrum feedback, intended to improve quality and lower distortion. A manual top-cut tone control circuit is also fitted; this is R11-C17. Power supply is by a substantial double-wound drop-through mains transformer with a centre-tapped HT winding for full-wave rectifier V5. The heaters of the receiving valves are supplied from a separate winding.

As for AGC, find R7 on the circuit. It is connected directly to the AF signal source and goes via R2 to V1 control grid and also, via IFT1 secondary, to the control grid of V2. The line is decoupled by C11. This is an important component as its function, together with R7, is to integrate i.e. smooth out AF signal fluctuations to produce a relatively steady DC voltage that drifts up or down with changes in received signal strength. In other words it is a source of grid bias that changes to compensate for signal strength variations, acting automatically, hence the name Automatic Gain Control (Automatic Volume Control).

What to watch for with the 494

The usual suspects are the tubular coupling and decoupling capacitors, especially but not exclusively C18 and C20 (the pentode tone corrector). C21 should be checked for condition as this output valve cathode bypass will often be found either dried up or short circuit. Its companion resistor R14 is always a low value – in this case, only 270Ω – and such low values tend to go even lower, initiating an increase in cathode current which overheats the resistor which goes even lower... this can eventually damage the valve, so the resistor must be checked.

Where the B8G valves are used, their thin pins corrode easily and this can cause numerous problems of an intermittent nature. The best method for cleaning pins is to use a glassfibre pen. The bases can be cleaned with switch cleaner, with the valve inserted and removed a few times to assist the process.

The AGC components R7, C11 and R2 should be carefully checked. As before, any high value resistors tend rise even further with age and should always be checked. Scale lamp and other chassis wiring should be checked for quality of insulation.

Noisy volume and tone controls should be cleaned as described elsewhere, i.e. switch cleaner, Vaseline and if essential a joggling of the metal slider contact to move it to a better position on the track. The wave-change switch will benefit from switch cleaner and a light smear of Vaseline.

Take especial care to replace any mains lead that feels lumpy through its braiding or that exhibits the slightest crumbling of the lead ends. The mains transformer used with the 494 is a substantial component and generally gives little trouble provided storage has been dry, except for the voltage tapping selector method. This consists of a short flying lead with a snap-on connector and these often do give trouble because they loosen with age and do not easily tighten up. Best method is to solder the lead permanently in place.

BUSH DAC90A

These little Bush sets are a perennial favourite with collectors and restorers. Their neat Bakelite cabinets, in mottled brown Bakelite or less commonly in white Urea, have an attractive vaguely Deco appearance. Their chunky control knobs and the angled illuminated scale enhance the overall appearance. Do not confuse with the similar-in-appearance but earlier DAC90. The DAC90A has a gold anodised metal loudspeaker grille.

The circuit design is conventional with 2-waveband coverage and a four receiving valve line-up. Power supplies are of the AC/DC configuration and here we meet for the first time a fixed capacitor C22 across the mains input, there to bypass mains-borne RF noise. There is no provision for an external aerial; the frame aerial windings L1, L2 are tuned and signals are mixed in V1 hexode section.

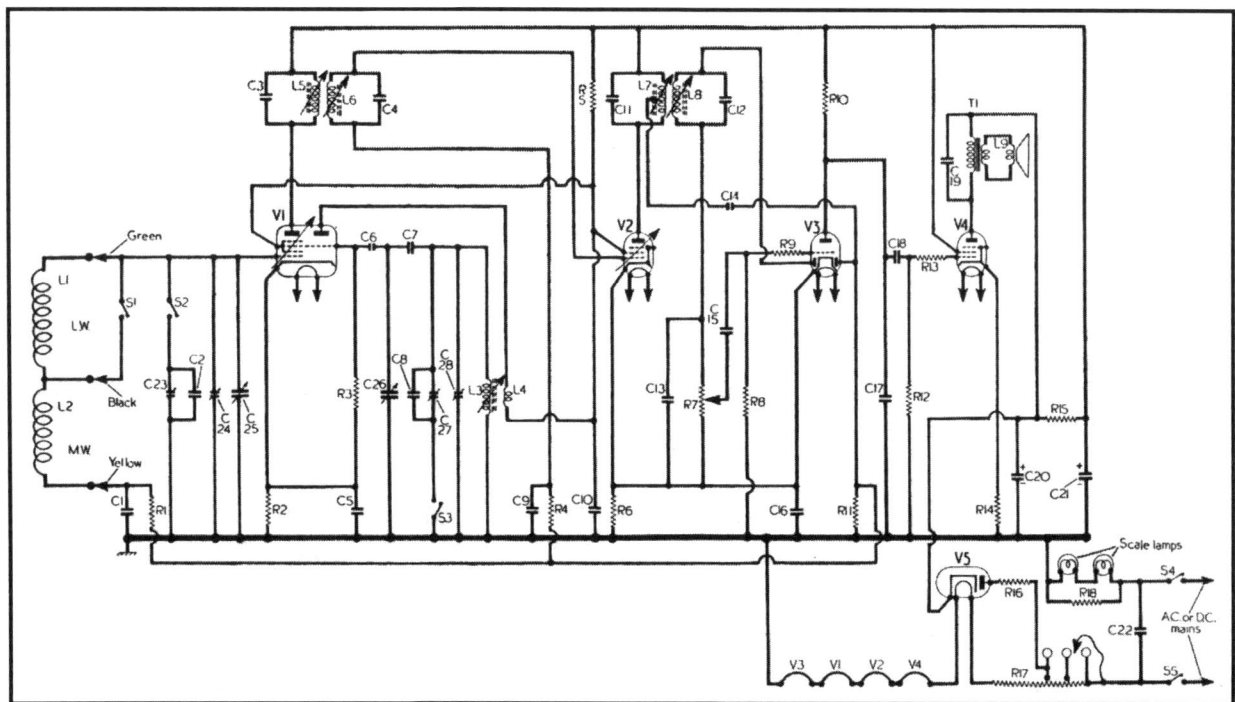

Bush DAC90A circuit diagram

The triode section is, as usual, the local oscillator. The oscillator tracks the frequency changes across C23 as the tuning is operated, keeping 465kHz spacing. 465kHz is of course the IF frequency.

The two IFTs are slug tuned and the demodulated AF signal appears at V3 control grid – but this time, a separate diode within V3 provides AGC potential. This is developed across R11 and fed back to the vari-μ valves V1 and V2. The volume control is R7. The output stage is basic: V4 feeds T1, the output transformer. C19 is the pentode tone corrector. The power supply is AC/DC and this has the chassis live to the mains. The end of the series heater chain is grounded to chassis from one pole of the two pole mains switch and the other pole reaches the chassis via the scale lamps and their shunt resistor R18.

What to watch for with the DAC90A

R17 is a vitreous (pot) wire-wound resistor, protected by green enamel and boasting several tapping points. Because the wire-wound passes the full current requirement for the heaters, it runs hot. This in turn tends to cause dry joint problems with the connections to it. The wiring itself is almost always unsafe, with sections bared and any remaining sleeving crumbling away at the slightest touch. It should be replaced with heat-resistive sleeved flexible wire. This is a very common problem affecting many AC/DC sets to a greater or lesser degree.

Another absolute must for replacement is C22 (if it still exists, as it often found to be shattered or missing). It should be replaced with a Y1 or Y2 series component – the 'Y' type capacitors are designed such that they fail safely. The set will work without the capacitor, though mains-borne interference can occasionally be troublesome.

Many restorers make it regular practice to change all of the wax tubular capacitors in the DAC90A. Most are mounted on a tag panel and as long as you exchange *one at a time*, should you choose to do so, you shouldn't make an error. R14 should be checked, as should R4 on the AGC line and R8 V3 grid return. It is probably safest to check all resistors for drift. Change C19, the pentode tone corrector, and C18, the grid coupler as failure of either of these can destroy the output valve.

The output valve itself is a slightly weak link, being a UL41 and prone to heater-cathode leakage which produces an annoyingly harsh-edged hum. Mullard valves were specified; different makes of UL41 can cause a problem because Bush use a nominally spare valve base pin as an anchor for components. Non-Mullard valves may actually use the supposedly non-connected valve pin to make an internal connection and this can give rise to buzzing and other odd problems. It is worth a check and if in doubt, isolate the pin by removing the components anchored to its holder tag, keeping their junction intact.

The wave-change switch is a simple device but somewhat flimsy. Clean with care.
The knobs are held by grub screws but these are accessible through holes beneath the cabinet (inside from the back for the wave-change knob).

The original mains connection method is in the form of a two pin chassis-mounted plug with the mains lead being terminated with a Bakelite two-pin socket. Connection can be made in either polarity, so it is a 50-50 chance whether the neutral is connected to chassis, or actually mains live (the set will work happily either way).

Bush DAC90A mains connection adaptation

Some restorers mark the plug to indicate the correct way around, but for user safety I prefer to do away with the plug-socket arrangement and wire a new length of lead directly to the on-off switch. This is done quite easily by removing the nuts holding the pins to the paxolin panel (the brown circular plate in the photograph above) – after unsoldering and completely removing the connection leads to the pins.
A hole to take a suitable size of rubber grommet is drilled in the plate at a point where it clears the chassis metalwork.

A new two-core mains lead is then fed through and connected up to the on-off switch tags. Plastic tie straps, one fitted around the lead immediately behind the hole and one to strap the lead down through a convenient chassis hole, help prevent strain on the lead. One final safety point concerns the metal grille mesh. Some restorers advocate fitting an earth to this, via a three-core mains lead, in case the grille inadvertently comes into contact with mains live. Personally, I doubt this could happen but if unsure, it must be better to add a little insulation around the grille edges on the inside of the cabinet. Fitting an earth to a live-chassis set seems wrong and potentially unsafe.

Finally, look for stress cracks, especially with the white urea case variant. The area at the top left as viewed from the front gets hot due to the dropper and the power valves beneath it and this can, over the years, discolour the plastic and cause cracks to appear. Urea is rather prone to this type of fault. The back covers, too, get fragile because of the internal heat build-up and may need repairing.

ULTRA CORONATION TWIN R786

This is one of a line of neatly designed little transportable sets, with the flexibility of operation from either AC or DC mains or internal dry batteries. The somewhat complex switching from battery to mains power occurs upon the fitting of the polarized mains plug. The circuit itself is a standard four-valve two-waveband superhet. The frame aerial L1 presents signals to the control grid of V1, which is a heptode valve. The oscillation is developed by 'electron coupling' within the grid structure of the valve – there is no separate triode oscillator. Effectively, two of the grids work as anode and control grid for the oscillator. There is no way to connect an external aerial or earth, nor should there be as the design is 'live-chassis'.

The IF frequency chosen for this model is a somewhat unusual 471kHz. V3 is a diode pentode, the single diode demodulating the signal with C15 and R7 filtering IF and loading the diode respectively. AGC potential is integrated and smoothed by C10 and R8 and a fixed voltage for bias purposes is taken via R10. The output stage arrangements are unremarkable; the main problem with working on chassis of this type is the compact size. There is always the danger of inadvertently bringing the filament line into contact with an HT source. This will instantly blow the valves, so – and especially when working on a powered-up set - take great care with metal probes, screwdrivers and the like.

Other than the actual switching, the power supply arrangements are fairly straightforward, considering the source flexibility. Mains power is applied directly, with only the neutral lead being switched. You might wish to change that to cut the live lead instead. MR1 is an air-cooled metal oxide rectifier with C24 and C24 reservoir and smoothing respectively.
The valve filaments are wired in series and, on mains, R20 acts as a ballast or dropper resistor to reduce the high mains potential to 7.5V.

THINGS TO WATCH FOR WITH THE CORONATION TWIN
The metal rectifier is likely to be high resistance, reducing both the filament and HT voltage level. This in turn will give distorted and low-volume sound output and a general lack of sensitivity and in extremis, a dead set. The rectifier can be replaced with a suitable solid-state diode.

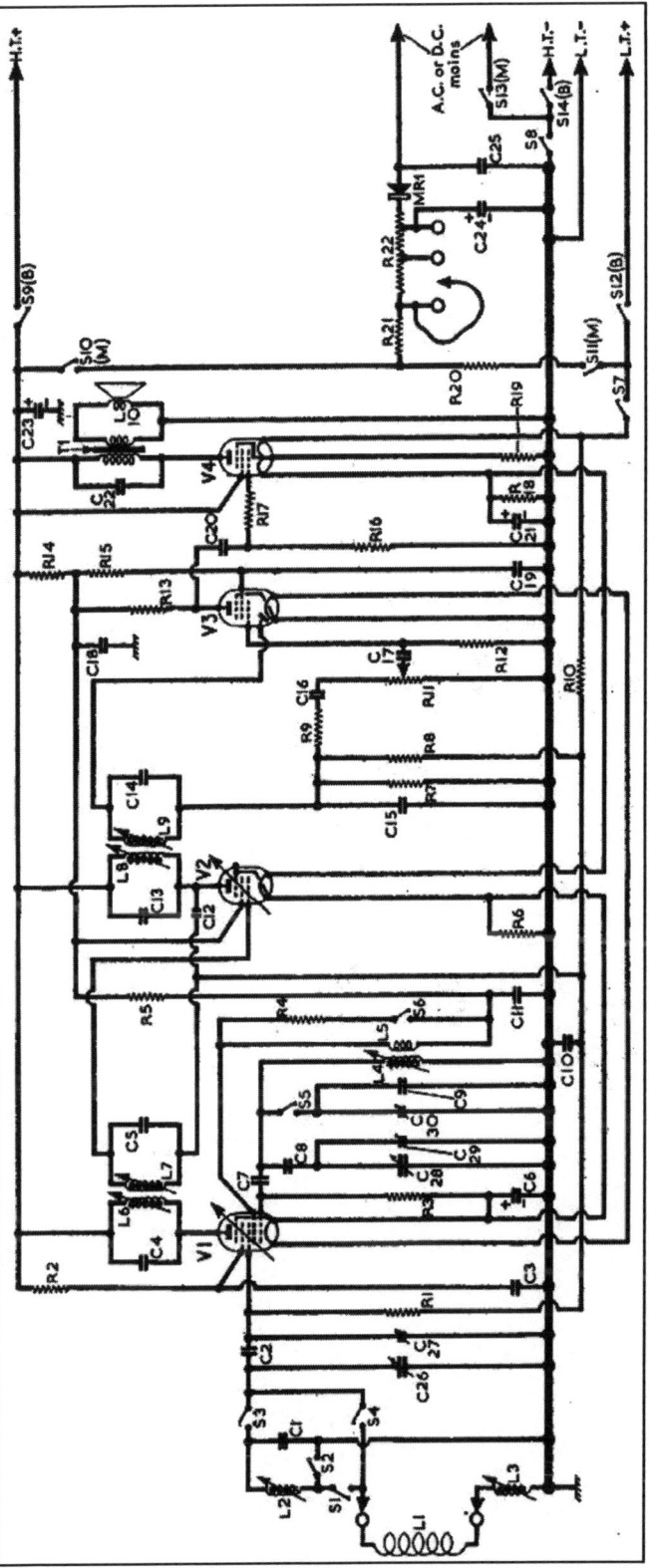

Ultra Coronation Twin R786 circuit

Components are more likely to exhibit age-related changes rather than direct faults, as the low current needs of the miniature valves generally provides for a cool running chassis. However, capacitors and electrolytic capacitors – and this includes C21 – always should be checked.

R10, at 5.6MΩ, might have gone high. R20 is likely to have worked hard and its connections should be checked for heat loosening. This applies also to R21 and R22.
Before purchase, ensure sure that the mains connector is present as inserting this activates the mains/battery switch. The little knobs are rather flimsy and prone to damage.

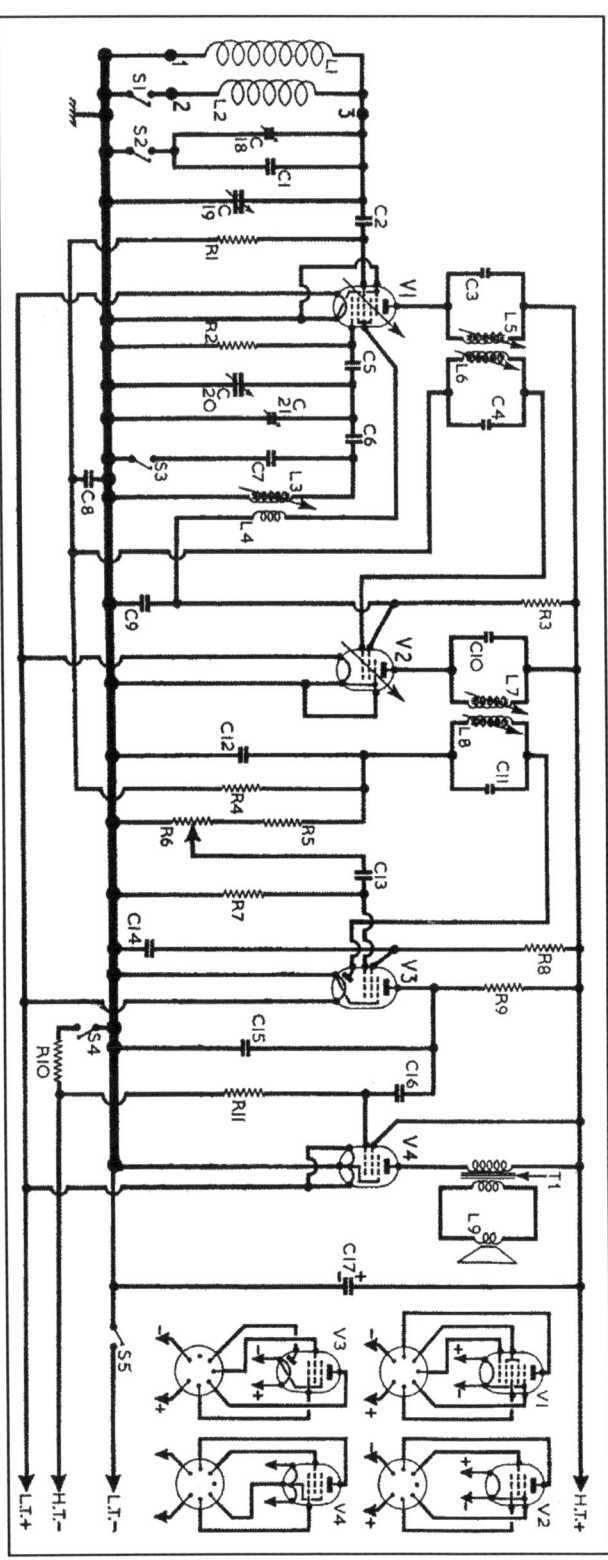

VIDOR CN414 ALL-DRY PORTABLE

This has been included for completeness. The receiver circuitry is very similar to that used in the Ultra 786 (above) and there is no need to repeat the description. There are divergences with the power supply, as this Vidor is battery only. Note the use of parallel filament connections, allowing a 1.5V cell to be used. These LT cells were physically large – they had to be to cope with the current drain.

Vidor CN414 circuit

The Vidor CN414 is quite typical of many 'all dry' portables of the 1950s. It was considered best to have portable radios that used two discrete batteries, as here, because if one wore out before the other – and it was usually the LT cell – only that one would need replacement, with a consequent saving of money. The usual warnings regarding wax–coated capacitors, electrolytic capacitors and carbon resistors apply here, though once again, as the sets used only modest current, the failures are likely to be age-related.

Nevertheless, makers persisted in combining HT and LT supplies into one package; after all, a large and profitable part of the business of both Vidor and Ever Ready was the production of batteries.

Sometimes these batteries will be found still in place within a receiver unused for many years. Natural exhaustion often causes the battery electrolyte (acid) to eat through the metal casing, then through the printed card covers to leak into the cabinet or even into the component area. This isn't good but unless the seepage is extensive, the corrosive acid can be neutralized with methylated spirits, after which a careful examination for damage should take place.

'All-dry' is a term used to denote the type of batteries used by a receiver. Before WWII, battery radios used 'wet cell' accumulators for low-tension filament supply. Post war advances in valve technology made low current consumption valves a reality and it is these that are known as 'all dry', running from dry batteries.

Left: Plus-a-Gram advert, circa late 1940s urged you to use the pick-up sockets on your radio

BUSH VHF80 AM/FM RECEIVER

We have now reached the most complex of the sets to be described. Released in 1960, this is a six-valve AC/DC receiver fitted with internal AM and FM aerials, with provision for an external FM aerial. Medium and long wave coverage on AM and 87.5-100MHz on FM. To simplify the description the circuit has been split into three parts, starting with the front-end tuning system. V1a/b is a double valve, a UCC85. The FM internal aerial is a simple wire with a balanced input across A1 and A2 sockets. Note that V1a is operating in grounded-grid mode with the input signal being applied to the cathode. If this arrangement seems a little strange to you, it was very popular with designers as grounding (earthing) the grid, through as short a lead as practicable, minimised grid-anode capacitance at the high FM frequencies. R2 is there to provide bias, but is a very small 27Ω. The circuit is naturally very low impedance which is the reason for the aerial matching transformer L1. L3 together with its associated components provides tuned anode coupling to the triode V1b, which is a self-oscillating mixer IF of 10.7 mHz appears at v1b anode and is tuned by IF transformer L6/L7.

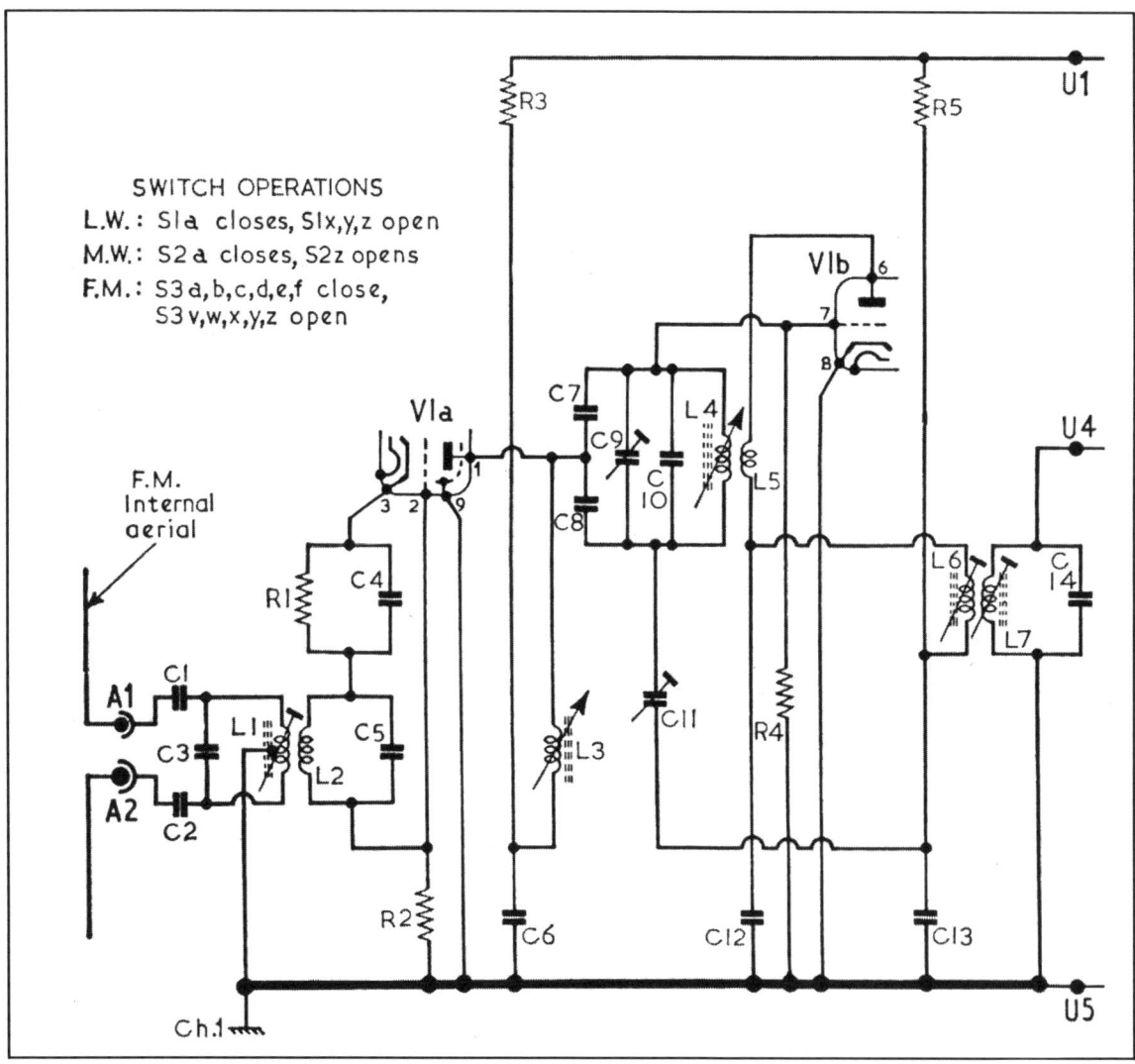

VINTAGE VALVE RADIOS

The IF signal is passed to the control grid of V2 when switch S3c is closed and the valve acts as an IF amplifier for FM. The signal is further tuned by L11/L12 and coupled via S3z to the heptode section of V3, the second IF amplifier, thence to the third IF amplifier V4. When S3x makes, V2 grid is connected to the AM front-end tuning system and ferrite rod aerial. The output from this valve is untuned and coupled to the heptode section of V2 via S3f. V3 triode is the local oscillator for AM and the mixing process produces an IF of 470kHz. This is fed to IFT windings L17/18.

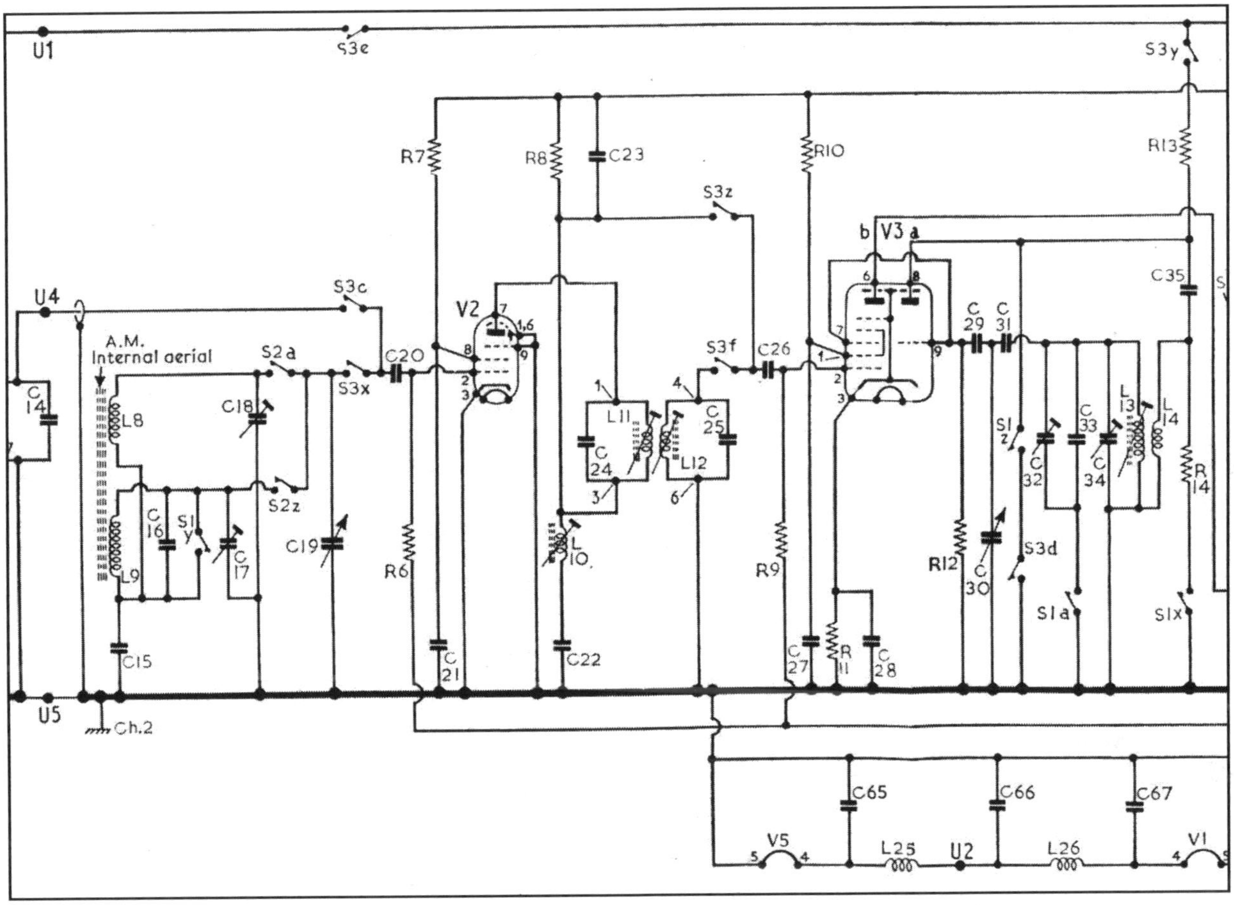

Bush VHF81, slightly later but very similar to the VHF80

V4 is an IF amplifier for both AM and FM. Note that the IFTs for both AM and FM remain in circuit at all times — each having very little effect upon the other. The detector diode for AM is V5c. The FM discriminator (detector, in effect) is V5a and V5b. V5 is an audio amplifier and V6 is a pentode AF output.

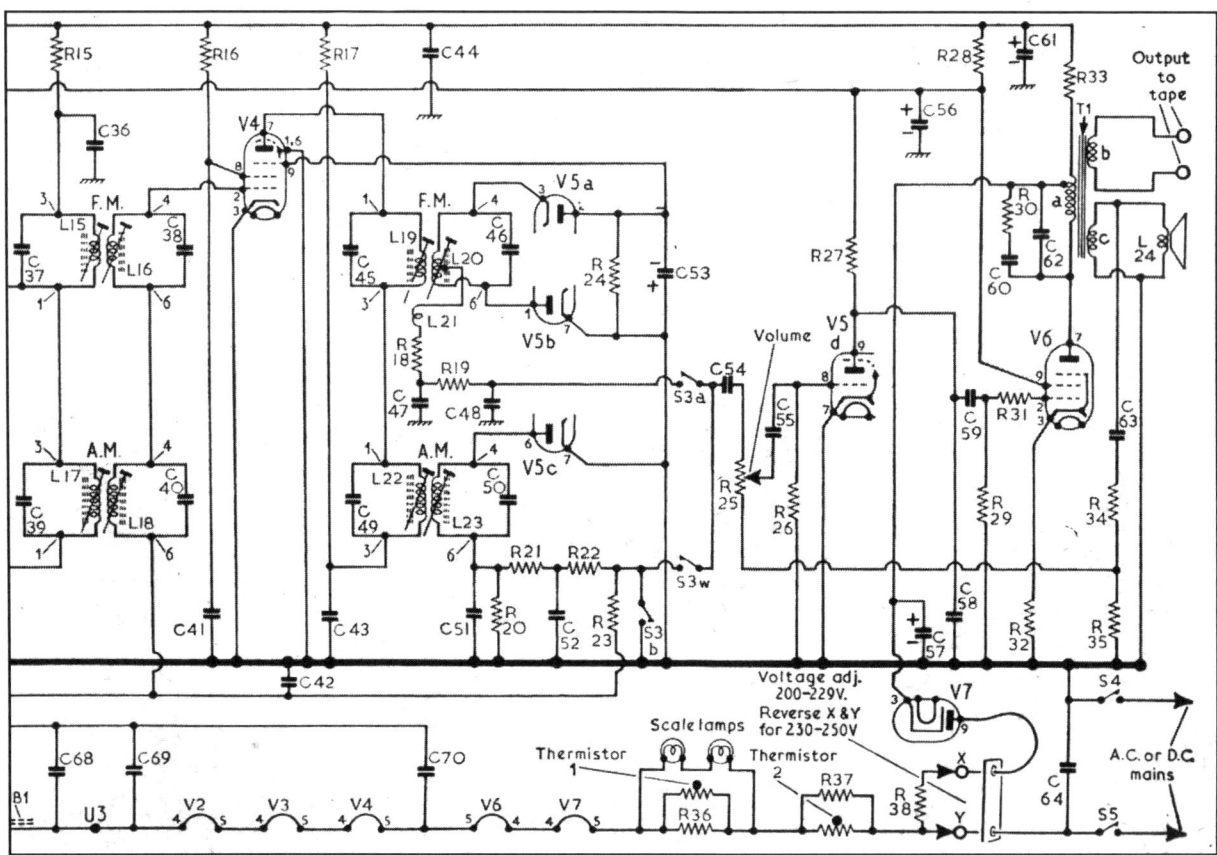

Circuit diagrams can tell you everything you need to know about a set. You may have noticed that the heaters of the valves in the VHF80 are in series, typical of AC/DC practice but notice also that the two scale lamps form part of the heater continuity — with a bypassing resistor in parallel with them, to limit the power applied across the lamps and a thermistor to limit current surges. Despite the thermistor, the lamps will often be found to have blown. The failure of either or both lamps will result in a non-illuminated scale, but because of the bypass resistor (R36), the set will work without the lamps.

You can see from the above very brief description that AM/FM receivers are built to a level of complexity well beyond the average AM only radio. The advice must be that you should not consider working on AM/FM receivers until experience and confidence has been gained by working on simpler receivers; but equally, do not let the apparent complexity put you off. Every radio can be broken down to discrete parts, each individually understandable and what today may appear impossibly difficult to master may well, tomorrow, prove not to be so hard after all.

EPHEMERA

Collecting items associated with vintage radio can be very interesting in its own right. Here are two examples from the author's 'Radio Luxembourg' collection.
Right: Radio Parade announces the start of the Dan Dare serial, 1951
Below: Hughie Green records 'Opportunity Knocks' for Luxembourg, circa 1950. The cast is notable: Green himself is centre-stage, flanked on his right by Bob Danvers-Walker and on his left by the producer Gordon Crier. Behind Hughie is bandleader Lew Stone.

MORE EPHEMERA

Over the years much printed matter was produced of historical interest on the technical side of both radio and television. Here are just a handful of examples. Wholesale catalogues such as Sloane Electrical Co's 'Slonetric' of 1935-6 were typical. All prices given in the catalogue are full retail, but it is doubtful that Sloanes would have supplied individual customers. The contents include radio receivers by Aerodyne, Alba, Cossor, Ekco, Ever Ready, GEC, Mullard and several other major makers.

'TELEVISION' is a booklet from the Science Museum, published in 1937 and therefore on the cusp of the creation of a high definition TV system.

This fascinating document covers the history and development of the technology up to the time and details the competition between the Baird system and that of Marconi-EMI. The transmission arrangements in operation at Alexandra Palace are also described.

'The Wireless Show!' is the illustrated record of an exhibition held in the Victoria and Albert Museum in 1977.

'The Birth of a High Definition Television System' is a paper read to the Television Society in 1952 and published by EMI Ltd.

'Aerodyne Radio' is a catalogue circa 1934

CHAPTER 6
CHOOSING YOUR FIRST SET

There it is, the old radio that you remember listening to as a child, or the one that has been in your family for several generations. Perhaps you can trace its purchase date in the 1950s, the 1940s or even the 1930s. It has stood mute in the loft for long years, waiting to live again and for you to restore to its former glory. Though neglected, it holds much sentimental value to you and others in your family. But wait. This is not the set you should be practicing on – for practice makes perfect and you, especially if inexperienced, may not yet have mastered the skills needed for a successful outcome.

Defiant, model unknown. A make best left alone unless you are confident of success

Even if you are skilled in today's electronics, it would be better to select some other old radio, purchased as cheaply as possible, to try out in practice the things mentioned in principle here. For preference, more than one old set should be thought of as an investment in your skill development: the small outlay will bring you rich rewards.

But which sets to obtain to practice on?

This is not an easy question to answer. It is perhaps better to ask which sets should *not* be selected. What you do not need is, to start with at least, is anything complex. Avoid sets with multiple push buttons, switchable AM/FM and more than four or five valves. Also you might prefer to avoid AC/DC receivers as these have live chassis, a complication that at first you can well do without. Very compact 'mantel' receivers, too, are more difficult to work on due to their component-packed chassis and (possible) miniature valves. Battery valve radios pose problems of power supply as commercial production of HT batteries have long been discontinued.

It is often thought that the relative simplicity and non-lethal voltages of battery receivers make for ease of restoration but remember that battery sets, at least the all-dry type, are compactly constructed almost to the point of miniaturisation in some examples. Then again, the delicate filaments of the valves used are all too easily destroyed and finally, there remains the difficulty of obtaining suitable sources of power (usually 90V HT and 1.5V LT). An HT battery can be assembled using sufficient PP3 9V batteries wired in series, but these issues add another layer of complication that the restorer might also prefer to avoid.

With the above in mind, you need to find a receiver that, ideally, has the following attributes:
- AC only, using a fully-isolating transformer. Note: there are some receivers that use a transformer for heaters only, deriving HT directly from the mains. This makes them live chassis; not ideal. There are others that use an autotransformer, which isn't really a transformer at all and offers little in the way of shock-protection. You can check these points with the relevant service data, generally easily obtainable from sources mentioned at the end of this book.
- Large cabinet with a commensurately large chassis, for ease of access.
- Post-war receivers are preferable for lower purchase cost and more straightforward restoration.
- Octal or B8G based valves for preference, but earlier bases used in pre-WWII such as B5, B7 and side-contact types are acceptable. It can be a little tricky to locate pin numbers on the small B8A 'lockfit' bases common in late 1940s sets.
- Physical construction should be straightforward; complicated tuning mechanisms and mechanical switch links only make life difficult. (So avoid Philips and Mullard receivers as the Philips Company had a tendency to over-engineer their controls; though for the more experienced, these sets make rewarding restoration material).
- Finally, the circuitry should be devoid of excess frills such as complex tone control networks, so this might rule out larger HMV and Marconiphone sets – but don't discount them entirely. The circuitry may be a little more complex than you need for starters but the sets are well-built and generally convenient to work on.

Actual makes and models that match entirely the above criteria are surprisingly few. Post-war receiver production tended to cut costs where possible and also had to be tailored to fit available supplies of components, valves and materials. So, partly due to enforced economy but also partly to the designing of sets to suit what little *was* available plus the existence of DC mains in parts of the country, many sets were made with 'U' designated chassis, which generally means they were capable of operation on either AC or DC mains. This in turn rules out the use of a protecting mains transformer (quite a saving for the manufacturer). Others, for example some of the Murphy range, opted to use an autotransformer which, with a single tapped winding was cheaper to make than a full transformer. This meant that the sets could only work on AC but still lost the protection of a double-wound transformer – a potentially 'live' chassis.

Fewer large sets were being manufactured after WWII and makers went in for the second-set market, so lots of compact AC/DC receivers filled the radio shop windows through 1946-1955, by which time a new innovation was making progress: the AM/FM receiver. The boost to trade sales provided by this broadcasting innovation slowed the gradual decline of the radio audience and allowed the production of some prodigiously large high-quality receivers, especially of continental origin, along with a range of more reasonably sized receivers from many British makers.

Good as they often are, none of these AM/FM receivers are truly suitable for the improver restorer to work on and achieve success. They are perhaps best left for restoration after experience has been gained. If restoring radios is compared to mountain climbing, the enthusiast new to restoring is in the foothills, looking up. With that in mind, here are a few sets that fit most of the stated criteria fairly well and should prove relatively straightforward for the improving restorer to tackle – and they shouldn't cost a fortune to obtain. I would suggest the Cossor models 470AC and 494AC are good candidates. The HMV 1122 and the Marconiphone T38A are among others worth considering.

Some larger Bush radios of the immediate post-war period are good prospects but the very beginner should avoid the smaller sets such as the DAC90 and the DAC90A as these are live chassis and though eminently suitable for restoration by the knowledgeable, especially the latter set, they may be best kept until you have gained practical experience. Most Pye receivers of the 1950s are also worth a look.

Some makes to avoid (at first)
'Defiant' was a brand owned by the Co-op stores. Usually very well built and with a quality of visual design to match most of the well-known brands, there is often a problem with both identification of a set and in obtaining service data. Until you have sufficient confidence to work blind, give the brand a miss.
'Westminster' was a chain store brand, sold by Currys. These would have been built by a variety of companies and again, service data is woefully absent. Beginners beware.
'Baird', the famous television name, was used by Radio Rentals on their rented radio sets. No doubt the chassis were well made, possibly by Plessey or Ekco, but again, service data is often impossible to locate.
'Noble' is one of a number of brand names on sets found in department stores. Sometimes – often, in fact – the chassis will be identical to one used in a known-brand set but you take a chance on this and unless you can verify the presence of data, these ranges again are best left for later.
Avoid kit-built sets unless you accept that these are almost always AC/DC or live chassis – no isolating transformer – and although simple in design whether TRF or superhet, they can and do use 'odd' valves and wayward circuitry; also the amateur build quality is variable. Remember these tips are for the beginner/improver. As you progress you will gain the confidence to tackle more complexity.

Other tips before buying
Take a careful look at this photograph. It shows the underside of an early 1930s AC mains TRF. The small choke has been added to the set, held precariously by a single loose screw with its clamp dangerously close to the poorly wired and incorrect mains switch. The large white wire-wound resistor is similarly loose, held only by its wires. The rotted insulation on the mains transformer has been ignored. Do your best to check whether a set seems untouched. Maybe it is full of dust and spider husks. Not a pleasant sight perhaps, but actually reassuring because it probably means that nobody has messed about with it. It is

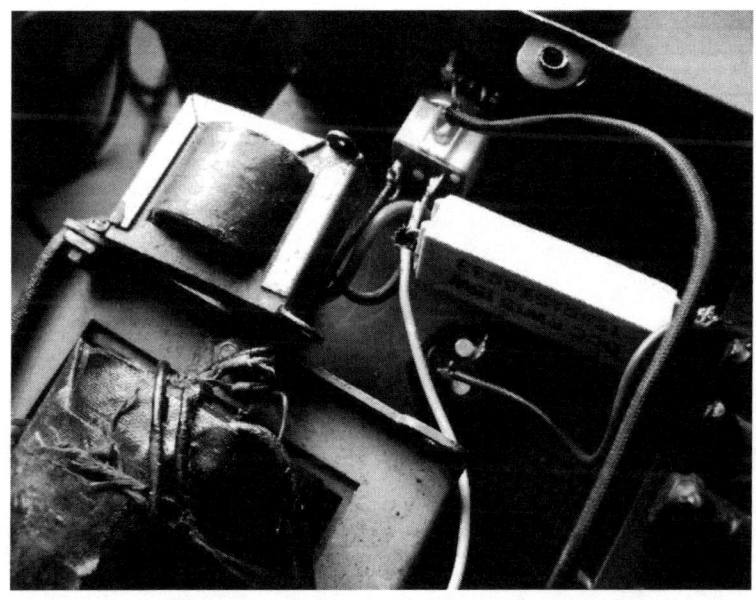

after all a big enough task to sort out the faults on any vintage receiver without having to cope with an extra layer of trouble, courtesy of the person often referred to as 'The Phantom', the meddler who wires diodes and electrolytic capacitors the wrong way around, forces incorrect valves into straining sockets, messes up the wiring to switches and slaps silver paint liberally all over a rusted chassis – usually without bothering to take the chassis out of the cabinet first. Far too many potentially good sets have been spoiled in this way. Strangely this seems to be a growing problem.

It can be hard to spot the worst atrocities, hidden as they may be beneath a cabinet that looks, superficially at least, benignly attractive. Get the back cover off if you can. Alarm bells should ring if the knobs don't match either the set or each other, or if a mediocre finish has been applied to the cabinet, for example brushed-on varnish stain. Grille cloth too should be original, even if rotted. New cloth might signal that the set has already been at least partly overhauled and as this is your purpose for buying, leave it for someone else to complete.

Has the set been 'got at' by someone in the past? See above for guidance.

Are the valves present and if so, are they the correct ones?

What is the state - if any - of the mains lead?

Does the rotary mains switch (often part of the volume or tone control) feel as though it is clicking over properly?

If all knobs are present, are they the correct ones for the model, and is their attachment method (grub screw, 'D' clip) functioning on them all?

What is the condition of the visible internal wiring, for example the loudspeaker connection leads? Usually, with elderly sets, the rubber insulation will have crumbled or hardened (self-vulcanisation)

Most of the above points would not rule a set out entirely, but it is as well to know what you are buying into. Besides, such detractions can be used as a lever to bargain the price down with. You need to keep initial costs down, if for no better reason than you have no way of knowing what the cost of restoration work will amount to.

INTERNET AUCTIONS

The phrase 'Caveat Emptor' (buyer beware) comes readily to mind in respect of these auctions. The first thing to check is the accuracy of the auction statement as provided by the seller. Is the radio *really* a 1930's model? You will often find that accuracy is lacking when manufacturing dates are mentioned. Often it may simply be an error on the seller's part, but the point is that there exists a world of difference in terms of value between a good 1930s set and a good 1950s set.

Trickery

Learn to recognize the tricks of the trade - terms such as 'Art Deco' do not truly apply to radios manufactured after WWII. The term was coined in the 1960s but it specifically refers to items built during the period 1925-1939 approximately. 'Stunning' and 'WOW!' really are meaningless and are there only to attract your attention. 'Found in an attic'. So what? 'Rare' is a matter of opinion, usually. Take notice of what is NOT said, rather than what is. Some of the sales pages are highly decorated with colour and fancy graphics, but you are bidding on a radio, NOT clever web site design. Don't be taken in. It is also surprising how many 'collectors' are seemingly disposing of their collections because their wives are threatening to leave them otherwise, or are downsizing their home or selling their deceased Granny's radio. Are these perhaps just cunning ways of avoiding giving the real reason the set is up for auction? Could be ... and you, as a potential purchaser, have no way to test the veracity of claims.

Honesty

What if the seller who claims not to know anything about radios? It is certainly true that some who sell vintage radio on the internet are being honest when they say that, but others use it as a 'blind', pretending not to know that the loudspeaker, valves or mains transformer is missing – and to sidestep 'awkward' questions. Check the availability of pictures of the set you are interested in. No pictures? Then the advice must be: don't bid. Instead, contact the seller and ask for pictures via email. If you don't get them, for whatever reason, reconsider your position.

Substitution

Sometimes the picture shown is not of the set you are contemplating bidding for, but one found on some other website or scanned from an advert (see later). If you suspect this kind of thing, ask for more pictures. If none are forthcoming, your suspicion is probably well-founded.

A picture is worth a thousand words – or not

What story do the pictures tell? I spotted recently an attractive looking Pye set from the early 1930s*. The seller (obviously a trader, to judge by his vast feedback) claimed to know nothing, not even the make of the set, though the rising sun motif should have given a huge clue in that respect. The pictures, of which there were two, were not very distinct. One showed the front of the set, the other one of the sides - but interestingly the blank one, not the side where the control panel was. I therefore emailed him to ask pertinent questions (in a polite manner, of course - I did not simply assume the worst). No answer of any kind was received so I did not bid and the set finally sold for over £70. I'd be inclined to bet that something was adrift with it - perhaps no control panel, or missing knobs etc. otherwise, why no photo, no answer?

You can usually check the seller's feedback (comments both good and bad left by previous purchasers) and this is helpful but it is not a cast-iron guarantee.

...a pig in a poke

Face it; buying via an on auction is akin to buying a pig in a poke. It amazes me that so many do so, being prepared to pay large sums when buying virtually blind. Finally, there are now lots of traders plugging their goods in these auctions. Nothing wrong there, but it is always good to know from whom you are buying.

Payment and security

So you've bid, and won. Now you must pay. Another old saying has occurred to me - 'a fool and his money are soon parted'. Don't rush to give it away. When paying, I prefer to pay by Paypal or send a cheque directly to the seller. With Paypal you have a measure of protection; if you send directly to the seller and you don't get the goods, at least you know who has your money. Remember - these are only my personal opinions. You must decide for yourself and accept the fact that the business of auction buying, whether on-line or otherwise, has its attendant risks whatever steps you take to minimize them. Having said all internet auctions are an interesting resource that there are many absolutely genuine folk selling regularly on them.

Buyer beware... again

Recently a number of vintage radio enthusiasts have found identical goods advertised on more than one auction. The obvious inference is that one of the 'sellers' is attempting to sell something he or she does not own. This has proved to be the case, several people losing money and as they never existed, not receiving any goods. When and if any monies can be recovered, you may find that a fairly steep processing charge of some kind is levied on you. It is quite possible that this kind of heartless scam is widespread throughout on-line auction categories.

*Avoid Pye portables from this period that have a side-mounted control panel as this is made from cast 'Mazak' pot metal that often self-destructs, crumbling into dust.

If in any doubt, email the seller, ask pertinent and preferably technical questions and for more pictures to be supplied. Base any further actions on the answers. Do NOT rely on a good feedback record: these are NOT a foolproof indicator of a seller's honesty.

More scams
Suppose you bid on an object but someone outbids you. So you've lost the auction. But wait: there's an email from someone offering to sell you the same item as a second chance offer. This applies if the winning bidder reneges on his bid! Great, you think, and send off your cheque. That proves to be a mistake; the seller has been sending second chance offers to all who bid originally on the item concerned. He doesn't own it and has no intention of honouring any deal. All he wants is your money.

A seller was advertising his Pilot Major Maestro for sale on an auction site. The photo looked familiar, and so it should have: it was my Major Maestro. He'd picked up the photograph from my website. Bit cheeky, especially as I'd displayed a copyright notice… however, that wasn't the worst thing. Clearly not the brightest of scam merchants, he made the mistake of posting a picture of his own set alongside my photo. His was not the same model as mine and the visual differences were very clear to see – or were to me, but then I knew what he was up to. Somebody bought the set, of course. His version of the Major Maestro was an earlier two-band version, with a tuning scale that worked differently - and a case in a far worse condition. The moral to this tale of woe? Check those photographs with care.

In case you think this kind of photo substitution is a rare occurrence, it isn't. It is however yet another example of just how crafty these spoof merchants and thieves are. Of course, not all second chance offers are scams - but it is up to you, the prospective purchaser, to check thoroughly before parting with cash or cheque. Be aware: there will be other scams masquerading as honest deals. Remember, *caveat emptor*.

TO SUMMARISE: THINGS TO CHECK WHEN CONSIDERING A PURCHASE
Has the set been 'got at' by someone in the past, or recently? (Very common)
Are the valves present and if so, are they the correct ones?
What is the state - if any - of the mains lead?
Give the set a gentle shake. Any rattling or looseness indicates poor workmanship at some point.
Does the rotary mains switch (often part of the volume or tone control) 'feel' as though it is clicking over properly?
If all knobs are present, are they the correct ones for the model, and is their attachment method (grub screw, 'D' clip) functioning on them all?
Is the scale glass intact, and is there missing lettering/station marking?
What condition is any of the visible internal wiring, for example the loudspeaker connection leads? Usually, with elderly sets, the rubber insulation will have crumbled or age-hardened. (self-vulcanisation)

Do NOT apply power to any unknown vintage set before checks and tests (outlined later) are carried out. Compromised by age, even a set that worked perfectly before storage is liable to have developed faults, some of which could be destructive when power is applied. Therefore, all the above should be done, in effect, by testing using touch and sight. Decision time… to buy or not to buy.

CHAPTER 7
WORKSHOP SAFETY AND EQUIPMENT

Mains powered radios fall into a number of groups but all require the presence of potentially lethal high voltages. As you may already have been made aware earlier, transformer-equipped sets can offer a greater degree of protection but whether the set is designed for AC mains only and possesses an isolating transformer, or is designed for AC/DC operation and is linked directly to the mains supply, there will be some point within the chassis assembly that is raw mains, i.e. directly connected to the mains with no protective transformer nor even a limiting resistor.

Protect yourself
Treat all valve-type mains radios with great respect. Your working area should have good illumination. Consider building a series-type test lamp. The floor should be made of or covered with well-insulated, dry material such as thick linoleum or carpet. On concrete, a wooden 'duck board' is a good idea. The workbench should be of wooden construction, with a wooden, plastic, thick linoleum or cork surface, definitely **not** uncovered (bare) metal. The use of a mains isolating transformer (1:1) gives a good measure of personal protection to the restorer. The use of a Residual Current Device (RCD) or an Earth Leakage Circuit Breaker (ELCB) will give good protection but **it is essential** that both the set you are working on and any test equipment in use is connected through it. Both RCDs and ELCBs are available as plug-in fitments, and a multi-way extension lead could be used with one.
Never put both hands into or on the chassis of a working set. Work with one hand only whenever possible. Never take chances. **Always** check the polarity of any fitted mains plug. To avoid inadvertent contact with hands, temporarily tape over exposed mains transformer connections or fuse-holders. Be especially careful if you wear a metal ring, watchstrap, bracelet or 'dangly' necklace.

TOOLS AND EQUIPMENT
There are five absolute essentials for the beginning restorer and these are: a soldering iron, an adequate test meter, a means of safely connecting 'doubtful' receivers to the mains (i.e. a safety lamp), a good source of light and the requisite service data. Let's look at each of these requirements in more detail.

Soldering iron
It isn't necessary to pay the earth for one; a basic mains powered iron of 25 watts or so can be obtained for a few pounds but be aware that you get what you pay for, by and large and a cheap iron will soon show its inbuilt limitations. For example, its metal casing may be earthed because the element within is working at full mains potential. This could, in certain circumstances, cause problems when working on live chassis equipment and could also, more seriously, earth *you,* the operator working on a live chassis, leaving you exposed to the possibility of a fatal shock. This is a very unlikely scenario as most modern irons should be double insulated and therefore not in need of an earth, but any risk that can be eliminated, no matter how small, surely should be. Another limitation will show itself when you attempt to unsolder a large multi-lead joint with a lot of solder involved. The low wattage plus the lack of a thermostatic control will cause the iron to lose heat, making such tasks slow and arduous. Soldering component with large metal tags will also affect the temperature and possibly leave joints that are 'dry' and less than perfect.

A better iron to purchase would be a 'soldering station' type, with a low voltage 40+ watt thermostatically controlled iron. These are inevitably more expensive than the basic iron types but are well worth the outlay. The station will consist of a double-wound isolating mains transformer. Such irons are safe in use, reach working heat quickly and maintain their tip temperature in use.

As for solder, avoid the modern lead-free type. This won't suit the tin/lead joints of vintage radios. It is still possible to buy reels of the traditional tin/lead alloy solder, with built-in flux.

Multimeter
The next essential item is a multi-test meter of some kind. Traditionally, this would be an analogue type, most commonly an Avo model 8, but nowadays there are meters with digital readouts that can be obtained at very reasonable cost and are extremely versatile devices. With either an analogue or a digital meter, you will be able to make the wide range of voltage, current and resistance checks needed for servicing the typical vintage radio.

Some digital meters have inbuilt extra facilities such as capacitor or transistor testers, though their value in practice can be questionable. Any meter will allow you to check, using resistance ranges, for shorted or open-circuited leads, components, coil windings and valve heaters and – with analogue meters, but not all digital types due to the need for a forward-bias voltage across transistor and diode junctions - you can also check the action of diode and transistor junctions for forward and reverse resistance by testing, reversing the test leads and retesting.

Safety lamp/limiter
Many restorers advocate the use of a variac as a safe means to connect sets to the mains for early testing. This is a device that provides a fully variable and controllable source of voltage, using the AC mains supply. Good as they are, they do not provide the protection or isolation that some think they do. A far cheaper (and I believe, rather better) way to protect sets from drawing excess current is to use a safety lamp. This can be as simple as a 60 watt mains bulb wired in series with the set's mains input. It must be a standard filament bulb, not a modern 'power-saver' type. Far more convenient, however, is a simple rig with switches, easily home-built. See below for construction details.

Light source
You cannot work in the dark, or in your own shadow. Your working area must be well and evenly lit and a bench lamp of some kind is almost a necessity. One of the low-voltage types with an inbuilt transformer would be suitable.

Service data
This can be obtained for almost any set you wish to work on, with the possible exception of some of the Baird (Radio Rentals), Westminster and Defiant models and a few sets made for sale in department stores and catalogues. See the 'sources' section in the appendix for suppliers. Data was made available from around 1934 for the great majority of makes but earlier data can be less easy to obtain, especially for minor brands. However these are often simpler sets, electronically at least, and with some experience they can often be successfully worked on without recourse to comprehensive data.

Other important items
At this stage you may be wondering why there has been no mention of oscilloscopes, signal generators, grid dip meters, valve testers and other devices.

In fact a beginning restorer would find only limited use for a signal generator and probably no use whatsoever for the others mentioned. When progress is made and knowledge gained a signal generator will be found to be very useful and an oscilloscope occasionally useful. As for valve testers, they are relatively scarce and so have become sought-after, raising their purchase cost far higher than their intrinsic value. For many restorers the most effective approach to valve testing is, if in doubt, replace.
Some types of fault can, in any case, show themselves with valves: flashing lights inside a working valve probably means there is an inter-electrode short-circuit. An unlit valve may mean that the heater or filament is open-circuit (test with test meter on low resistance setting). A white deposit inside the glass envelope probably means that the vacuum within has failed. A blue glow inside suggests a poor vacuum.

Other than those obvious things, low emission through age is a major factor in determining whether a valve is past redemption and a buzzing or humming when a set is working could indicate a partial cathode-heater short (but it could also indicate lots of non-valve causes, too – see fault finding at component level). So, all things considered, a valve tester, though useful at times, is far from essential. A lot of valves would have to be purchased before the cost of such a tester was approached. Bear in mind that valves generally have long lives and problems with many sets are due to components having failed through age, so do not jump to conclusions by assuming 'It must be a valve' when first faced with a fault. That said, the local oscillator valve can lose emission and stop oscillating, rendering a set 'dead' and the rectifier valve may lose emission, causing HT voltage to fall below the level needed for the local oscillator to work.

SUGGESTED LIST OF HAND TOOLS

Soldering iron. Although this has already been suggested, for serious work a soldering station, preferably low-voltage and thermostatically controlled, will give excellent service.
Solder: 60/40 tin/lead flux-cored solder. As mentioned earlier, do NOT try to use modern lead-free solder on old joints. It won't work.
Solder sucker. This is a vacuum device, very simple and low cost, used to clear tags of solder before removing components. Melt the solder with the iron, place the nylon nozzle close by and press the button. The solder is sucked into the reservoir and can be ejected by resetting the spring-loaded plunger ready for the next task. An alternative to the solder sucker is solder wick. This is a length of woven wire that draws the molten solder from the joint by capillary action.
Pliers: several types are needed. Radio pliers have a long thin nose and are useful for reaching in between wiring. Standard box-joint pliers come in handy when a good grip is required.
Side cutters: buy a good quality pair. I find side cutters more convenient than face cutters for snipping components out of sets.
Wire strippers: for removing insulation. 'Pliers' style are good.
Screwdrivers: an assortment of these, to include crosspoint and flat-bladed radio/electrician's screwdrivers and at least one flat bladed larger type.
Box spanners or nut spinners (or both): box spanners are tubular with different sizes of box on each end, turned by a tommy bar. Nut spinners have screwdriver handles and shafts with socket ends. All types should be BA (British Association) sizes, as this was the standard during most of the British vintage period. Metric spanners are poor fits for BA components though they can be useful for continental receivers.
Open ended spanners: again, BA sizes are perhaps most useful.
Saws: a junior hacksaw and a full-size hacksaw are at times invaluable.
Drill bits: a set of bits, ideally both BA and metric (or British 'fractions of an inch' types.)
Power drill: I have both battery and mains types but due to convenience the former gets the most use. If you can afford it, a good investment is a bench drill (drill press).

Vacuum cleaner: the most effective way to clean out cabinets.
Bench vice and/or clamp-on miniature vice: very useful as an extra pair of hands.
Files: needles files in a set, also a 10" fine flat file.
Pop riveter tool and a rivet selection: occasional use.
Heavy duty tacker/stapler: occasionally handy for fixing grille cloth.
Mole grips: sometimes a vice-like grip is called for.
Paintbrushes: very small glue-types are useful for minor painting tasks. A ½" and a 1" brush are handy for chassis cleaning.
A bench grinder is handy for sharpening screwdriver tips etc.
Wire wool and small wire brushes help clean corroded metal.
A mini-drill such as the Dremel can be useful, if only rarely. A headband with interchangeable magnifying lenses is well worth while obtaining. Some come fitted with a battery-powered lamp.

BRIEF SUGGESTED LIST OF MATERIALS

- Bake-O-Brite polish, T-Cut, Brasso: all may be used to clean Bakelite cabinets.
- Wet and dry paper: used wet with soap, various grades will de-rust chassis, remove marks from wooden and Bakelite cabinet surfaces (very fine only, e.g. 1000 grit, used wet with block soap lubricant).
- Rust treatment chemicals: various types, liquid and gel.
- Paint stripper. Nitromors is a reliable brand. Choose spirit soluble rather than water soluble.
- Aerosol paint: choose to suit your need, including clear high gloss for polished wooden cabinets, and primer for chassis. Car accessory shops are useful for this type of product. Consider grey primer and clear semi-gloss lacquer for chassis refinishing.
- Resin repair materials: for repairs to damaged Bakelite cabinets (see description of use in section 10). Again, car accessory shops can supply.
- Two-part fillers including Milliput and wood repair types. Two-part high performance wood filler is far better than conventional Plastic Wood and can be obtained in a small range of wood colours.
- Wax stick for cabinet repair: this is a product sold in wood tones and available from DIY stores. It can be melted into damaged areas on wooden cabinets and when set, scraped or rubbed level.
- Switch cleaner in aerosol form.
- WD40. Do not use this for switches and if possible avoid contact with thermoplastics, but otherwise this product is a useful cleaning, penetrating and lubricating agent and can help free rusted-on control knobs.
- Foaming cleanser. Obtainable from component suppliers, this product is effective at cleaning the many years worth of dirt covering all types of cabinet.

COMPONENTS TO STOCK

It is convenient to have a range of capacitors and resistors on hand. All non-electrolytic capacitors should be high voltage working, say 450VW, for general use. A high working voltage component can be used in low voltage situations but the reverse is definitely not the case.
A list of suggested values of tubular plastic and electrolytic capacitors, used to replace vintage capacitors is given on the following page.

OLD VALUE	REPLACE WITH	OLD VALUE	REPLACE WITH
0.001 µF wax tubular	**0.001 µF**	0.1 µF wax tubular	**0.1 µF, 0.015 µF**
0.01 µF wax tubular	**0.01 µF**	0.25 µF wax tubular	**0.22 µF**
25 µF low volts electro	**22 µF 50 VW**	10 µF 350VW electro	**8-10 µF 450 electro**
25 µF 350VW electro	**22 µF 450 VW electro**		

Note that high voltage electrolytic capacitors used for smoothing and especially reservoir purposes should have a ripple rating printed on the case. Ripple is the proportion of AC still present after rectification and is sawtooth in form, hence the need for capacitors to be made to withstand this ripple, which causes heating. It is prevalent at the reservoir but less so at the smoothing capacitor. Physically very small high-value capacitors are likely to be unsuitable for reservoir use.

There is a link between ripple factor and ESR (equivalent series resistance of a capacitor). As a rule of thumb, in a typical radio a ripple current rating of anything over 100mA should be fine.

PicoFarad (pF) value capacitors will be found in the RF and IF sections of receivers. These tend to be more reliable than the tubular µF types. In any case it is more of a problem to have these in stock as the values used vary considerably, so the best plan may be to purchase as needed though if you can find a 'kit' of various values on offer it would be worth obtaining.

Resistors come in a range of preferred values and in wattage ratings from fractions of a watt to 3 watts. For vintage work 1 watt types will be found to be the most useful and as they are physically smaller they can replace lower wattage vintage ones. When replacing resistors in values higher than 3 watts it may be easiest to use wire-wound resistors. Remember to support wire-wound resistors securely and locate apart from other components as they will generate heat.

Some resistors may be hard to replace with exact resistive value; choose the nearest preferred value or make up the value using two resistors in series. In practice it will be found that often quite wide variations in value have little effect – after all, standard old carbon stick resistors were made with a tolerance of 20%.

Useful odds and ends

These items may be found from suppliers on the internet:
Scale cord for re-stringing scale drives.
Quantity of B.A. sized nuts, screws, washers and star washers.
Tag strip. This is a strip of paxolin with a series of tags spaced along it, every fourth tag being extended and folded into a chassis-mount form and useful for mounting replacement components such as rectifier diodes and wire-wound resistors.

BUILD A SAFETY/LIMITER LAMP

This simple but invaluable device is extremely useful to the restorer. It allows power to be fed safely to a radio in order to test for potential problems with mains transformers, smoothing capacitors or rectifier short-circuits. The device works like this:

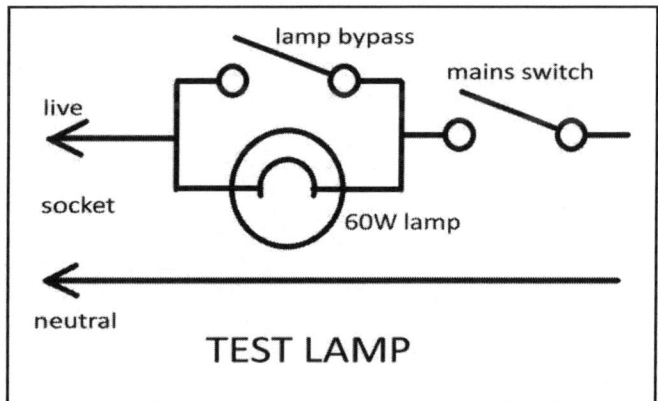

The power is applied to the set under test in series with a 'proper' conventional 60W lamp*. Once satisfied that no danger of burn-out or catastrophic failure is likely, the switch is thrown to short out the lamp and apply power directly. It's that simple - and that useful. I never test without it. For instructions in the use of the lamp limiter, please turn to p.100.

*Never apply power through lamp limiter or direct until you have ensured no obvious short-circuit or other power supply fault exists. Do not be tempted to use a modern low-consumption lamp.

List of components and materials for the safety/test lamp
1 X 60W mains lamp
1 X batten holder to suit above lamp
1 X one-way mains-type surface mounting light switch and pattress box, plastic
1 X surface mounting switched 13A socket and pattress box, plastic
1 X choc-bloc, at least 3 way @ 13A, for facilitating lamp wiring
A quantity of timber is required to form a 'chassis' for the test lamp and you can use whatever is to hand, but as a guide, the original uses a 9mm ply top panel with 15mm MDF side rails. Woodscrews to suit pattresses and rails.

Suggested construction method.
Cut timber to size after laying out the switches, lamp holder and pattresses as shown in the photograph. Two vertical rails can be made from 1½" X 1"softwood, glued and screwed through the plywood top. Using the top components as a guide, bore holes through the top panel to pass the wiring through.

Mount the choc-bloc under the top panel clear of the holes. Wire as the diagram. A good length of flexible 3-core mains lead should be fitted. Add labels on the switch to indicate lamp and direct. Secure the wiring to the side rails with cable clips or straps to prevent strain on connections. Check the wiring carefully before testing under power. Use a 3A fuse in the mains plug.

CHAPTER 8
STARTING FAULTFINDING: 'COLD' TESTS

With your newly-acquired radio on the bench or table in front of you, it is time to make a start. But what to do first? I contend that before any restoration should begin and surely before any cabinet work, the chassis itself must be brought into some kind of working order, in other words made serviceable. This type of work is not restoration as such; that follows afterwards. This initial exercise is to find out just what problems you will be faced with and how to correct them, even if on a temporary basis, to ensure that the time, expense and effort involved in subsequent restoration work will be well spent.

Visual checks
Often, a valve set will have been put aside and stored in a loft or a shed for many years. Many of the components will have suffered through lack of use, adverse storage conditions (damp, sunlight, dust and dirt, contaminants) and simply age. It should be assumed, then, that unless you are certain of a set's provenance – and likely, even when a set has been kept in 'ideal' conditions – that at least some components will no longer be within specification. Coils, transformers and especially capacitors may have picked up damp. Coils may suffer from so-called green spot copper corrosion (aggravated by damp) which can cause an otherwise at-a-glance perfect component to have one or more open-circuit windings. Capacitors may fail simply through age as their internal dielectric insulation, often waxed paper-based, absorbs moisture and becomes 'leaky'. Another source of trouble is the insulation on wiring and especially the mains lead if present. As a generalization, pre-war sets should have their mains leads very carefully checked as the rubber insulation within the flex may have perished. This usually takes the form of age-hardening – self-vulcanization of the rubber – and the resultant brittle crumbling and cracking can render such leads lethal in use. In its most severe form the rubber becomes dust.

Having visually examined the set for broken or missing valves, loudspeaker, top-chassis components or mains lead, a start can be made with a series of 'cold' (i.e. no power connected) tests. You should be searching for power supply problems such as open or short circuits across the mains input, the mains transformer windings if fitted, the heater chain (depending upon the set) and the HT+ to chassis resistance.
Innate electrical failures need a different approach. PM or energised loudspeakers can suffer from sticking cones caused by rust in the speech-coil gap. This fault cannot be seen but can be felt: gentle finger pressure on the cone evenly at each side of the magnet should sense if the cone is free to move or is very stiff, perhaps making an audible scraping noise and a grittiness that is felt, indicative of corrosion within the speech coil gap.

Measurements with an ohmmeter
I must make clear at this point that some of the faults able to be located by resistance tests as mentioned below may also, and perhaps better, be located by power-on tests. Take for example the presence of a dry soldered joint. Whilst it is true that such a fault could be isolated by cold testing, gentle prodding with an insulated tool whilst the receiver is operating is a much surer way of isolating the fault. Do bear this in mind as you read on.

Energised loudspeakers may also have open circuit field windings and as this winding acts as a power supply choke for the set's HT supply, the result under power is a 'dead' set. The cold test for this is by resistance reading, using your multimeter set to 'Ohms X 1'. You should find a reading of 500-1000Ω – but having maker's data to hand is invaluable. Metal rectifiers of both the finned and the contact-cooled types tend to go high resistance with age. This lowers the available HT level, perhaps to a point where the valves cannot function. The resistance of these may be read in both directions through the rectifier by changing the meter leads over. A high resistance in both directions indicates a possible problem. When carrying out this test, the component connections must be removed or a false reading is likely.

This resistance testing process is not limited to loudspeakers and rectifiers. Simple though not always conclusive tests can be applied to mains leads, switches, variable resistors and almost any part of the chassis where wiring is used: leads to the loudspeaker, to the scale lamps, to the aerial and earth etc. As pointed out earlier any vintage receiver must be expected to have faulty components, although this fact may not prevent the receiver from working.

Resistors may read perfectly accurately on test but under the stress of working conditions may change in value, usually going higher in resistance. Voltage checks as described later can be more effective in pinpointing this type of problem.

Other faults with both resistors and capacitors come down to physical damage which may be visually apparent upon close (magnified) inspection, such as the rivets on mica capacitors becoming loose or the wire loop connections at the ends of resistors cracking and losing contact or going intermittent.

It may be that some drift in the value of a component will have little or no discernable effect upon a set's performance but in order to ensure optimum working, these are best changed if more than, say, 20% out. Example: nominally 100Ω but reads over 130Ω should be changed. This is a personal recommendation, however. Many restorers leave the resistors alone until other avenues have been explored, in particular checking for capacitor faults.

Resistors of low value tend to work hard (pass heavy current) and these may be found to have drifted down in value and are often charred as a result. Replace with the correct value – and in the case of low values, as close as possible to the original value.

Dry solder joints with resistors are quite common, especially where components have run hot.

Other cold checks where the ohmmeter comes into its own: the heaters of valves may be checked for continuity, but be sure when checking filaments of battery valves that the resistance range you use is not powered by a battery of much higher voltage than the valve filament or you may inadvertently destroy the valve. The action of on-off switches, the continuity of coils, a search for a shorting vane on an air-spaced tuning capacitor, poor contacts in valve-holders and wave-change switches, these are just some examples of the usefulness of an ohmmeter.

Essential final cold checks
Ensure by testing that no short-circuit exists across the receiver's mains input circuitry. Check too that there is high resistance from the HT+ line to chassis. Finally, check for short-circuits across the primary of the output transformer as a short here will damage the output valve, possibly fatally.

As valves are expensive, all other avenues should be explored before replacing (unless you have to hand a spare valve, known to be serviceable).

CHAPTER 9
TEST EQUIPMENT

The most useful item of test equipment – so useful that it is fair to say that it is indispensible to the restorer, is the multi-test meter (multimeter). These come in two main types, analogue and digital.

The analogue multimeter
The analogue multimeter, perhaps the most well-known of which is the Avometer, has a scale calibrated in volts and ohms across which a needle swings during testing. Selection of 'range' allows the user to choose a suitable range where the needle can be expected to traverse half or more than half of the scale: readings where the needle is crammed to one or other end of the scale tend to be inaccurate. So, for resistance, the Avo will give you 'ohms', 'ohms multiplied by 100' and 'ohms divided by 100'. There is a selection of ranges for AC and DC voltage and current.

The author's much-used and venerable Avo model 8

Advantages: smooth movement of the needle is helpful when measuring rising or falling potentials and when using the multimeter as an output meter in conjunction with a signal generator. There were numerous cheaply made analogue meters on the market at one time; there are still one or two, seemingly made for automotive checks.

All the Avo models have a rugged construction and can give a lifetime's service. For vintage radio work, I suggest the model 8 in any of its marks is a good choice. The model 7 has a lower meter resistance and in some circumstances this can lead to falsely low readings, although many of the older vintage service sheets state that recorded voltages were taken using a model 7.

The digital meter
These have digital displays – numbers – rather than a meter scale. They can be obtained at a reasonable cost and even a low-cost cheap one will usually be found adequate for most general purposes. The disadvantage is, depending upon the quality and the facilities offered by the meter, that the displayed numbers tend to jump around somewhat. Flimsy construction is typical with the economy types. The low priced ones understandably tend to have fewer ranges. Autoranging is sometimes available (the meter finds its own suitable range). By and large, no digital meter will withstand a great deal of rough handling.

They are very good for quick, accurate testing and as you get an instant numerical readout, so you do not have to do any (admittedly simple) calculations that you sometimes have to carry out when comparing the scale reading of an analogue meter with the selected range setting.

Both types of meter are, therefore, useful. Start with a digital but if you really get into vintage work, also look for an Avo or similar analogue test meter at vintage auctions. A digital meter isn't useful for checking the forward and reverse resistance of diodes and transistors; for this you need an analogue type. A couple of points when considering the purchase of an Avo or similar analogue meter: check that the needle can swing cleanly across the scale, that the needle isn't bent and the movement is intact (test by reading a battery with the meter). If you can, look into the battery compartment to check for corrosion due to a leaking battery. Finally check that the rotary switches work smoothly without and roughness or sticking.

Signal generator
These devices allow you to generate a continuous signal over any desired frequency within the broadcast bands, including IF frequencies.

AVO signal generator. Bought at a bargain price, once renovated this old generator has proved both reliable and useful

The signal can conveniently be modulated with a tone. This allows you to hear the signal as you align the set, starting perhaps with the IF transformers, where you will inject a signal suitable for the IF frequency of the receiver, perhaps 465 or 470kHz, then working your way forwards toward the aerial, injecting signals at selected points on the tuning scale on the medium, long and shot wave bands. By this means, each adjustable trimmer within the set can be carefully aligned to give maximum output, indicated on a meter connected across the loudspeaker transformer. The generator can also be used as a fault finding tool, injecting signals in the same way until a point is reached where the signal is no longer heard; by this means you can narrow down the faulty section within the set.

Signal generators can be small and battery operated, such as the tiny 'Nombrex' generator of the 1960s, or they can be large, heavy and mains-powered devices such as the Taylor, Advance or Heathkit models. There's usually a few generators entered in radio auctions and you can find them on stalls at radio fairs such as those hosted by 'The Radiophile' magazine and the British Vintage Wireless Society.

Test lamp
No apologies for repeating this device; so simple, so effective, easy to build, easy to use. Construction was described earlier. An essential safety and testing device, in the author's opinion. See p.100.

Oscilloscope

The oscilloscope produces a visual representation of a signal, a voltage or a current. This can be useful for fault tracing in conjunction with a signal generator and can be a convenient way to help alignment of RF and IF stages when used as a visual display of the output signal. However, unless you can find one at low cost, the oscilloscope should be seen initially as something of a luxury for straightforward valve radio work.

SIGNAL TRACER/INJECTOR and DIODE PROBE

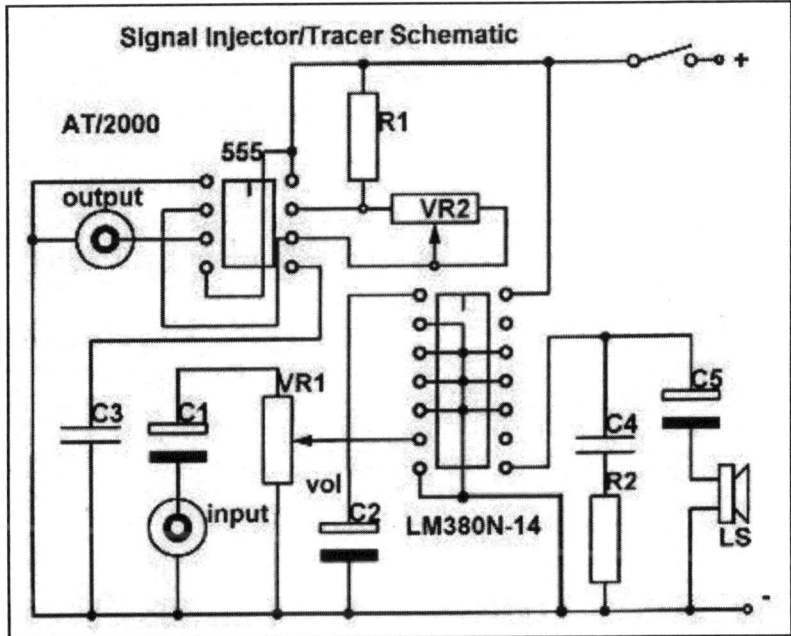

This design by the author is in the form of a compact square-wave generator together with a small amplifier. The square-wave means the generation of a signal rich in harmonics which will cover in one go most of the broadcast bands. This can be fed in at the aerial and the tracer amplifier can be applied to various points working back from the output valve until the detector stage is reached, when a series diode needs to be introduced into the tracer input lead in order to detect signals from the square-wave generator. The diode probe can be moved steadily toward the aerial although a point may be reached at which it becomes too insensitive to be of practical use, in which case the generator can be moved in from the aerial stage by stage.

The aim is to find the point at which the signal is either detected by the diode i.e. made audible, or the point at which it disappears, whereupon the location of the fault is, if not exactly pinpointed, at least it is narrowed down to a manageable stage of handful of components.

Testers of this type were made by some test equipment manufacturers but it is relatively easy to make one for yourself, using a simple amplifier circuit (perhaps a small silicon chip type) and a square-wave generator circuit (again, a small chip of the 555 timer type).

A circuit diagram of a useful tracer/injector is shown above. It is wise to place a capacitor of around 10nF in series with the oscillator output, with a high working voltage rating, say 400VW. This is to protect the oscillator against inadvertent high DC input. This can be constructed on matrix board or stripboard and should be built into a non-metal insulated box.

A diode probe (germanium type – the P-N junctions of silicon diodes require too high a potential to allow low-level signals to be reliably detected) can be fitted into an empty ballpoint pen case to act as a test prod if required. See diagram on previous page.

Circuit function of the signal injector/tracer
A 555 timer chip is connected in astable mode, the frequency being determined by the time constant network R1/VR2/C3. The output is to a coax socket. VR2 allows adjustment of the time constant and therefore the pitch of the audible sound when fed into the amplifier section either via the radio under test or direct into the amplifier input socket.

The amplifier is an LM380N-14, a low cost and efficient little chip. It is a DIL-14 pin package. The 555 standard is DIL-8 so there is no chance of confusion. To minimize possible damage and make life easier if a change of chip becomes necessary it is prudent to use chip holders rather than soldering the chips themselves. A screened lead should be made fitted with a coaxial plug, with a test prod to the centre conductor. In use, the outer screen should be clipped to chassis.

The optional detector probe described on the previous page should allow the detection of signals in the IF stages up to the detector diode itself (usually one diode of a multiple valve). With IF stages in order, it should be possible to hear radio programmes over the tracer internal LS. Don't expect high fidelity, however. Though a standard marker pen case is fine, the probe can more easily be built into a thick marker pen case. The switch allows the probe to be used with the amplifier for AF circuit checks.

COMPONENT LIST for the signal injector/tracer
C1,2,3: 10µF electrolytic
C4: 100nF
C5: 470µF electrolytic
R1: 1k
R2: 2R7
VR1: 10k
VR2: 47k preset
Loudspeaker: 8 ohms

PROBE
OA90 or similar germanium diode
180pF RF type capacitor
10nF
Plus small panel of SRBP, i.e. stripboard or a PCB to support the components and a marker-pen case to house them. A short length of welding or brazing rod will make a suitable test prod.

CHAPTER 10
FAULT-FINDING

The very first thing to do with any unknown receiver is the visual check, as described earlier and although this can be limited to what can be seen with the back cover removed, to begin with at least it may not be essential to remove the chassis from the cabinet. Next, check using an ohmmeter (multimeter set to Ω X 1) the resistance across the mains input live and neutral. For this cold test, ensure the set's on-off switch is set to 'on' **but not connected to the power supply.** It is worth remembering that on-off switches commonly fail in open-circuit mode. A mains input resistance test where the switch is faulty will read infinity. Sets using AC/DC heater chains with resistive droppers should register around 1kΩ or perhaps a little more. This proves that the heater chain is intact. Open circuit indicates a complete break somewhere along the line, perhaps in the mains lead, the switch or the ballast resistor arrangement but don't forget that a missing valve or one with an open-circuit heater will affect the reading. Completely open circuit reading means a faulty on-off switch or mains lead.

Low or very low resistance readings suggest a short circuit: there may be such a fault in one or more decoupling capacitors from the heater line to chassis. Also it may be that a cathode-heater short has occurred in one of the valves or perhaps the rectifier valve has developed an internal short-circuit. When readings are open or short, further cold investigation should be carried out (see below). Only when readings are 'normal' should testing under power be contemplated (but **not yet** - see later).

With AC only sets using a fully wound and isolating mains transformer, any cold reading across the mains input will be influenced by the inductance of the transformer primary winding and this is going to read as quite a low resistance on your DC-powered test meter, perhaps 40-50Ω. Anything very much higher or lower than that would indicate respectively an open-circuit or shorted primary winding. The mains tapping points can be suspects in the former case and any RF bypass capacitor fitted across the mains input can cause the second. An AC/DC receiver should provide a reading at least as high as the dropper resistor resistance and this should rise when any valve is removed, breaking the series heater path.

HT line resistance

Assuming that so far everything reads about normal, a resistance reading needs to be taken from the HT line to chassis to check for HT short circuits. This may be done by accessing the under-chassis through a hatch that is present in some cabinets, or you may be able to locate the tag strip of the output transformer where mounted on the top deck or attached to the loudspeaker, reading from the primary tags to chassis. You should expect to find around 10KΩ. Much higher would indicate an open-circuit between the transformer and the HT+ line. Very high at one end indicates an open-circuit primary. Readings of much less than 10kΩ would suggest a leak to chassis, possibly because of a faulty reservoir capacitor or tone-control components of the top-cut type where a capacitor is connected between the anode of the output valve and chassis (via a variable control).

Sometimes a wound choke is used between the reservoir and smoothing capacitors; at other times and more commonly it is a wire-wound or physically large carbon resistor. Either of these can go open-circuit. With sets using mains energized loudspeakers, the field winding doubles as a choke and this could be open-circuit and unfortunately will quite often be so.

Any faults found should be investigated by continuing the cold-testing procedure as far as possible.

TESTING UNDER POWER. Numbers in brackets refer to example circuit on p. 107.

Sets that show no obvious problem can be tested under power but **definitely not by direct connection to the mains.** The test lamp or a variac (variable voltage source) must be used, the former for preference. Assuming the test lamp is in use, upon switch-on the lamp will glow brightly for a second or two but then it should dim right down to a feeble glow as the set warms up. If it remains bright there is a problem, most likely an HT short-circuit. After thirty seconds or so it should be possible to discern a hum from the loudspeaker, though this may not be very loud and you will need to place your ear close the grille to be sure.

Absolutely 'dead' receiver

With no illumination at all from the test lamp, dead silence with no noticeable hum would indicate a lack of HT or possibly AC power. AC can be measured at the mains transformer secondary or from the tags of an AC/DC set's dropper resistor. After the rectifier, HT+ can be measured at the reservoir and smoothing capacitor terminals (1). Nothing at either means that the rectifier valve is faulty or there is a break in the connection from the rectifier valve holder to the reservoir capacitor.

Unfortunately there are no cast-iron guarantees with fault-finding. In the above paragraphs I have suggested some of the most likely causes of total silence but these are generalisations and there are other paths, should the methods suggested prove fruitless, to be followed. For example, the loudspeaker itself could be open-circuit, as could the output transformer – usually the primary winding (2). With the power disconnected, the loudspeaker can be checked on Ohms X 1, directly across the speech coil terminals. A click should be heard as you touch the meter leads on the connections. No click is worrying because this can mean a burnt-out winding but it is possible that the winding is jammed in the gap and incapable of movement; test for this by pressing gently with fingertips on the cone. It should move slightly.

The secondary then the primary of the output transformer – and the various connecting leads to it, including and arrangement for the connection of an extension loudspeaker – can also be resistance and continuity checked before applying power once more.

DC Voltage checks

If voltage is present at the smoothing capacitor, check for it on the output valve anode and screen grid. Then switch the set off and disconnect it from the mains before touching the output valve and the rectifier valve envelope (glass). If HT has been generated, both valves have been passing current and both will be very warm. If the rectifier is barely warm it may be faulty, assuming that its heater was glowing under power. If the rectifier is hot but the output valve is cool, switch the set on again and check for voltage at the cathode of the output valve. If this is very high, check the cathode resistor for open-circuit. By these means you should be able to narrow down the cause of the fault.

Live set but no stations audible

Assuming you have hum and/or faint crackling, then rotating the volume control (3) should cause a rustling noise and is a fair test to ensure that the AF stages at least are operating. If the set is fitted with pick-up sockets **AND is AC only with a full transformer (do not risk touching pick-up sockets where fitted to an AC/DC receiver),** a fingertip on one or other of the pick-up sockets – **free hand not in contact with the chassis** - should give rise to a loud 50Hz hum, providing the volume control is fully advanced clockwise. Again this is a good test of AF stage function. Check that 'gram' has been selected, if the set is fitted with a switch as part of the wave-change switch.

No crackle from the control and no hum from the fingertip test both indicate AF amplifier trouble. Lightly tap the output valve with your fingertip to check again if it is hot and so is passing current, and is therefore probably OK.

Perhaps the easiest way to double-check this is to take a small screwdriver and scrape it on the output valve grid terminal, on the valve base. This should, assuming the valve is passing current, give a modest crackle in the loudspeaker with volume at maximum. If this is present, nothing here points to the fault being localised to the output stage. For all the above tests, 'rock' the volume control to ensure it isn't the cause of the lack of signals.

The chassis will need to be out of the cabinet from this point on, if it isn't already. Check voltages around the output valve with respect to chassis: screen grid, cathode. Refer to your data but as a rule, the screen should have a high HT level and the cathode somewhere between perhaps 10-20V. The control grid (4) must be negative with respect to the cathode, by about the cathode voltage: so if for example the grid reads zero volts and the cathode 15 volts, the grid is effectively negative with respect to the cathode and that's how it should be. Excessive positive voltage on the grid with respect to chassis would suggest either a leaking coupling capacitor (very common), a 'floating' grid (open-circuit grid resistor) (11) or a failed valve. Leaking couplers lead rapidly to failed valves, so you might be looking at both faults.

Assuming the tests show that the AF and output stages are working, rotate the wave-change switch (5). You should hear a healthy crackling. If this is weak and no stations can be heard as you tune across any band, take a deep breath and switch the test lamp supply to direct (be ready to switch back to bypass should anything untoward occur). This action will increase to output of the rectifier valve and improve the emission of all the valves including the frequency-changer. At this point you should be able to make that wave-change switch crackle loudly and, with a screwdriver or short length of wire for an aerial, expect to hear at least some signs of life in the form of local stations on medium, morse, mush and far-flung foreigners on short, radio 4 on long.

If no stations are received, valve voltage checks should be made starting with the frequency-changer. Service data is essential for this. One thing rarely mentioned in data is the slight negative 'kick' provided by the local oscillator grid (5) as the test meter, set to DC volts, touches it. This is best checked with an analogue meter and is a sure sign that the oscillator is functioning, though not conclusive that it is running at the correct frequency.

Local oscillator
Oscillator problems can be tricky to isolate but all faults eventually succumb to a logical and painstaking approach, never rushing, never missing a check that seems to obvious to bother making.

The local oscillator (frequency changer) valve is one that may well be a candidate for replacement as a drop in emission to the point where the oscillator section won't run may mean a complete lack of signals. Occasionally a clue to this may be gained from the fact that long wave works, others don't. This is when the oscillator manages to run at the lower frequencies of long wave but just can't produce the higher ones of medium and short. Don't discount the capacitors in the frequency-changer stage, either. These are very small value types and are often overlooked in the search for faulty components. Though less troublesome than their wax-coated relatives their innocence is not to be taken for granted.

Note that low HT+ voltage can also cause the local oscillator to cease functioning entirely or partially on some or all bands. Most AC-DC sets should have an HT around 180-200V and most AC only sets with full-wave rectifiers should have HT+ well above 200V.

Potential divider resistor networks should be carefully checked too, especially those supplying screen voltages. This includes IF amplifier valves. No signals but a negative 'kick' on the oscillator grid might point to IF transformer trouble (see below).

Problems with valves

In a mains radio, hum and noise may be caused by any valve that has poor or failing heater-cathode insulation. The cathode picks up the 50Hz mains ripple from the heater. The only realistic cure is replacement of the offending valve, but that can be difficult to pinpoint without a valve tester or – better still - a set of known good valves for substitution.

Heaters may be open-circuit. In an AC mains set, if one of the valves does not glow, the chances are that the heater has failed. This is easily tested with an ohmmeter. Set to 'ohms X 1' and check across the heater pins for continuity. In an AC/DC set, if none of the valves glow, this could be any one of the valves with an open heater, or indeed, with some models at least, a scale lamp with an open filament. Again, best check is with an ohmmeter. Check heater decoupling capacitors where not all valves are lit with an AC/DC set.

If the problem with the set is low gain, possibly distorted at full volume setting, the emission of one or more valves, especially in the AF or output stages, could be the problem. Valves often have a long life, but all have a finite one. The oxide layer on the cathode eventually erodes away and the gain of the valve drops. Before assuming a given valve is faulty, check voltages, especially the high tension (HT), as the lack of sufficient voltage can cause the same symptom. Of course, such a lack might well point to another of the valves – the HT rectifier. A blue glow inside any valve indicates that the vacuum is impaired. The glow is caused by gas ionisation within the envelope. As is so often the case, the only cure is replacement.

Checking electrolytic capacitors

Electrolytic capacitors with a high value, i.e. those used as reservoir or smoothing (1), may be checked by disconnection from the circuit (simplest way is to remove the connection to the tag being tested) and taking a reading with the meter set to 'ohms X 100'. The needle – or reading, in the case of a digital meter – will immediately show a low resistance but should rapidly climb into a very high resistance level.

The charged capacitor may be discharged by temporarily placing a resistor of any value between 10kΩ and 100kΩ across the leads or tags and then a second reading can be taken, which should show a similar result to the first reading. Assuming readings are as stated, the capacitor may be judged satisfactory in that no excess leakage has developed, nor is it open-circuit or low emission due to electrolyte failure. This test does not measure equivalent series resistance (ESR) but at least you will know that the component is serviceable and will not cause damage when the receiver is under power. Conversely, readings that remain stubbornly high resistance or remain low resistance indicate a problem with the capacitor.

Resistor faults

Resistors on older sets will often tend to have drifted upwards in value. This is especially so with higher value carbon composition resistors, the cheapest and therefore most common of types. Resistors, like capacitors, may look perfectly OK but don't be fooled – check with the meter, using the same technique as described above for capacitors. Resistors hardly ever go 'dead' short.

'Motorboating' and instability

These are related audible effects and are usually due to failed decoupling capacitors. Motorboating sounds rather like a motor launch travelling up a river.

Instability is a cacophony of squeals, howls and other noises varying in frequency, usually loudly.

Check any HT decoupler by bridging across it with a known good component from HT line to chassis. If one isn't fitted, fit a temporary one of, say, 0.02µF and see if the problem is cured. If it is, either leave the temporary fix in place – make it permanent – or replace the smoothing capacitor which originally would have been expected to reject radio frequencies that other wise might reach the HT line and feedback to other stages. With age, electrolytic capacitors function less efficiently at RF.

If the added decoupling makes no improvement, check that any screened valve is truly screened, i.e. that is screened coating is grounded to chassis. In larger valves such as the octal range this is usually achieved by means of a fine loop of wire around the screening where the glass joins the base. This loop is internally connected to a valve pin and thence to chassis. The wire loop commonly breaks free and causes instability but it can be taped or glued back in place. Valves that have lost their screened coating can also cause problems and may need to be replaced, though the 'faulty' valve may work well in a different receiver. See 'instability' below for repair techniques.

Check the small resistors adjacent to control grid connections, either on the valve base or in some cases upon or within the valve cap. These are called grid stoppers, and their name is to some extent self-explanatory: they are there to stop parasitic oscillation (instability). Check the condition of any capacitor immediately connected between the output of the detector stage and chassis, as this will be fitted to prevent residual RF from entering the audio stages and causing instability.

Check the condition of any screened leads to grids in the RF/IF sections of the set. Replace if in doubt. Ensure that coil and IF transformer screening covers are in place.

Microphony and howling

These problems stem from positive feedback in one form or another. Microphony occurs when a valve becomes sensitive to physical vibrations. It can give rise to odd echoing or pinging effects, especially when the valve in question is tapped but even when the cabinet is tapped or the volume is loud and the valve picks up audio vibrations from the loudspeaker. Most valves have some sensitivity in this respect and special vibration damped valve-holders are sometimes found in the RF or IF stage. Obviously, if the valve-holder's damped mounting has become compromised due, for example, to a tight connection to the base of the valve-holder or to the rubber suspension age-hardening, the valve itself may be perfectly OK.

Instability in the form of loud howling can occur where octal valves of the RF type with a screening coat have either lost most of the metallised coating or the loop of fine wire connection from the coating to an earthed valve pin has failed due to the glass envelope becoming loose in the plastic base (very common). The glass may be re-glued but this isn't always the best answer and generally, a repair is better effected by fitting a replacement couple of loops of fine wire around the screening, held by glue dabs or tape and taken either down the outside of the base to the earthing pin originally used or otherwise to a convenient earthing point on the chassis. For the latter, allow additional flexible linking wire to facilitate later valve removal from the socket.

Hum problems

Hum can be troublesome with many sets. Apart from power supply faults, usually cured by replacing the reservoir and smoothing electrolytic capacitors, poor screening of AF wiring around the volume control and the pick-up sockets can create problems. Sometimes something as simple as moving a capacitor or a lead a few degrees away from its location can effect a startling cure.

Other times, it is a question of replacing screened wiring or adding it where plain wiring seems to be a culprit.

Buzzing noise – a rather rough hum – that is only present when a station is tuned in may indicate a cathode heater leak in the output valve. Continuous buzzing may point to a faulty valve-holder causing 'tracking' of voltage from one pin to another. Tracking can sometimes be seen as tiny sparks in subdued light.

Intermittent faults
Faults of an intermittent nature can be the most trying to locate. Unfortunately these can be caused by almost anything active within the set but usually a single resistor, a capacitor or a valve may prove to be the culprit. If you suspect a valve of creating an intermittent problem, the only certain way to check is to replace it as even a valve tester may be hard pressed to test for such a fault. After replacement, 'soak' test by running the set for a few hours and noting if the fault is still present.

Failing access to a spare valve and before purchasing one, try gentle tapping of the suspect valve, using the handle of an insulated screwdriver. Remember, *gentle* tapping! This action might provoke the valve into showing the fault – but bear in mind the possibility that the fault may be in the valve-holder itself, or any of the connections to it, and these might also be affected by such tapping.

This same procedure can be followed for any component you suspect, unless gentle prodding with an insulated tool has managed to push the component into failure mode. Also, this prodding technique can be used to pin-point a common cause of intermittency – dry solder joints.

Noise, hissing or rustling in the AF stages, perhaps even with the volume control set to minimum, can be caused by control tracks (3) and noisy resistors (7). Controls can be treated with switch cleaner, ideally followed by a smear of Vaseline on the track. Screen resistors should be checked first by temporary substitution (disconnect one end and solder a known good resistor in place). If the screen resistor(s) prove blameless, keep hunting as any resistor can cause the problem, even the most innocent looking one. Crackling caused by arcing across valve-holder or switch pins can be troublesome but might show up if viewed under low lighting, as mentioned under 'hum'. Do not overlook power transformer leads when searching for the source of crackling, especially with very old transformers (1930s receivers).

General faults (valves check OK)
Distortion, instability, poor quality sound, low gain: capacitors acting as AF couplers (8) and decouplers (9), usually between 0.001μF – 0.1μF, should be checked as a matter of course, as this action alone will locate a great many problems. Poor tonal quality may be caused by the pentode tone correction capacitor (12).

Every resistor should be checked, whether they look as if they have had a hard life or not, especially cathode and screen components. These can also cause an increase in noise or hiss. Resistors can change value, usually by an increase in resistance, quite naturally over time, so even new old stock resistors should be checked for accuracy before use – do not rely upon the colour code markings. The higher value resistors are quite prone to this.

Valve-holders should be cleaned with lubricating switch-cleaner, as should wave-change switches and volume and tone potentiometers. Sometimes you have to dismantle rotary volume and tone controls to clean them adequately as it may be a tarnished silver-plated slider that is the cause rather than the actual carbon track. Whilst apart, a touch of automotive grease on the spindle will help the smooth operation of the control. The carbon track itself could be given the very slightest smear of Vaseline.

If an on-off switch is combined and there is difficulty in switching on and off, the outer can usually carries the switch section and once the can is levered off the Bakelite case, the forked lever for this can be seen through the actuator hole. A slight nip together of the fork – don't overdo this – plus a squirt of lubricating switch cleaner usually cures problems.

I.F. Transformer problems

The general method of adjusting an IF transformer is covered under 'test equipment'. Refer to circuit data for specifics. IF transformers can and do suffer from a number of faults. Windings are fragile and can become open-circuit. If this is at one end of a winding, perhaps where the wire is soldered to a thicker support or to a tag, repairs can be effected relatively easily – though care should be taken to ensure the finely covered wire is properly bared and tinned. Magnifying glasses are very handy for delicate work such as this. The parallel tuning capacitors (10) usually fitted inside the screening cans may go open circuit, short circuit or drift in value.

A few transformers have compression (variable capacitance) trimmers instead of cores and fixed capacitors. Others may have brass inserts instead of iron dust slugs. The latter are fragile and succumb to careless handling by cracking, making them impossible to adjust properly. They may also become critically loose in the threaded tube, moving up or down it as the chassis is turned. This gives rise to a perplexing scenario where the set works with the chassis on one position but not in another. Finally, remember the Phantom – that elusive meddler who can by his clumsiness and ineptitude introduce a variety of faults never seen by the original radio engineers. IF transformers seem to be a particular target of this gentleman and out-of-position or broken cores are the usual result of his ministrations.

Most faults with IF transformers show when the attempt is made to align the transformer; it simply will not peak up satisfactorily. When this happens and cores and windings are intact and windings show continuity on the ohmmeter, suspect the parallel capacitor.

LOUDSPEAKER PROBLEMS

By the beginning of the 1930s, the horn has given way to the cone-type dynamic loudspeaker. This consisted typically of a stiff paper cone, the apex of which was attached to a thin metal rod. This rod was in turn fastened to an iron armature which moved under the influence of current passing through a coil or coils. The current was derived directly from the audio output valve anode – no output transformer, the coil forming the anode load – and like its predecessor the horn, the cone loudspeaker was sensitive, requiring only modest output power for ample volume. This was ideal for the limited power of valves of the time. The only real fault that can happen with either cone or horn units is the failure of a winding, either shorting to the outer metal casing or becoming open-circuit.

When power output valves such as the Mullard PEN4VA became available, the high sensitivity of cone loudspeakers became less important and their innate lack of a good frequency response and poor audio quality made them useful only in economy receivers.

Moving-coil loudspeakers

Meanwhile, the moving-coil loudspeaker had been developed and these have never been bettered in terms of audio range and sound quality. Less sensitive than earpiece driven horns or vibrating reed cone loudspeakers, PM loudspeakers, especially the early ones, required a good power output valve (or valves, in push-pull) to drive them. There are two basic types of moving coil loudspeakers: permanent magnet (PM) and energised (field winding) units. The modern PM units are fitted with very powerful magnets that maximise sensitivity.

Faults with both moving coil types include torn cones, off-centre speech coils and corrosion within the very narrow speech coil gap. Sometimes it is possible to dismantle a unit, clean up the gap surfaces and re-centre the cone: some units are fitted with a central 'spider' which is adjustable to minimise rubbing when the cone is moved.

Field winding problems
Because of the very fine winding wire, the field windings fitted to energized types can and often do go open-circuit. Only rarely does this happen close to or at a wire termination point, allowing repair; more often, the fault lies irreparably buried within the mass of wire and is a very difficult rewind task due to the very fine wire needed. It is simpler to replace a faulty energised loudspeaker with a PM unit of the same physical diameter. If this is opted for, the missing field winding then must be replaced either with a choke of more usually a wire-wound resistor of 1-2KΩ.
Open-circuit speech coils may be repairable if the break is visible at the flexible wire ends.

Repairing a Loudspeaker cone

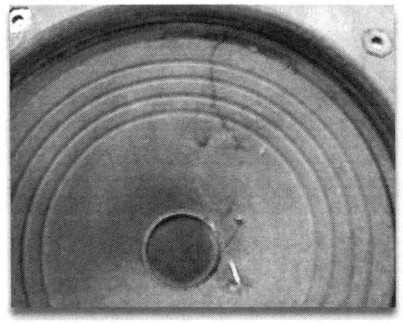

The cone of the loudspeaker on the left is torn. A reasonable repair can be effected by first taping across the back of the tear with masking tape (above right). Note that the tape should be repeatedly taped down to a surface and released in order to kill some of its adhesive power. Failure to do this may cause the cone to tear upon removal of the tape.
At the front, a thin layer of Copydex latex adhesive is brushed across the crack.

The tape should be removed when the adhesive on the front of the cone has set (changed from milky white to transparent). A further thin layer of adhesive brushed across the back of the repair will help strengthen it (below right).

Why Copydex? It is latex-based and remains semi-flexible. Any adhesive with flexibility should be suitable, however.

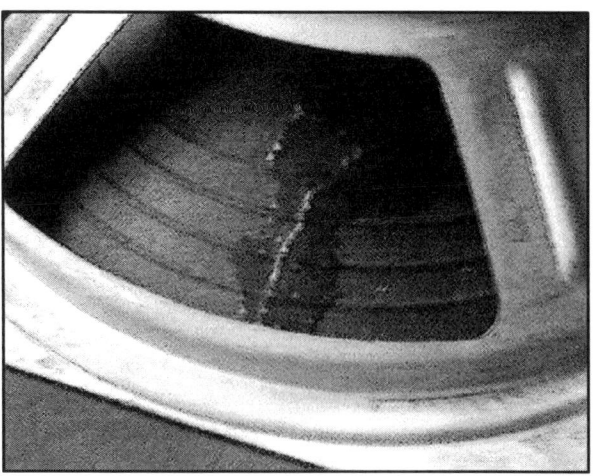

VINTAGE VALVE RADIOS

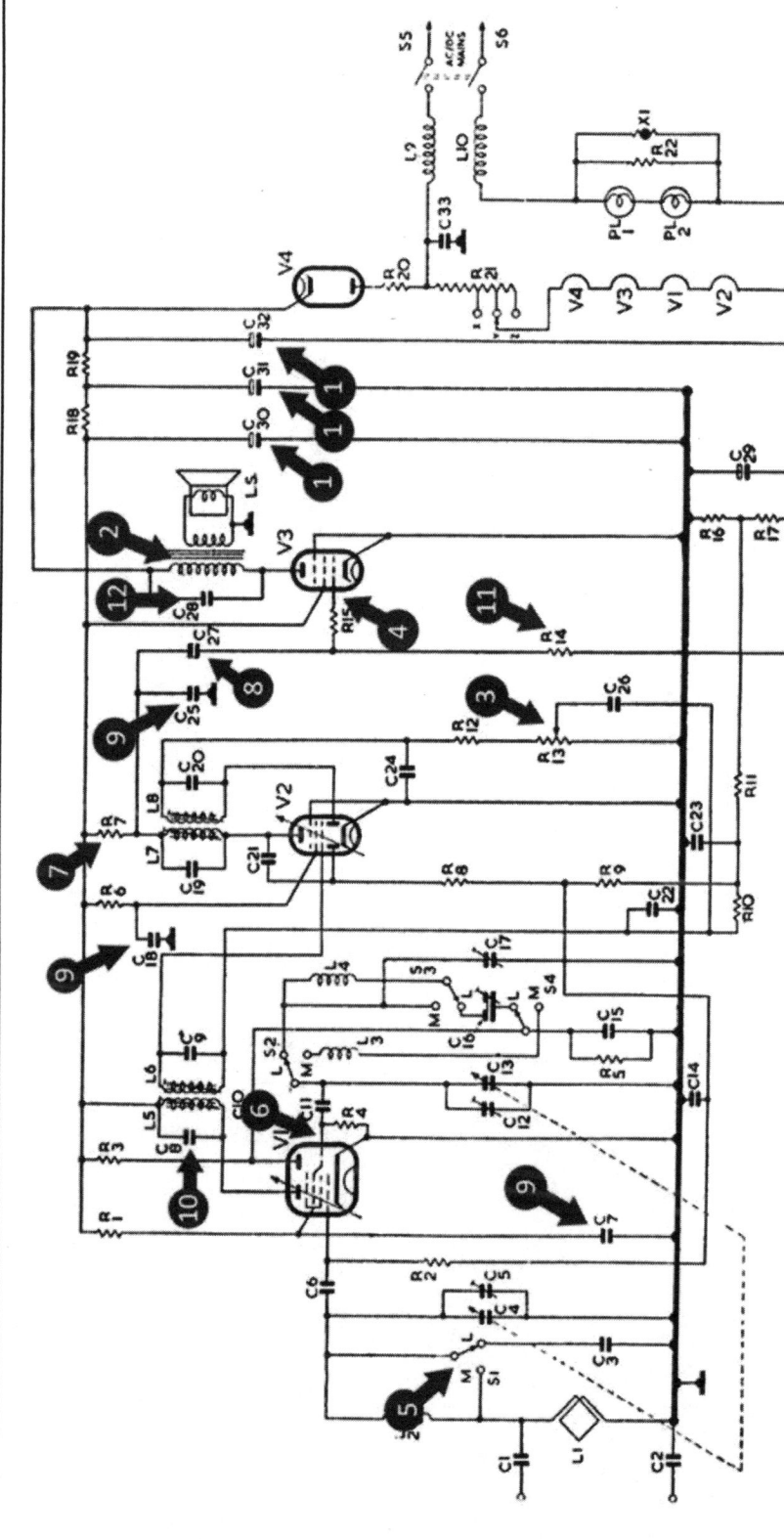

Example circuit. The numbered components are referred to in the text

This circuit has been chosen for its simplicity. There is no separate IF amplifier stage and this is therefore what is often called a 'short' superhet. Another form of short superhet is one where the detector and the AF output stage are combined in one valve – no separate AF amplifier. No earth on this AC/DC Chassis. For reference, C1 is an external aerial coupling capacitor, C2 is a chassis decoupling capacitor. These two capacitors provide essential isolation from the 'live' chassis and C2 MUST be replaced by an 'Y' rated component which in the event of failure will open-circuit. L1 is an internal frame aerial, C33 is the mains RF bypass capacitor, C14 is the AGC filter capacitor and C29 is a grid bias reservoir capacitor (unusually, no cathode bias is used. C29 polarity is important.) R21 is the tapped mains dropper resistor.

VINTAGE VALVE RADIOS

VINTAGE MAGAZINES
Of the 1930s

Vintage radio magazines such as the three shown here can be a great source of information about early radio as well as being both nostalgic and fascinating in their own right.

CHAPTER 11
STARTING RESTORATION

Once the chassis has been made to function, however imperfectly, true restoration can begin. Restoration may be conveniently divided into the two main categories of cabinet restoration and chassis restoration. After this rough division comes the fine tuning of the individual restoration project, as each project is to a greater or lesser extent unique: from minor work, more a quick service than a restoration in truth, where the cabinet and chassis are surface cleaned and only the faulty components replaced, through to a complete cabinet and chassis rebuild; cabinet stripped and major panels replaced or re-veneered, new knobs cast or found, scale plate remade or repaired, loudspeaker repaired or replaced. Chassis stripped back to bare metal with all components removed, followed by a painstaking repaint and rebuild, hiding new capacitors within the shells of the old and ending with full tuned circuit alignment using a signal generator and either an oscilloscope or meter as an output measuring device. These two extremes are relatively rare and most work is somewhere between, with minor work being perhaps the rarest as vintage radios rarely have but a single fault and almost always consist of a series of minor faults crowned with one or more major problems. Full chassis stripdowns (bare chassis) is probably best reserved for the most elderly of receivers such as late 1920s-early 1930s TRFs.

The value of notes and photographs
These are essential as a record of your work and as a guide for reassembly in cases where several components have to be removed together. However, it is definitely best to replace components one at a time, retesting after each change as this minimises the likelihood of introduced errors.
It also pays to make rough diagrams of the connections to some components such as the mains or output transformers, coil banks and IFTs before disconnecting and removing them. Label the removed component, too. The sketch should note the mounted orientation of the component and the colours of leads together with their destination within the set: i.e. 'to output transformer primary' – with an arrow.
In this author's opinion you simply cannot have too many clear close-up colour photographs as reference material. If in doubt, take the picture. Today's digital cameras are a boon.

Although the next section assumes you've taken the plunge and purchased a set and have brought it into a working state you should bear in mind that at least some of the following points raise questions that should have been asked **before** you parted with your money.

Restoration ethics
Perhaps this section should be called 'what to restore - and what to leave'. People find it hard to agree on details. There are more questions than answers in this section! The biggest problem is with wooden cabinets. Do you treat them as antique in the sense that they are old and should show their history in their patina, in the scratches, in the stains, ring marks, woodworm holes, rotting loudspeaker fabric? Then there's the electronics to consider.

Should the valves be changed for more modern types, with replacement valve-holders and modified wiring to suit? Or should all efforts revolve around locating original valves?

Should the electrolytic capacitors be replaced with similar types, perhaps very expensively, or should they be removed and modern types fitted? Resistors of the old style carbon stick form can still be obtained, at a premium, so should these be used, or newer, smaller types fitted? These are points to ponder.

Essentials

Not everything is open to debate. Logically, some things simply *must* be changed or modified regardless of the damage to authenticity. Mains lead is a prime candidate for replacement in almost every elderly set. Chassis earthing arrangements must be checked and if necessary modified for safety. Mains input plugs and sockets need careful thought, too: a fixed mains lead is inherently safer, in my opinion.

It's all a matter of degree. Some things can be left, but woodworm infestation can't, especially if it is a live infestation – and how can you be 100% certain that it is dead? If you value the furniture – and the structural timber – within your home or that of anyone who may subsequently acquire the set, then treatment surely is a must. (Why did you buy the set, if woodworm attack is obvious?)

Loudspeaker fabric that is ripped or rotted must be changed for the sake of appearance. If the chassis is badly rusted, then treatment and possibly painting or even re-plating may be needed. If the missing or broken valve you need is unobtainable, a suitable replacement must be fitted and the set adapted to suit.

However, this does not resolve the fundamental dilemma with renovation; namely, how far is too far? It is impossible to say, though the slighting epithet 'over-restored' applies generally to poorly-conceived restoration work – metal grille where cloth once was, painted or over-varnished cabinet (deprecatingly known as toffee-apple effect). I can, though, give you my views. Remember, this is only my personal opinion, as are most of the comments in this section and should be read as such. You have every right to your own shade of opinion, which may differ greatly from mine and yet be just as valid.

No rule book to tear up

There is no published set of rules or guidelines for restoration*, so you must create your own. Here is the main question I ask myself: would I put this radio on display in my own home?

It seems to me to reasonable to compare vintage radio restoration to vintage car or traction engine restoration. How often do you see a vintage car at a rally covered in rust, with a rotten tonneau cover and crazed glass, or a traction engine rusted and splattered in filthy soot-encrusted grease?

That said, if a wooden cabinet is clean and only lightly marked and bearing signs of being cared for, then it's probably best to leave alone. Very marked, stained or badly damaged cabinets need more thorough restoration. Bakelite sets seem naturally to lend themselves to a good clean-up, using 'Brasso' metal polish and/or Bakelite polish. This applies to Bakelite knobs and trim, too.

Radio sets are not typical antiques. In addition to visual appeal, sets should work well and be safe in use.

It is important to distinguish between restoration and conservation, a term implying that items are preserved in the state which they are found. Conservation is best kept for museum exhibits.

*Unless you count this book as containing such guidance, of course. Guidance is the operative word, however. There are not and surely can never be definitive fixed rules for such a subjective process, beyond the essential safety aspects.

Cabinets for radios fall generally into three categories: wooden, Bakelite and fabric/foil covered. Wooden types are almost always built from veneered ply sheet, perhaps with solid hardwood additions. Bakelite cabinets may be a one or two-piece moulding, sometimes with ply additions such as a loudspeaker baffle or a bottom plate. Fabric and foil covering, perhaps found together where the fabric is a loudspeaker grille cover, may be over a plywood or (less commonly) a metal casing. Radios toward the end of the valve era and into the transistor age may have thermoplastic cabinets or detailing. Assuming you've bought and are ready to restore the chassis to its former glory, a considerable knowledge of valve function and radio circuitry is required and is essential for safety, both for the restorer and for the final user(s). Mains powered radio chassis use high voltages. Beyond the technical aspects of restoration, an ability to work with materials as listed above will lift your restoration to a higher level of quality.

This image shows an Ekco A144 before (right) and after (left) cabinet restoration. It may seem hard to believe but both photographs are untouched and original. The effects of ageing on the surface finish show in the faded, crazed and scratched veneer. The cabinet was stripped – primarily by scraping with a metal cabinet scraper, the easiest way in this case as the microcrazing made the surface extremely fragile (far worse in fact than the photograph can show).
The plastic grille was a haven for dirt and it too had been partly bleached by sunlight. A good clean was followed by a respray in an almost exactly matching paint. The knobs had as usual picked up much dirt in their ribbing and this was cleaned out with foam cleanser and a toothbrush.
Once fully stripped, the cabinet was very lightly sanded along the grain with fine wet and dry paper, used dry. The new lacquer finish was applied by HVLP (high volume low pressure) spray equipment and finished by flatting with 1000 grade wet and dry, used wet with soap lubricant, then polished with metal polish. No stain or toning was used, despite the fact that the finished cabinet looks considerably darker; this serves to demonstrate the extent of the fading, most of which was probably caused by exposure to sunlight over a long period, perhaps in a shed or outhouse. The set has, visually at least, been brought back to life.
The question is: which would you prefer to have in your home? Before, or after?

AC/DC chassis are almost always non-isolated - in other words, the chassis metal is live to the mains. It follows that should the mains plug or the wall socket be incorrectly wired, touching the chassis would result in a severe, perhaps even fatal electric shock; the reason why the novice restorer has been recommended to avoid them when starting out.

Of course, having read this manual through to this point, you are equipped with a passable understanding of the task and how you can with safety undertake the work involved. A common error is to assume that the valves are probably the cause whenever a set is inoperative or is exhibiting a fault. This is understandable, as valves are often the first thing people think of as likely to need replacement should a radio not function satisfactorily. In truth, however, although valves certainly do lose emission over their lifetimes, causing a lack of gain, low volume, insensitivity etc, and certainly can develop other more baffling faults, there is the strong likelihood that other components already discussed may be the culprits: in particular, the capacitors. These are more often than not of the waxed paper variety and as pointed out earlier are notorious for leakage. Remember, a good capacitor should not pass any measurable DC current. Leaky ones definitely do, resulting in distorted or low volume sound, inability of certain valve stages to function and a possible shortening of valve life. Especially important to check in this respect is any AF coupling capacitor between the AF amplifier anode and the output valve control grid as a leaky capacitor here can greatly shorten the life of the output valve. This is a very common fault.

Under-chassis components may be replaced with modern equivalents, but the purist may wish to go to the lengths of cutting open the old ones, emptying them and hiding a new, tiny modern component within. This is to maintain the appearance of originality. My personal view is that replaced components on the top of the chassis should where possible be made to appear original. Under the deck is not so important.

Typical top deck components that fail include the valves themselves, the smoothing and reservoir capacitors (often combined into a single metal tubular or rectangular block) and transformers, both power and audio output.

Combined capacitors of this type may be cut open and modern smaller replacements slid into the case, with due regard for insulation. The cut open section can usually be hidden with the clamp that holds the component in place or, as in the photograph (left), the top cap carefully sawn off and refitted.

Rebuilding an electrolytic capacitor (see also photograph on p.116)

Wiring is commonly found to have deteriorated with impaired and crumbling insulation and/or corroded conductor wires. For mains leads, replacement is the only safe option in such cases and should be scrutinised for this problem. With under-chassis wiring of the rigid type – i.e. with a solid core conductor – it is possible to disconnect at one end and slide new sleeving over the crumbling old one. This is a task made easier if you use heat shrink sleeving, available in a range of colours, as an internal diameter can be selected to slip easily over, after which warming with a hair dryer will shrink it tightly in place.

On-off switches, where single pole types are used, will commonly be wired into the mains neutral lead. I always rewire these into the live conductor. The mains fuse – the one in the plug, that is - should be no more than 3A. Throw out the 13A fuse that comes as standard.

Restorable chassis faults in radio sets fall into two types: electrical and mechanical. Sometimes, in fact often, a fault may be a combination of both types of problem.

Mechanical problems

These are usually quite apparent. Broken dial drive cords, for example, result in a complete lack of movement of the tuning scale pointer and often a 'loose' feel to the tuning control. Mechanical wear is also fairly easy to spot; loose knobs and/or wobbly control spindles tell their own story. Physical damage to cabinets, especially the rather brittle Bakelite types, usually occurs as a result of the set being dropped or knocked off a table or shelf. Broken scale glass is another worrying sign and I would rarely pay much if anything for a set with cracked glass unless it was something special.

Valves don't enjoy impacts, either, so it may not just be the cabinet that is cracked. The plastic bases and top caps of the older valves will often be found to be loose. This is common and is not always a sign of trouble, but valves with an external metallised coating should have their grounding wires checked. This is usually a fine wire bonded to the coat and running to a pin within the base.

Manual controls and switches are subject to considerable mechanical wear. Wave-change switches can become noisy or even cause a complete lack of signals. Volume and tone controls can crackle badly when operated. Faults of this nature can often be cured by application of lubricating switch cleaner. Loosening of the cement used to fasten the valve envelopes to their bases or to the top caps is a common occurrence in old receivers. Severe corrosion or extensive physical damage to a chassis or cabinet, caused, for example, by poor storage or the accidental dropping of a receiver may also be met with.

Combined electrical/mechanical problems

These can be less obvious and unfortunately more common; loose connections in or poor connections to valve-holders, dial bulb holders and fuse-holders, corroded connections to ballast wire-wound resistors due to years of heat/cold cycling, dust or dirt in the vanes of ganged tuning capacitors, loudspeaker speech coils rubbing and crackling, frame aerial wire damage, broken ferrite rod aerials.

Corrosion evident in this Pye P76

The core laminations of mains and output transformers can be damaged by damp and this will be evident in the form of a swelling and distortion of the transformer shape. This can mean a drop in efficiency of the transformer, or even complete failure – but it can also be that despite appearances the component will work satisfactorily. In such cases it has to be accepted that purchasing the afflicted receiver carries a risk, with perhaps a subsequently downward-amended offer.

Capacitor faults

Wax-coated capacitors are notorious for 'leaking', that is, becoming resistive and passing DC, the one thing no capacitor should do. This is a function of the age of the component but is influenced by adverse storage. Some restorers change certain makes of these components on sight, preferring not to wait until the component actually fails, believing that it is only a matter of time before it does so.

Right: Typical wax capacitor. This one is the mains RF bypass component in a Bush DAC90A and the partly melted wax suggests that it has been getting warm. The surprising thing is that it actually still exists; these RF bypass capacitors usually fail explosively. It has, however, been snipped out of circuit and removed from its close-to-dropper retaining strap

There is a point to this, in my opinion, but as far as the likelihood of failure by specific makes I have found that several makes of the same type of waxed capacitor fail with regularity due to age. It is prudent then always to check these, especially the one coupling the AF amplifier anode to the output valve grid as a leaky component here will quickly destroy the output valve. A low-cost digital meter can be used to check capacitors. Ideally one end of the component to be tested should be disconnected for a reading to be accurate.

However, if resistance readings are carried out both ways, swapping the test leads around, and the highest reading accepted as being nearest correct, any significant leak should show up. It should be understood that such a rest cannot check the component under the stress of its working conditions and there are those who would advocate the use specialised equipment for testing capacitors under power, but the simplest and safest way is, if in doubt, replace. One at a time; it is not wise to change several components at a time. Change the one you suspect, having found it to provide a doubtful test-meter reading, then carry on to others, one at a time. To do otherwise is to risk making errors by introducing faults. Do not pay for so-called 'audio quality' capacitors. Standard new components of the correct or nearest preferred value and a suitable working voltage are all you need.

Tuning indicators

Tuning indicators (T.I.s) are a special type of valve designed to provide the listener with a visual indication of precise tuning. Green 'leaves' grow larger until at their maximum, the chosen station is correctly tuned.

Bush VHF61, complete with 'magic eye' tuning indicator, with a decorative escutcheon (top right)

Sometimes called 'magic eyes', these devices can be circular, with the display at one end, or tubular, with the display along the length of the valve. Unfortunately the display of most tuning indicators seems to weaken with age and use. They will be often be found to work only dimly if at all and replacements are becoming very scarce and expensive. There are other earlier visual tuning aids to be found in mid-1930s receivers.

Further problems with resistors

A physical examination of the older type of carbon stick resistor may lead you to think that their rather charred appearance indicates a fault. Well, it might – but then again, it might not. The same applies to mains and HT droppers (ballast resistors). Physical deterioration of resistors does take place, but it is best located with voltage and/or resistance tests (probably voltages first, to pin down the problem area). In general, if a carbon resistor looks fine, it often is, other than age-related changes in value.

In the case of a low to medium value resistor, say between 100Ω – 100kΩ, if it looks as though it has been working very hard, check the voltage across it. Go by service data whenever possible. If the voltage drop is excessive, check associated components such as capacitors and valves for short circuits before switching off and disconnecting the set from the mains after which, ideally, disconnect one end of the resistor to prevent false readings from parallel circuitry and check across it with the ohmmeter. Any large variation should lead to substitution of the suspect component. If a voltage drop is much less than expected, check any parallel components – usually capacitors – for leaks or short-circuits.

With higher value carbon types, say from around 150kΩ to the MΩ values, the best test is temporary substitution by disconnecting one end of the suspect and tack-soldering a temporary good component in place. The high values are usually found in the RF/IF stages and around the AGC circuits, also where tuning indicators are used. As a generalisation, high values tend to go higher as they age and low values tend to go lower. Check large resistors for mechanical problems such as loose end connections.

Wire-wound types go completely open-circuit when the resistance wire fails. This usually happens in dropper resistors as a natural result of ageing, but check for any excessive load (short-circuits) before replacing. Take care around droppers. Remember that some of the sections on a multi-section dropper may very likely be carrying raw mains and the possibility of a very nasty shock is high for the unwary.

VINTAGE VALVE RADIOS

Further problems with capacitors

Some basic problems have already been highlighted, but capacitors are, more than any component, subject to age deterioration. I always suspect wax-coated paper-dielectric capacitors. These are found in most sets as coupling and decoupling components in the AF and AGC circuits, and decoupling valve screens in the IF stages. If in doubt, replace. Always replace the capacitor coupling AF signals to the output valve control grid as a leak in this one will overrun and destroy the output valve and possibly the output transformer.

Do not assume the tiny RF capacitors are above blame. These are pF values, often assemblies of silvered mica plates. Failure is not common, however, and when they do fail it is usually by going open-circuit. If these are tuning an IF transformer, a faulty one will show by the fact that adjusting the core of the transformer has little effect upon its gain.

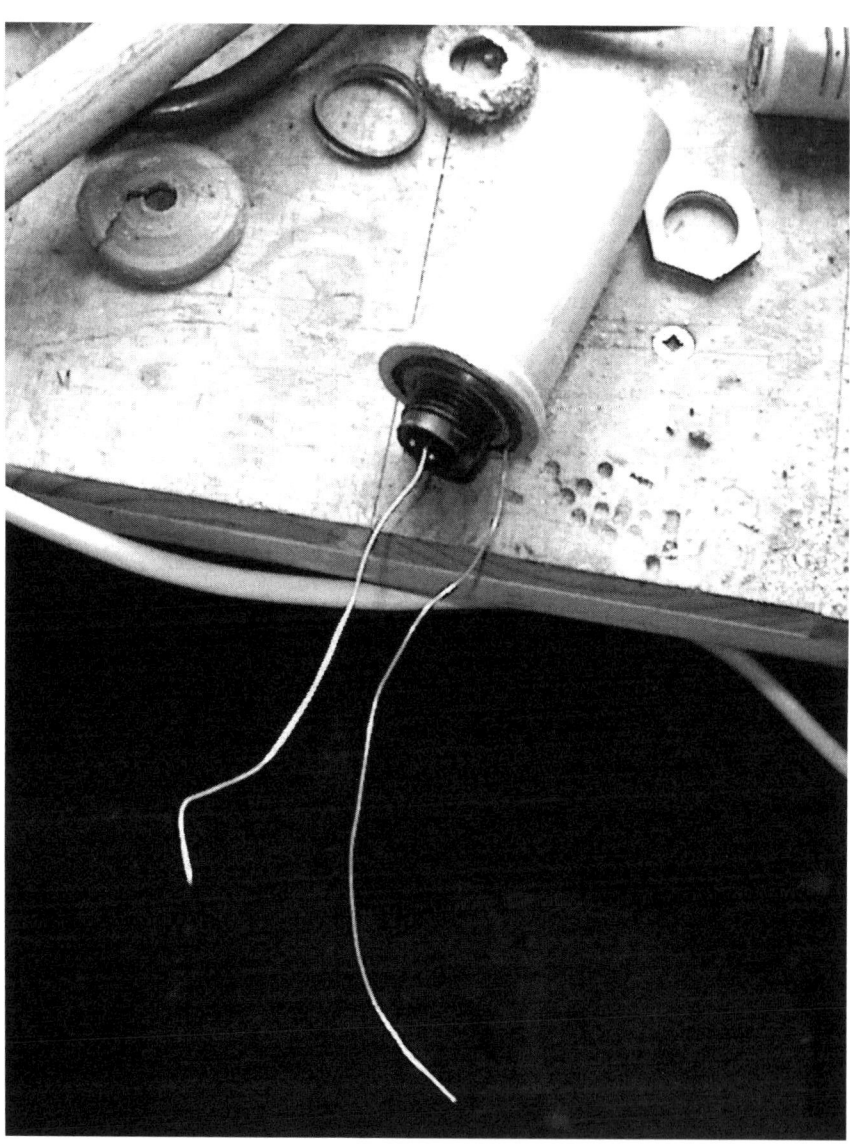

A rebuilt wet electrolyte capacitor. Once fitted, this component will look entirely original – from the chassis top

The main HT smoothing electrolytic capacitor may also act as an RF bypass for the HT supply. As electrolytics age their impedance – equivalent series resistance (ESR) – increases, sometimes to the point at which their capacity to bypass RF fails, even though they perform their primary smoothing function perfectly well. The result is instability due often to the IF amplifier valve oscillating. This causes distortion and other squeals and whistles. Bridge the smoothing electrolytic with a good 0.1μF plain capacitor to prove the point. Note that the same effect may be caused by poor decoupling of the IF amplifier screen.

Problems with inductors

Mains transformers and smoothing chokes can be damaged through excessive current due to short circuits in rectifiers or reservoir capacitors. Disconnection, shorted turns or actual burn-out can result. The only answer here is to replace, but be sure to fix the problem that caused the damage in the first place. Bear in mind that transformers can fail for no obvious reason, though, so if you can't find one, replace anyway but to be sure, power up through the test lamp.

If a mains transformer runs very hot in the absence of HT short circuits, it may be suffering from shorted turns. Replacement is the only reasonable option but again, check that no fault remains present that caused the damage in the first place.

Age and poor storage, the twin ills that beset vintage radios in general, affect wire-ended types of mains transformers. Check the lead-out wires for rotted insulation, in particular receivers from the pre-WWII period that used rubber as the insulating medium. This commonly fails by self-vulcanisation, crumbling into dust. It can be replaced with a modern sleeving, perhaps of the heat-shrink variety, or one of the woven types that have the look of the original.

IF transformers can also suffer open-circuit contacts or windings and sometimes the fault can, confusingly, result in a loss of gain rather than no signals. The test is to measure the continuity of the windings, using data if possible.

Any and all inductors can suffer from 'green spot' which is basically copper corrosion. This can cause a coil to become open-circuit. If it is visible at the coil connections it is usually possible to repair the problem but if it is buried somewhere within the windings the only answer may be a rewind or a replacement coil.

Components such as capacitors wired in parallel to IFT windings can be the cause of shorts, but this is rather rare. Broken cores in the IFTs are far too common, sadly, indicating that some ham-fisted person (or the aforementioned Phantom) has tried to tweak the cores for better gain. The cores are made most commonly from brittle ferrite and do not take kindly to a metal screwdriver blade. As they are often locked in place with a dab of compound or paint, the core breaks as an attempt to turn it is made.

If you suspect the IF alignment is at fault, use a proper alignment tool or at least a plastic knitting needle filed to a good fitting screwdriver tip shape. Cores may be damaged beyond redemption. If you possess scrap transformers that use similar cores, they can be pressed into service as replacements. As IFTs have upper and lower cores, you can usually remove one core fully to gain access to the broken core for removal and replacement. Failing all else, resort to drilling out the damaged core – but this is a tricky task and one slip can inadvertently ruin the transformer, so it is not something to undertake lightly.

Lack of use brings problems of its own

When a radio has been stored under adverse conditions such as high humidity, components can quite quickly deteriorate; but even ostensibly reasonable storage will cause problems through age and inactivity. Electrolytic capacitors, especially, are prone to failure through lack of use. To be accurate, they should be reformed before power is applied to a set, if a very long period has elapsed since last used. This unformed condition causes them to present a relatively low resistance at first switch-on and it is this that can do the damage – to the electrolytic and/or to the major components of the power supply. A rough and ready reforming can be carried out by powering the set through the test lamp described earlier. Leave it running for half an hour or so, with the lamp in circuit, before switching to full power. Of course, long before this time the lamp should have been virtually extinguished. If it remains rather bright then do not risk full power but investigate for HT leakage.

Resistors fare reasonably well under adverse conditions, though HT ballast wire-wound types may lose their protective coatings to expose the resistance wire core. It is impossible to be specific about makes and types but in general carbon resistors have a tendency to drift in value. This drift is almost always upwards but in the case of low-value, high-current resistors the drift – caused by use, not by age – is downward.

The types of insulating materials used in many older sets will also tend to deteriorate through adverse storage or simply through age. Once the flexible insulated coverings on components, connecting wire and mains wire becomes brittle and cracks, it can cause DC leakage (especially where several conductors are grouped tightly together within wide sleeving or screening) and, in RF stages, RF loss through leakage too. Replacement is perhaps the only cure. Given that a set appears to have suffered in this way through poor storage, it is in any case often cheaper in the long run to replace most of the possible suspect capacitors in a radio rather than check and replace individually.

Other common problems
Volume and tone controls quite commonly suffer from poor or intermittent contact. These rotary variable resistors often have a sufficient gap in their metal casing to allow the ingress of the cleaning fluid and this can be tried first but if ineffective, the case can be removed and the sliders 'joggled' to both increase tension and allow for a fresh part of the track to come in contact. Gentle tensioning, a spot or two of switch cleaner and a light smear of Vaseline or grease on the track often works wonders with these. Volume controls that do not respond to this treatment are likely to have pitted carbon tracks or a break at the end of their track and so need replacement. Generally speaking, for volume controls use logarithmic law types, not linear ones. Replacing a half-megohm control with a 1 megohm pot is generally unlikely to affect performance noticeably, so there is some leeway with the large values. Note that some modern potentiometers have plastic cases and where they are used to replace a pot with an earthed metal case, some hum pick-up may occur. Best where possible to replace with a metal-clad component.

Corrosion of contacts such as the ones found in wave-change switches or the sockets of valve-holders are commonly found to give trouble. In both cases, cleaning can generally consist of an application of switch cleaner/lubricant and a judicious 'tweak' of the tension of a contact or pin socket where necessary. Valve pins may require cleaning and the ideal tool for this is a glass-fibre brush/pen. Wire wool should be used with care and the valve examined afterward to clear any fine strands clinging around the pins.

Dry joints have been mentioned with regard to resistors but this malady can affect valve-holders and effectively any soldered connection within the chassis. Often easily found by the prodding action of an insulated tool, the slightest movement of the affected wire or tag causing intermittency. A faulty valve can produce the appearance of a dry joint – tapping almost anywhere in its vicinity can make the intermittent fault appear.

SAFETY CONSIDERATIONS

There is, with any vintage radio, an aspect of importance regarding safety; that of the potential user. Remember that no vintage radio can be expected to reach today's exacting safety standards but that said, it is the responsibility of the restorer to do his or her utmost to ensure that the receiver, once restored, is in a safe condition for others to use, whether these end users are members of family or the set is sold on as having been restored. Let's start with the mains lead.

Replacing mains leads: AC only receivers with a double-wound (isolating) mains transformer.
Most sets of this nature either have or **definitely should have** a three-core mains lead with an earth connected to the chassis metalwork. If there is only a two-core flex – a common situation with many vintage radios – then a three-core must be fitted, with the earth to the chassis as suggested.

If the mains switch on the receiver has only a single pole, it will most likely be switching the neutral. When rewiring, this should be made to switch live. Unfortunately this may occasionally result in an increase in hum due to the field around the live lead, but careful dressing or re-routing of the lead may minimise this.

Replacing mains leads: AC/DC sets (live chassis) or AC sets with single-wound (autotransformer) or heater-only transformers (live chassis)

These types of set should **never** have a three-core mains lead fitted as the **chassis must not be earthed.** When fitting new leads, ensure that the switching is to the live, as described above. Some makers used autotransformers regularly, for example Murphy. Autotransformers have only a single tapped winding and do NOT provide isolation from the 'raw' mains supply. This should highlight the need for correct service data.

Knobs, metalwork

Ensure that all knobs fitted with grub screws have them well recessed into the body of the knob. With AC/DC sets using grub-screw attached knobs, the essential gap between the top of the screw and the outer body of the knob should be filled with suitably coloured wax; cabinet maker's beaumontage wax sticks are available from DIY stores and woodwork suppliers such as Axminster, in a range of wood tones.

With knobs that are held by spring clips, there must be no chance of them working loose. It is useful to save scrap knobs of all types for re-use or as a source of stronger spring clips. Even better is the drilling and tapping of knobs to take a grub screw which can be made to tighten down into a blind hole drilled in the control spindle, as this is a more secure fitting than any spring can provide – **but fill the tapped hole in the knob with insulating wax as already described.**

Back covers, labels, emblems

The object of removable covers is to ensure, as far as possible, that no contact can occur between fingers and metalwork. The backs of many sets suffer badly. Especially prone to crumbling are the back covers fitted to small AC/DC receivers as the excess heat from dropper resistors tends to slowly burn the fibreboard until it chars so badly that it breaks up. Such covers need repair, either by fitting parts of scrap covers or by the fabrication of replacement covers. Standard hardboard is useful in this respect but if you can obtain the thinner board as used by some picture framers, it will make for easier cutting.

Another useful material for back covers is 3mm MDF sheet. Slots can be made using a router. This is a somewhat laborious task but it does make for a neat final product. When cutting slots, ensure that no slot is wide enough to allow a child's little finger to pass through. The new back cover for a wartime civilian receiver was made in this way, using a router fixed to a table. Note that as the set is fully isolated, the new back was made to match the original as closely as possible. This meant that the rear chassis runner remained exposed, though safe and earthed via the mains lead. The label, shown below, is also a facsimile, produced on a computer to match perfectly the appearance and text of the original.

As a guide to the kind of things that can be needed to make a restoration complete, overleaf are copies of the inner valve list and the cabinet top label for the wartime civilian set. All are recreations of originals. This type of work is ideally suited to the computer.

Waterslide transfers can also be made where needed, for example with logos such as HMV. The limitation of inkjet printing is that it cannot print white or gold, two colours commonly found on the brand logos of many radios.

VINTAGE VALVE RADIOS

THIS RECEIVER IS FOR USE ON
200/250 VOLT. A.C. SUPPLY
50-100 CYCLES

WARNING
DO NOT REMOVE THE BACK UNLESS THE RECEIVER IS COMPLETELY DISCONNECTED FROM THE MAINS.

A.C. MODEL WARTIME CIVILIAN RECEIVER INSTRUCTIONS

CONTROLS. Switch on by the small toggle switch at the back right of the chassis.

The receiver is tuned by the right-hand knob, and to receive a particular station the moving mark should be set opposite to its name or wavelength number on the dial. Choose a nearby station for your first trial. When you hear the station, turn the knob gently to and fro, and you will notice two points at which the station sounds shrill. The correct setting for best quality is midway between these two points.

The volume is controlled by the left-hand knob. Volume increases when the knob is turned to the right.

AERIAL AND EARTH. A normal type of aerial and earth should be used. The earth lead should be connected to the socket on the back of the chassis, marked E, and the aerial to A1, unless you live near a powerful transmitter, when socket A2 should be used.

MAINS VOLTAGE. This receiver is designed for use on 200-250 volts, 50-100 cycles, ALTERNATING CURRENT supplies, and serious damage will result if it is connected to direct current (D.C.) mains or to alternating current mains of the wrong type. If uncertain of your mains supply check details on electricity meter or consult the Electricity Supply Company.

To adjust the receiver to suit the voltage of your house supply, remove the fibre back and you will see, on the left, a small panel which is engraved 200-225 and 225-250V., and has two terminals. The lead connected to one of these terminals must be connected to the terminal corresponding to your supply. Thus, if your supply is 230 volts, it must be connected to the 225-250V. terminal.

For your own safety, take the mains plug from its socket before removing the fibre back of the set, and on no account switch the set on while the back is off.

VALVES
1. B.V.A. 273, 274, 275, 276, or 277.
2. B.V.A. 243 or 246.
3. B.V.A. 264, 265, or 266.
4. B.V.A. 211, 214, 215, or 216.

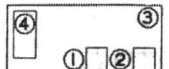

IN THE INTEREST OF WARTIME ECONOMY SWITCH OFF THE SET WHEN NOT IN USE

WARTIME CIVILIAN RECEIVERS.
MAINS MODEL.
Valve Replacements.

Valve position	BVA type	Equivalents
1	B.V.A. 274, 275, 276.	Osram X.61M, Marconi X.61M, Cossor OM10, Ever Ready ECH35, Ferranti 6K8G, Mullard ECH35, Brimar 6K8G
2	B.V.A. 243, 246, 347	Cossor 6K7G or OM6, Ever Ready EF39, Ferranti 6K7G or VPT62, Mullard EF39, Brimar 6K7G
3	B.V.A. 264, 265, 266 and 267	Ever Ready EL33, Mullard EL33, Brimar 6AG6G
4	B.V.A. 211, 214, 215 and 216	Osram U.14 or MU.14, Marconi U.14 or MU.14, Cossor 431U, Mazda UU5, Ever Ready AIID or SIID, Ferranti R.4, Mullard DW4/350 or IW4/350, Philips 1561 or 1867, Brimar R2 or R.3

Above, top: back panel information plate. Above: internal valve information. Below: mains version

CHAPTER 12
RESTORATION PROCEDURES

Earlier, the rebuilding of a tubular electrolytic capacitor was described. Some 1930s sets use a different form of multiple capacitor, combined within a metal or strong waxed card casing. The capacitive elements may be electrolytic or paper dielectric. It is impossible to find replacements for these, and because they are usually on the upper chassis and therefore quite visible, many restorers prefer to keep the appearance as original as possible.

Fitting new capacitors inside original cases
To do this, the faulty multiple capacitor is removed from the chassis and the innards removed to leave an empty shell. There are several ways this may be done and much depends upon the construction of the capacitor but as a rule, a cut may be made around the edge of the metal or card casing, just above the 'peened-over' end where the tags or wires emerge. A Stanley type knife can manage this, but it is a slow laborious task. The area may be hidden by the clamp that holds the component in place on the chassis. Once the casing is opened the innards can – usually – be persuaded to come out of the casing. If this proves difficult or if the internal components are embedded in wax or pitch, heat from a paint-stripping heart gun may be applied to melt out the fixing material. This can be a messy job, however and care must be taken to protect eyes, skin and lungs by the wearing of goggles, face mask and working gloves.

Stripped-out Tubular 'wet' electrolytic capacitors from a 1940s Philips receiver.

After cleaning up, new components of a suitable rating and with connection wires attached can be insulated with tape or with thin foam plastic (I use the type of material designed to cushion floating wood flooring). To complete the job, the side may be folded back into place and metal types re-soldered, card types glued where possible. With careful work, once the can is back on the chassis, nobody would suspect that it had been updated.

Tubular can-types may be opened either by sawing or filing the peened-over flange, subsequently hidden by the chassis mounting clamp or, as in the case of the Philips types shown on p.110, levering the top free. Replacement modern-style capacitors will fit easily into the empty cans and because of the loss of terminals their connecting wires can be fed into the chassis. With the Philips type wires may be fed into the chassis via a hole drilled through the threaded plastic mounting flange. With wet electrolyte capacitors, take care when opening the can by sawing to stop once the case is penetrated by the saw, to pour away slowly and carefully the liquid inside before completing the sawing. This weak acid is unpleasant stuff and it is preferable to wear latex gloves, old clothes and eye protection.

A main double reservoir and smoothing capacitor remade by the insertion of new components within the emptied case. The connecting wires have been brought out to the original tag end plate which was then secured in place with insulating tape (necessary in this case because the capacitor was the negative pole and was above chassis potential in the receiver concerned).

Wax-coated tubular capacitors

Most wax-coated tubular capacitors are situated beneath the chassis and can be changed for new types without too much concern, unless you are especially keen to get the appearance 'right'. Occasionally, however, such components are on view on the chassis top and here are two methods of rebuilding them.

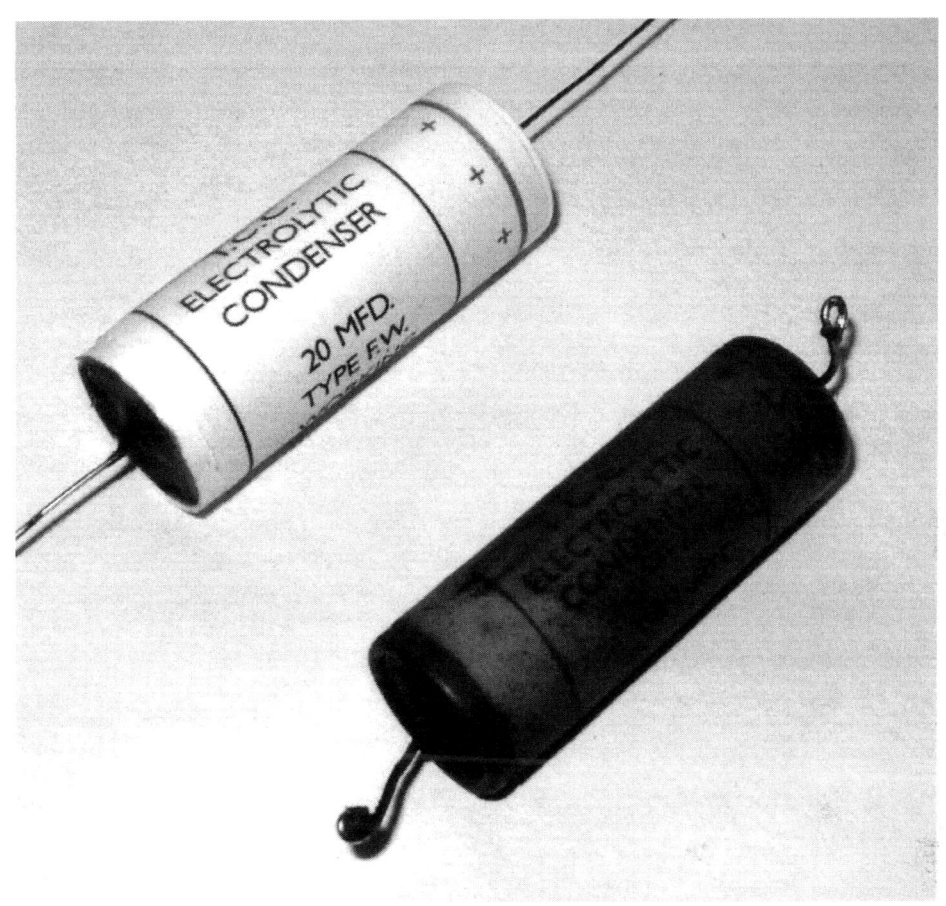

A copy electrolytic using a paper roll and a sleeve printed on computer

The first is to slit the old capacitor open along its length. Take care not to over-open or you may crack the casing. It should now be possible to extract the inner foil spiral together with the end discs that the connecting wires pass through. Free the discs.

The new component can be fitted by threading its wires through the holes in the discs and bulking up the new cap thickness with masking tape until it sits snugly in the cradle of the casing. The case can now be re-closed – it can be rejoined and sealed with superglue, or melted wax from a scrap capacitor, applied with the soldering iron.

The second method follows the same procedure for extracting the disc ends but in this case a new body is made from paper or thin card rolled around a suitably thick pen case and glued with Pritt Stik. A label can then be composed on the computer and printed with an inkjet printer before being glued into place.

The disc ends, especially if newly cut, can be coated with melted black crayon in order to improve the appearance.

If desired, the completed repair may be rewaxed by dipping in hot melted beeswax – but take care, this is a tricky procedure and is best done with a double-walled container, the outer being filled with water to limit the heat to that of boiling water. Paraffin wax – candle wax – is far too soft and too white.

For further examples see p.130

Substituting valves

Sometimes it is either difficult or prohibitively expensive to replace a faulty valve with a new (old stock) identical type.

Original layout of EF9 side-contact base

Conversion to a different type of valve with similar characteristics but a different base can be one answer to such a problem.

Side-contact valves are becoming scarcer and consequently more expensive; but that low-emission EBL1 can be exchanged for a good EBL31 (same characteristics, different base). Similarly the EF9 can be replaced with an EF39 – and so on. The photographs show one such modification. When converting from side-contact to octal, you have the choice of fitting an octal holder in place of the side-contact type or obtaining a side-contact plug to wire an octal base to. Where could you find a side-contact plug? Possibly, the base from the faulty side contact valve you intend to replace.

The replacement octal base for the EF39. Although the side-contact chassis hole is larger than the octal holder, slots were made using a warding file to take nuts and bolts, the added washers of which proved to be secure enough to avoid the need for a blanking plate with a new hole

The following is an example of a conversion process using a valve with slightly different characteristics, but with any such replacement work bear in mind the following: once converted, the set will no longer be fully original, so conversions should best be carried out in such a way as to allow the back-converting to the original specification.

IMPORTANT. Before considering conversion, you will need to locate adequate technical data for both the original and the new valve in order to make informed comparisons for workability and long-term reliability.

UL41-UL84 conversion

A B9A valve-holder plus a replacement cathode resistor is all that is required for this modification. Found in numerous post WWII AC/DC receivers, The UL41 is notorious for developing faults due to build up of deposits between valve pins inside the envelope, and cathode heater insulation failure. Other series heater 'rimlock' valves are sometimes prone to this too, but not quite to the same extent. The inevitable result is that good UL41 valves are becoming scarce and expensive. It is possible to fit a B9A based UL84 instead. These are still cheap, plentiful and importantly more reliable.

Right: UL84 valve on its home-made base adapter

The UL84 is easily capable of passing the 35mA or so required for this set and the heater current and voltage are identical to the UL41. In fact the maximum current will have to be restricted to prevent damage to the output transformer. The cathode resistor for the UL41 may not provide quite enough negative bias for a UL84. It is of course perfectly possible to replace the rimlock holder with a B9A type but this at best is a tricky operation. Besides, as already recommended, when any modification is carried out it is useful to do it in such a way that it is easily reversed. The B9A socket for the UL84 is the same size, and has the mounting holes in the same position as that for the UL41. Solder lengths of wire to the B9A pins, using sleeved wire of different colours – noting which colour is connected to which electrode. There is plenty of room to mount the new socket with the solder connections inside the original's skirt, and secure it with studding or long screws and nuts. Because the rimlock holder has a relatively large central hole, the insulated and colour-coded connecting wires can be threaded down through it. Under the chassis the emerging wires should be cut to about 50mm (2") to avoid pick up of stray mains and soldered to the relevant tags of the original output valve socket. The small amount of slack can be pushed back up the hole. Any additional resistors etc. can be added between the original connections and those of the new socket. A cathode resistor in the order of 200Ω should be all that is needed. With this reversible modification, all the de-modifier will have to do is remove the B9A base, unsolder the wires and plug in a working UL41. The new socket can be mounted above the old one using stand off pillars robbed from a scrap rotary switch, or lengths of threaded rod. The original valve-holder nuts were used to secure the pillars under the chassis, and screws in the tapped pillar tops used to fix the new socket. Some improvisation may be helpful here. The aim is to secure the holder firmly by whatever means.

Although the UL41 and UL84 have different anode load requirements, I found in practice it made little or no measurable or discernable difference to performance.

Cleaning and restoring chassis surface

Some chassis respond well to a good brushing and vacuum cleaning and probably a wash down with WD40, also brushed, particularly where the dirt is encrusted and hard to move by brush alone.

Be sure to dry off the WD40 with absorbent cloth such as old toweling. Try to avoid letting it come into prolonged contact with valve-holders or switches: it may be harmless but it is best not to take the chance. Chassis with rust should be cleaned as far as possible and all loose surface rust cleared using a small wire brush or abrasive paper before treating with rust killer. A sharp scraper can also be used. An improvised one can be a Stanley knife blade held at a slight angle to the metal surface, or perhaps a wood chisel, preferably one you have no plans to use subsequently on wood! Rusted areas should turn black or dark grey, indicating treatment is complete. Some type of protective finish, perhaps paint or clear lacquer (or both) is then advised.

One important point: many chassis were electroplated with metals such as Cadmium. Using abrasives on these can give rise to airborne particles which are dangerous to health. Therefore, when abrading or scraping, wet the surface and use wet and dry papers wetted with either WD40 (or turpentine substitute) or soap and water. The latter is recommended if you have an old hair dryer to hand to remove all traces of residual damp left after toweling.

This chassis has been partially stripped in readiness for cleaning and repainting. The IFT cans have been removed but the IFTs themselves and the valve-holders remain in position and will be protected with masking tape before spraying. Holes through to the underside of the chassis will also be blocked with tape and the open spaces between the chassis runners will be protected with newspaper

This particular chassis wasn't too rusted and abrasive paper wetted with WD40 was used to flat the surfaces prior to the preparation for spraying, which was done using aerosol cans. Several light coats of grey primer were finished with a light spray of clear semi-gloss to enhance and protect the paint (see overleaf for completed chassis)

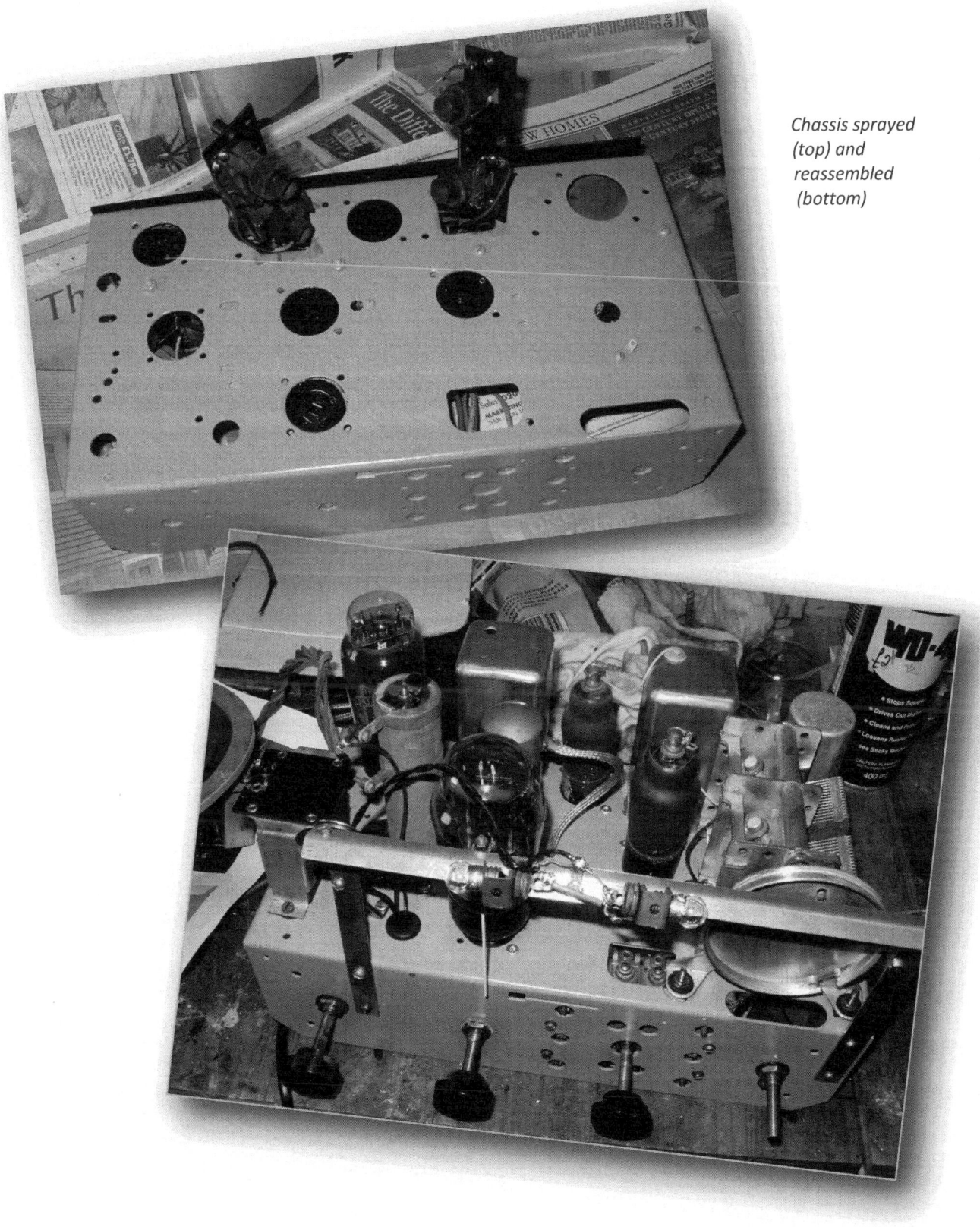

Chassis sprayed (top) and reassembled (bottom)

Internal woodwork

Restoration often involves skills beyond those required for electronic work. It helps if you already are multi-skilled but if not, it isn't impossible to develop them. It is just a matter of thinking through the problem in hand and working steadily and with care, never rushing.

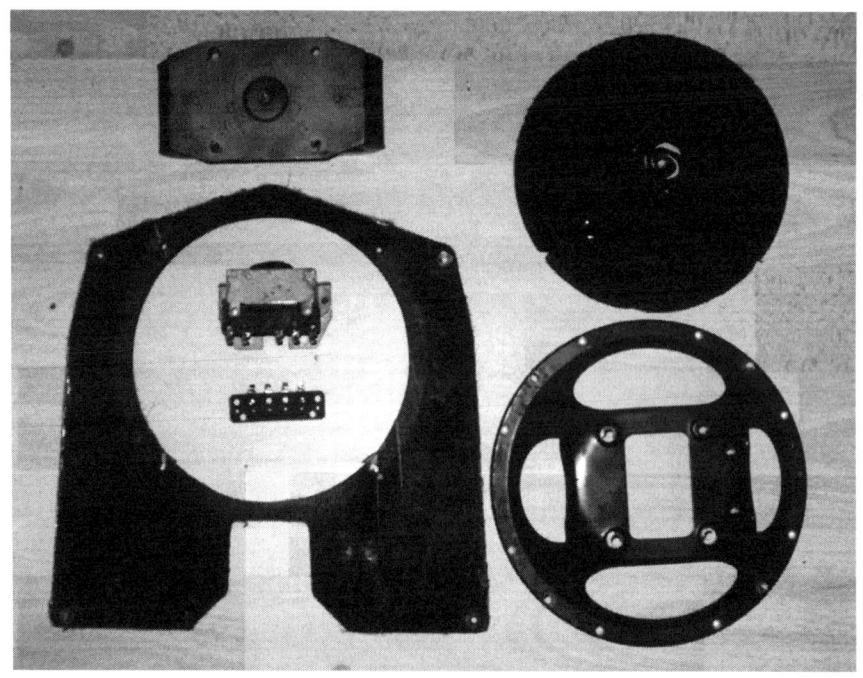

The baffle panel, chassis, transformer and magnet assembly of a mains-energised moving-coil loudspeaker fitted in a 1932 Ekco M23 dismantled for repair and rebuild

This baffle panel was split at the loudspeaker mounting holes and had warped quite badly, so a replacement was made in plywood. Considerable care was needed when drilling fixing holes to ensure they line up with the threaded holes in the Bakelite cabinet.

A new baffle cut to match the old one is temporarily fitted into the cabinet of the M23 to check accuracy before painting matt black

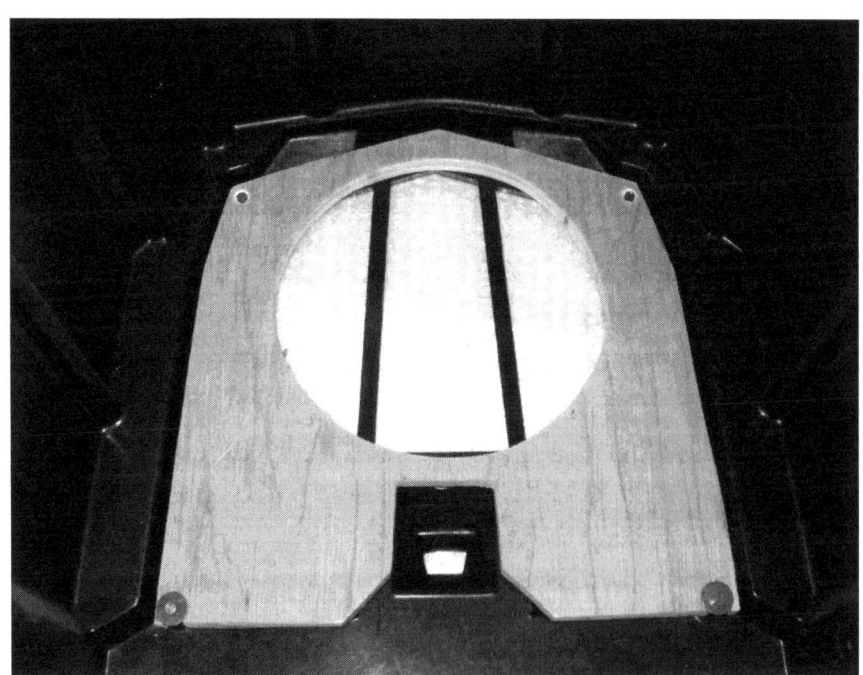

VINTAGE VALVE RADIOS

The simple design of the typical early 1930s TRF receiver lends itself to a comprehensive rebuild. Battery models in particular use very basic circuitry. Here is an example of one such rebuild, a K-B set dating from around 1932. The model was unknown to me at the time of restoring but the circuitry was similar to the rather later K-B model 333.

The chassis had, typically, been 'got at' by persons unknown. In particular they had daubed grey paint rather sparsely over the chassis. Several capacitors of modern vintage had been fitted and extensive rewiring had been carried out. Altogether the chassis, both externally and internally, was an untidy mess.

Above: grey paint - applied with a toothbrush?

Left: the underside of the chassis as found

Below: the chassis during stripping

A complete strip-down seemed the most straightforward was to sort the chassis out. As always, work began with a series of photographs to use as an aide-memoir for the rebuilding process.

With the tuning components removed it was possible to see that beneath the rust the chassis was originally silver

After a through rub down with wet/dry abrasive papers, wetted with soap and water, the chassis was treated to rust killer then sprayed with red oxide primer then steel grey gloss paint. An alternative would have been smooth Hammerite silver. The big advantage of Hammerite is that there is no requirement for priming first: two or three even coats of the finish are more than adequate to hide a thousand sins.

Chassis stripped and cleaned

Meanwhile, all the major components were checked and cleaned. Valve-holder tags were cleared of solder. A suitable capacitor of the period was found to use as a template to create 'new' cases. Strips of card were cut the length of the capacitor then rolled several times around a convenient marker pen barrel and secured using a glue Stick. New labels were created on the computer and printed onto cream paper before being wrapped around the card tubes.

The resprayed chassis

The TCC badge, copied from wax capacitors, wasn't easy to emulate; the closest to it was Gill Sans Bold with an added drop shadow. The remaining component information was set in a modern serif face. The label was copied and multiple pasted (in Photoshop) to fill an A4 page.

The innards of the few remaining original capacitors were removed complete with the end solder plates still attached. These plates were unsoldered and attached to a suitable modern and physically smaller component. This assembly was then refitted into the open casing. Closing the casing was easy enough; one I sealed with the scraped-off wax, the others I didn't need to. I have used superglue for the same task in the past. The slit can be positioned out of sight when the component is put into service.

The home-made 'kit' for capacitor rebuilds. Centre bottom of the picture is the slit and opened TCC wax capacitor that was used as a template

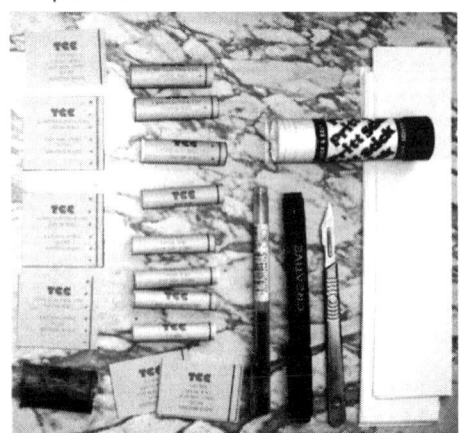

Above: the cleaned and restored components

Rewiring was done as far as possible with the original systoflex sleeving slipped on to new solid-core tinned copper wire. Battery and loudspeaker connections were made using colour-coded flexible stranded sleeved wire.

The underside of the chassis was left unsprayed; this simplified the task of ensuring good connection to all chassis earth returns.

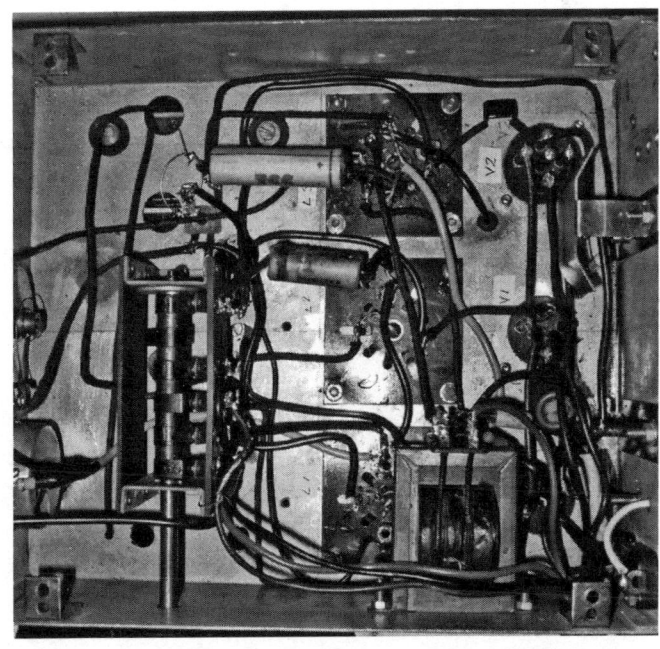

The finished K-B chassis

This kind of restoration work can be very rewarding but don't let the circuit simplicity lull you into thinking it is always going to be plain sailing. The band-pass coils used in the front-end of most TRF sets must be carefully labelled and a note taken of their orientation in the chassis before they are removed. In this case an added difficulty was that the open circumference of the cans holding these coils was peened over to grip them to the chassis.

There is no substitute for logical work with plenty of close-up photographs and notes and diagrams of parts before any dismantling takes place, or the risk is that you may end up with a small mound of unidentifiable components, coils and transformers that provide no obvious indication of how they should be wired.

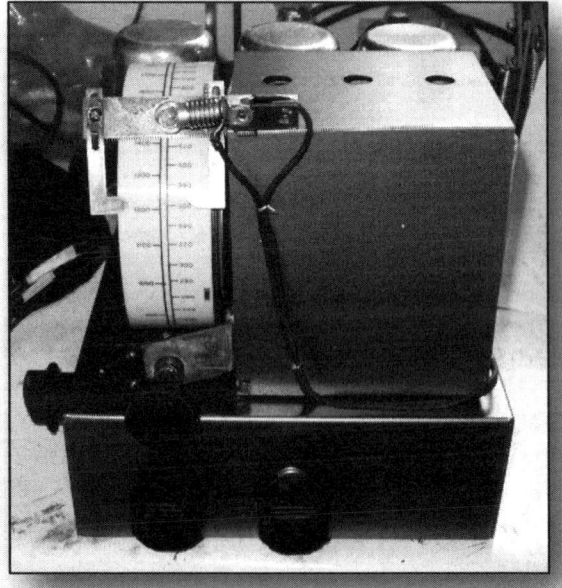

CHAPTER 13
CABINET REPAIRS AND RESTORATION

Whether housed in Bakelite or wood or covered in paint or textured sheet materials, a major part of any vintage radio restoration involves its appearance. All cabinets may suffer damage through adverse storage conditions or accident. Fortunately there is usually a way to correct such misfortunes.

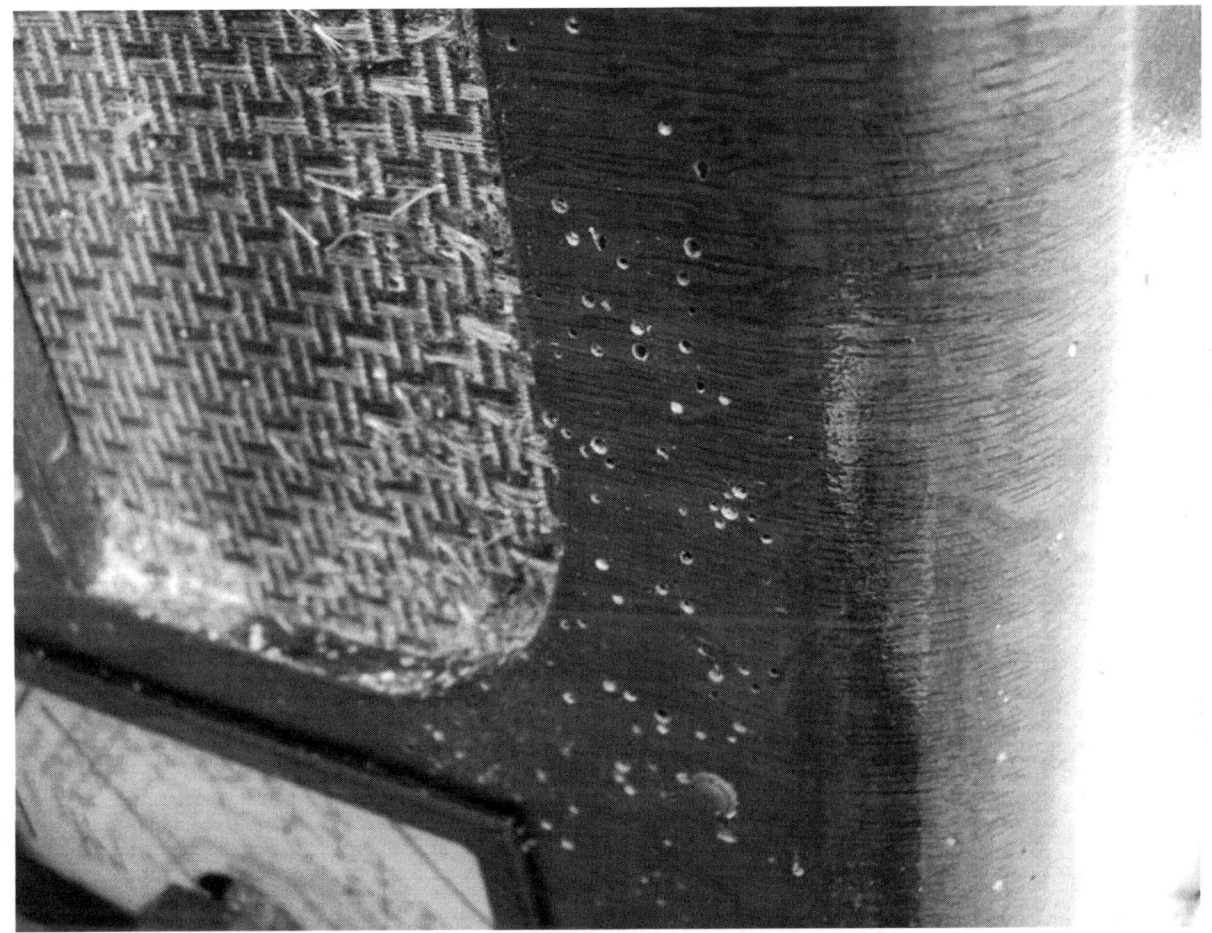

Woodworm took a liking to this 1930s Alba

There are exceptions, however. The Alba receiver shown above was so badly worm-eaten that the cabinet could not be saved and it literally fell into dust when the back cover was removed. In truth it was purchased for the parts it contained, which included a good set of valves, valve-holders, mains and output transformer and a useful energised 'Rola' loudspeaker. The set was brought home sealed into a plastic bin bag where it stayed for some months until the bag was opened out of doors, when it was given a quick and liberal dose of woodworm killer. Once the chassis and cabinet fittings were removed, the remains of the cabinet were burned. Not every woodworm attack is quite so far beyond redemption.

Wooden cabinets and woodworm

Annobium Punctatum is the scientific name for the common furniture beetle, the larvae of which are the cause of the holes we know as woodworm. These little creatures will attack perfectly sound wood and are extremely common in all temperate climes. Wooden cased radios are a prime target for them, so if evidence of infestation is noticed I recommend the following initial procedure, or something along similar lines, in defence: an external wash with 'five-star' or similar combined wood protection and woodworm killer should be given, before covering the set securely by placing into a sealed bin liner bag for storage in outhouse, shed or garage until restoration can be carried out. This is to prevent any escape of the flying insect that causes the damage. This avoids the risk of infection of other sets, wooden furniture and the structural timbers of workshop or house.

Remember that Bakelite cabinets often have a ply loudspeaker baffle board or a cabinet base board, both of which seem to attract woodworm infestation. This may be due to the Scotch (animal) glue used in old play veneers.

When examining sets for signs of woodworm, look carefully for holes in the grille cloth, as though someone had used it for darts practice. Also examine along the edges of the ply at the back and the feet of the set. The latter may be of softwood and especially prone to attack. It is said that active woodworm betray their presence by leaving small mounds of wood dust; this may be so but it doesn't cover the deliberate removal of the tell-tale dust by those wishing to sell the set. The best advice is to assume woodworm is active and treat accordingly.

Bakelite cabinets

Bakelite cabinets cannot be attacked by woodworm but they can be and often are damaged by poor storage, the main two problems being damp and ultra-violet light (sunlight). The fillers used in Bakelite during the moulding process can pick up moisture and swell, eventually breaking the surface. This can be seen as a lack of sheen and felt as slight roughness. In the worst cases it is visually very obvious. Little can be done to counteract this problem.

Ultra-violet light can, over time, have a bleaching effect, lightening any cabinet surface continually exposed to it. It is also possible the UV light increases brittleness. Again little can be done about it. From new, Bakelite is hard and brittle and a dropped cabinet can crack or shatter. It is possible to repair some of these. Stress-cracks can occur spontaneously, perhaps where the material is above a source of heat such as a mains dropper, or from a sharp corner or angle in the moulding. Urea Formaldehyde, a thermosetting plastic akin to Bakelite and often called so, is white or creamy-white in colour. Though possessing similar qualities to Bakelite, Urea is rather more fragile and more prone to stress-cracking.

Cabinets of portable receivers may be made from wood or metal, painted or covered with embossed vynide, vynaire or with early items, a leatherette-type material such as Rexine. Some of these coverings are tough, backed with woven fabric and last well: others are thinner and perhaps paper-backed. These can easily fray at corners or become quite badly soiled. Record players are most usually of ply construction with a covering fabric of some kind.

Starting the restoration

When first placed upon the bench, a careful general inspection of any set should be carried out to decide whether restoring is practicable and if so, just how deep such a restoration should be. During this examination, digital photos may be taken and a record made of any missing knobs, back covers, damage to loudspeaker escutcheon, fabric, woodworm past or present, damaged or missing emblems, scale glass problems, feet, chassis holding screws.

Though skilled refinishing is something of an art, remarkable transformations can be achieved with a little care and thought. Here we have a Pam TR30 in desperate need of attention (or of throwing in a skip).

A challenge? Certainly – but let's go through it step by step. First thing to do is to sort the chassis out. It is a waste of time to work on a cabinet only to find that for whatever reason, the chassis cannot be made to function. Assuming then that the electronics is good to go, we can turn our attention to the empty cabinet.

In dire need of repair, this cabinet was literally falling apart; the glue had failed extensively, probably due to many years of damp storage. Little persuasion was needed before the front moulding dropped off, followed by the inner contrasting parts.

Even the cabinet shell joints needed re-gluing, for which purpose ordinary woodworker's PVA glue proved suitable.

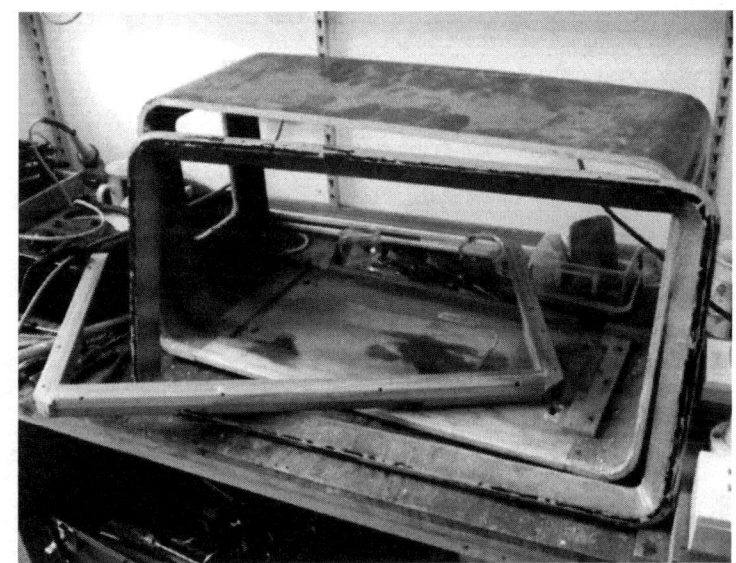

All surfaces and sections were stripped down to bare wood using gel paint stripper.
Wire wool helps stubborn finish removal, but strong rubber gloves should be worn to prevent unpleasant skin burns. Protect eyes, too.

Below: the front beaded surround has been stripped and cleaned and is shown being bonded to the shell. Note the extensive use of masking tape in lieu of potentially damaging clamps

Right: the main cabinet shell after stripping and during the cleaning up. Doesn't look too inspiring, does it...

After stripping, the action of the stripper was killed with turpentine substitute (white spirit) which was allowed to dry overnight before a clean up with fine abrasive paper, working at all time along the grain, never across it. The general inspection and minor repair process came next; steaming out dints, re-gluing joints, repairing damaged grilles and so on.

VINTAGE VALVE RADIOS

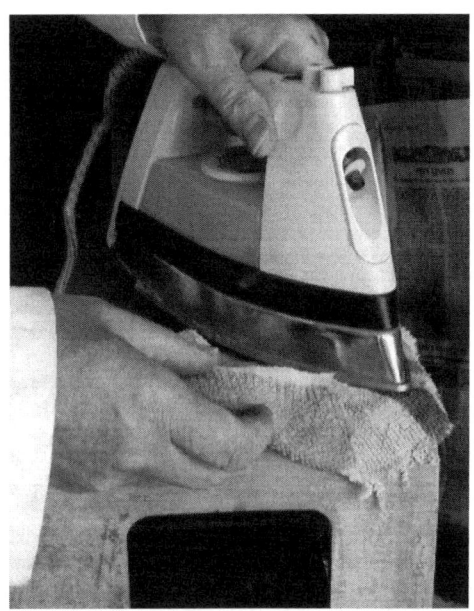

Left: one method of removing or at least minimizing dents where the wood fibres have been crushed but – importantly – not broken, is to steam them out.

This can only be done on bare timber and before the application of new finish. A cloth is wetted and placed over the depressed area, then a domestic iron set to a medium heat (not too hot or you risk melting the animal glue securing the veneer) is placed over the cloth.

The resulting burst of steam softens and helps the wood fibres recover their former position. The process may need to be repeated. The whole area will require fine sanding to level the now raised grain

After removal of any remaining wood dust using a 'tack rag' (proprietary sticky cloth) or a lint-free cloth damped with cellulose thinners (allow to dry), the first coat or two of aerosol clear gloss lacquer was applied. A light rub down with fine wet/dry paper helped to flatten these initial coats. The first clear coats sealed the wood grain.

Above: the finished cabinet, after toning and re-cellulosing.

Toner aerosols were then used to shade the cabinet as desired, using marking tape to protect areas that must remain as a contrast. Toner should not be applied directly to the wood, though it is tempting to do so, as differences in the porosity of the veneers may lead to a patchy effect. Besides, it can 'stain' into the grain, making it impossible to clean off in the event of a catastrophe – such as a severe run, known as 'curtaining' – in the spray finish. It is important to avoid the use of a power sander when cleaning up a stripped cabinet. The veneer used is always extremely thin and power sanding will all too easily cut through to expose the substrates of the ply. This is especially risky along edges.

The toner can be very lightly rubbed down after two to three coats have been applied but take great care near edges as it is all too easy to cut through the toned finish to reveal lighter wood, thereby ruining your work and necessitating a re-strip (one of the catastrophes mentioned above).
A finishing couple of gloss coats were flatted with 1000 grade wet/dry then brought up to a fine gloss using metal polish. T-Cut is an acceptable substitute for metal polish, as is car body cutting compound. A final light waxing completed the work.

Restoring Bakelite cabinets
Bakelite lends itself to a straightforward cleaning and polishing process, for which 'Bake-O-Brite' polish may be obtained (see Radiophile magazine details in the appendix). Many restorers prefer to use Brasso metal polish, which works very well though it and other car paint restoring compounds tend to leave a whitish deposit behind which builds up in corners, the traces of which are difficult to remove. T-Cut car polish also works well, but is slightly more abrasive than Brasso and perhaps best for cabinets that have become badly dulled. Some marks can, with great care, be removed by the use of fine wet/dry paper but there is the ever-present danger of creating a light patch on the surface.

Suitably coloured wax sticks can be obtained from woodworker's suppliers and Do-It-Yourself outlets. Although these sticks are intended for wooden furniture, it is possible to melt the wax into dents or chips in the Bakelite surface, using a clean soldering iron.

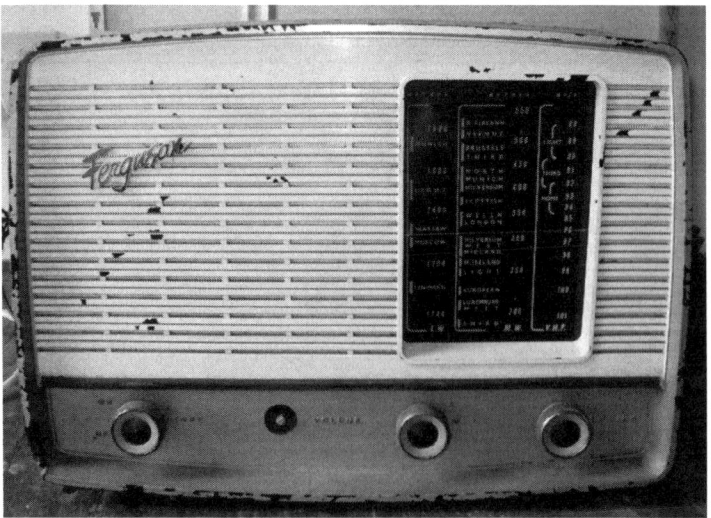

Right: the cabinet of this Ferguson 'Flight' has suffered from ill-treatment

Missing sections of shattered cabinets may be rebuilt using Milliput. I prefer the superfine white variety, obtainable from stationers and craft/model shops. It is a two-part product in stick form. Once set it can be carefully levelled using a craft knife blade held in the fingers, then gently buffed. This is not ideal for cracks which must be reinforced, but it works well when missing edges and sections need replacement. *See opposite for repairs to the Ferguson cabinet*

Milliput is used extensively here. The original silver paint was stripped from the cabinet then the shattered corners and the cracks were cleaned thoroughly then dried before starting work. Milliput was pressed into place, roughly building up the missing wall sections.

After this had half-hardened – a process which can take several hours or even days, depending upon ambient temperature and the age of the Milliput – a scalpel was used to shape the material to follow approximately the cabinet contours. When hardened, the repair was sanded to the finished shape. **Tip:** wetted fingers and cutting/shaping tools make working with Milliput much easier.

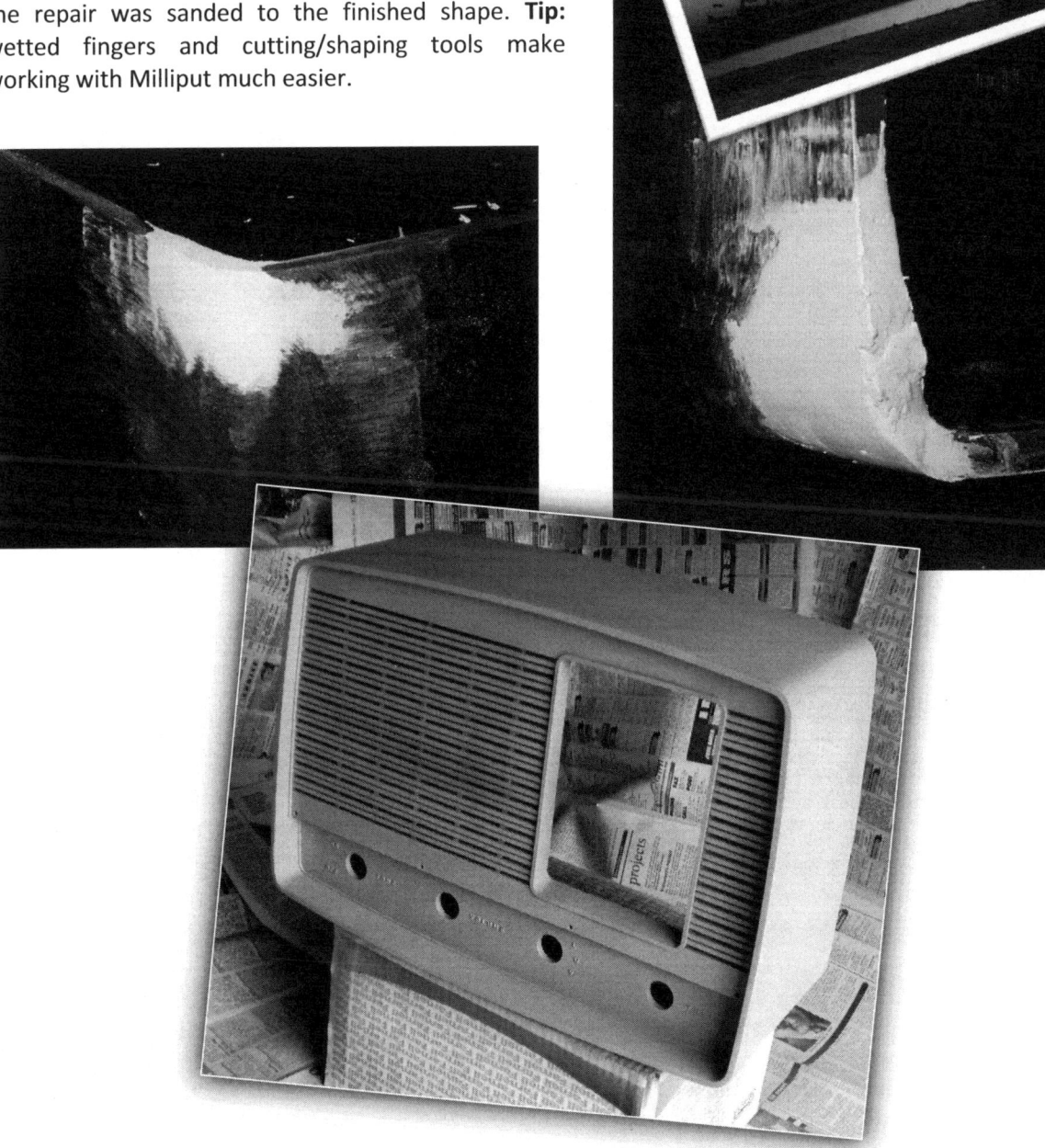

Milliput is quite easy to use. Equal amounts of the plastic and the hardener are kneaded thoroughly together, then pressed into place and moulded with the fingers into an approximate shape. Remember, if sticking occurs, wet the fingers.

After it has hardened sufficiently (it is a slow process which can be speeded somewhat by application of heat from a hair drier) it can be shaped using a variety of tools: I like to use a small scalpel to gently peel slices away. After it has set rock hard, it may be finished using wet/dry abrasive paper, best used wetted with soap and water.

The finished cabinet

Repairs with Milliput have to be painted to match the Bakelite, unfortunately, but with original spray-painted sets that is not a problem. There are similar products from other makers.

Cracks may benefit from support within the cabinet by bridging on the inside with resin and fine aluminium mesh or alternatively woven glass fibre mat. Key the surface first using coarse abrasive paper. All products mentioned except Milliput can be obtained from car accessory shops where they are sold as body repair kits and materials.

Aluminium mesh bedded in resin: note sticks to hold in place until resin sets

Cracks with voids (missing sections) in Bakelite can be rebuilt in the following manner: superglue along any crack edges then pull the opened crack edges together with strong tape such as wide masking tape. Allow time for the superglue to work. Don't worry if it beads up along the crack as it is pressed together; it will be possible to level this later by careful scraping using a craft knife blade. Bridge the void internally with mesh as shown above and right, then follow the filling method outlined on p. 143.

This Champion looks reasonable from the front, but the sides and top show characteristic – if unusually severe – stress-cracking of the Urea casing. The cabinet was self-colour Urea but the decision was made to paint it when repairs were completed in order to hide the extensive repair work. The process followed is described here as a step-by-step procedure applicable to any similar cabinet restoration.

The first step was to strengthen and stabilise the cracks from inside, using the embedded aluminium mesh or woven fibreglass matting method described earlier. The use of rough abrasive paper to key the inside surfaces surrounding the damaged area will help the resin to grip.

Strong adhesive tape (duct tape) was stretched across the cracks to pull the edges together as far as possible. A piece of matting – ideally, aluminium mesh or woven fibreglass matting for ease of working, but chopped strand glass fibre will work – was cut to a size that allowed around an inch (25mm) or more around the damage. A Mix of resin and hardener was made, following instructions supplied with the product. This was applied to the roughened area. The matting was placed on this and a stick was used to embed it in the resin. More resin was added as required. After allowing time for the product to cure, the supporting tape was removed.

The repaired 'Champion' cabinet

If you use this method you will make strong and permanent repairs to any crack. To complete the work, and make the cracks disappear they may be filled with Milliput. Superglue can also fill the cracks if the edges are in close contact. Break-outs and voids will have now have glass mat support and can be filled with Milliput as described above. Flatting of the entire cabinet with wet and dry paper, used wet with soap lubricant, will prepare it for spraying.

Not every Bakelite set is suitable for spray-painting.
When repairing brown 'Walnut' effect Bakelite cabinets, you can experiment along the following lines: prepare two small amounts of resin plus hardener in separate containers. Mix into one of these a very small quantity of brown and red pigment. Powder pigments can be bought from craft suppliers or you can try brown and red 'Humbrol' modelmaker's paint. Stir in black pigment or paint with the remaining resin/hardener mix. Surprisingly little paint is needed - limit the quantity of pigment or paint or you will risk failure of the curing process. Feed the brown/red mix into the void. Using something pointed, perhaps a sharpened matchstick, add a little of the black tinted resin, gently flowing it into the brown/red mix to imitate the swirling pattern of 'walnut effect' Bakelite. Do not overdo this action or the colours will blend into one and defeat the object. Fine wet and dry paper, used wet with block soap lubricant, will level the filling when set. Tape around the repair with masking tape, allowing about 10mm clearance, to avoid too much of the 'good' original finish being abraded. Finish by polishing with metal polish or T-Cut.

The same process but with only one mix – brown, cream or black – can be used on plain Bakelite cabinets. It is important to accept that getting an acceptable colour match is not easy and single-colour cabinets are even more of a problem to match than are mottled 'Walnut' types. Plain brown paint can be too light and you might have to mix a little black into the brown/red, or even use a touch of deeper red where the tone seems wrong. It is all a matter of practice and when a cabinet is badly damaged, you have little to lose by having a go. It can always be broken out and readied for a second or third attempt.

Difficulties with deeply textured Bakelite
Break-outs often occur along vulnerable edges and corners. These can prove tricky to repair invisibly. Here is one example. The missing cabinet corner of this Ekco M23 is all too obvious, jagged edge and all. Making an effective repair to such severe damage is far from straightforward as the graining and border design has somehow to be matched.

The work began by straightening the jagged break line to make it easier to fit a replacement section. The replacement was made by copying an area of the cabinet that had identical texturing and edging. This was situated some way above the break and it was moulded using Alginate compound, again obtainable from modelling sources. The compound is mixed with water and poured onto the area required.

Right: the break as presented

Some form of 'dam' or container must be built around the area to prevent loss of the liquid Alginate; this can be card, plasticine or a combination of both.
Resin, tinted with paint, was cast into the Alginate mould and when set, was cut to size to fit the cleaned break and bonded in place using superglue. Slight gaps were filled with Milliput and then the whole area was flashed lightly with a combination of spray paints in an attempt to match the original finish.

VINTAGE VALVE RADIOS

The Alginate mould

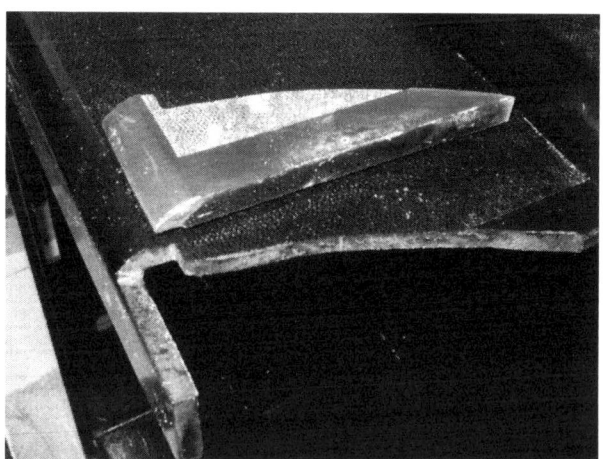

The resin cast being fitted

The final effect, although noticeable upon closer inspection, certainly is far from obvious as a repair and of course much better and surely safer than seeing the exposed metal chassis within.

VINTAGE VALVE RADIOS

Some repair work requires much thought. One of the loudspeaker grille bars on this Pilot Major Maestro was shattered and the broken pieces long lost. The task was to make up the missing piece and integrate it into the grille sufficiently well to make an acceptable repair.

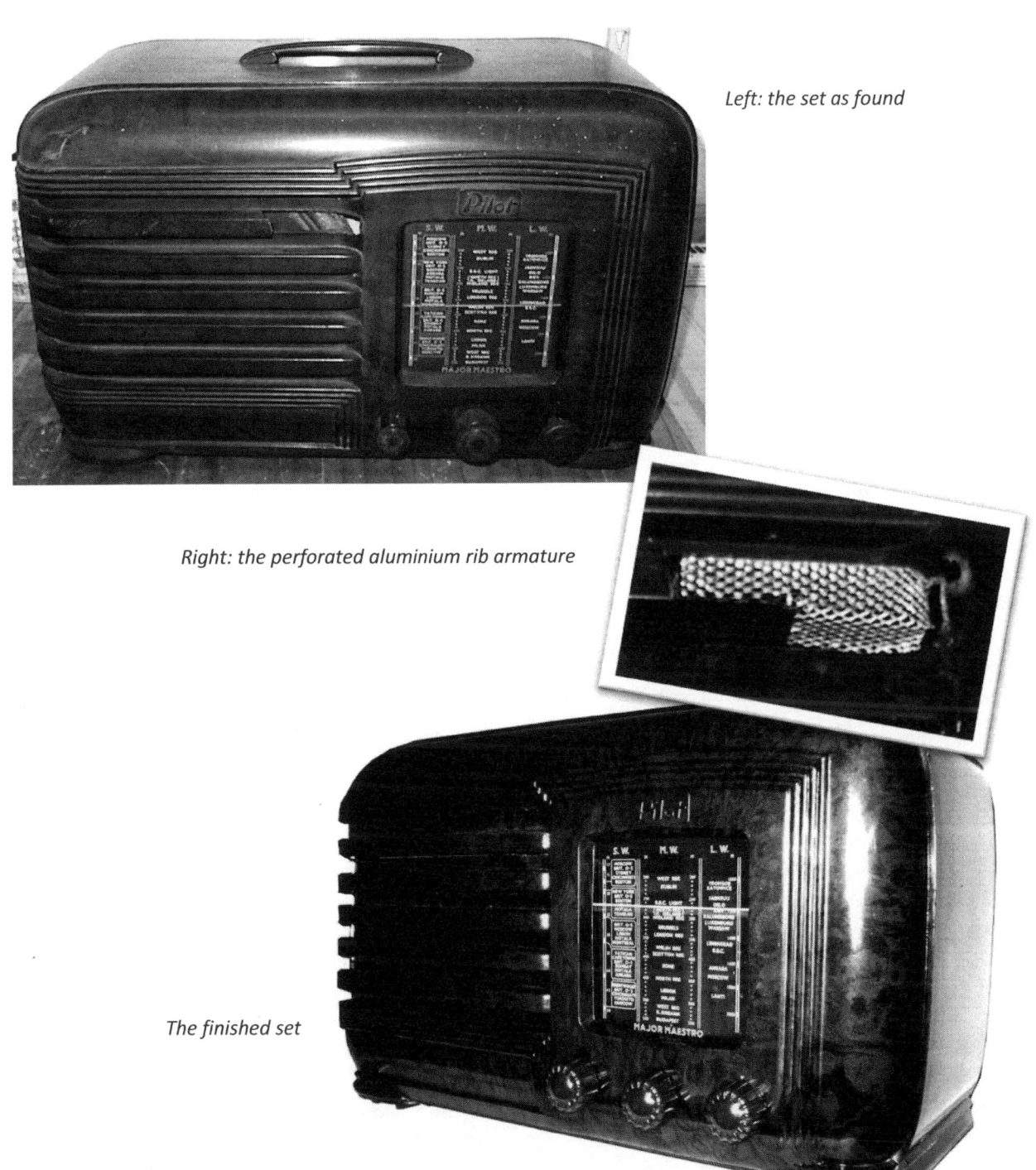

Left: the set as found

Right: the perforated aluminium rib armature

The finished set

The Major Maestro cabinet repair process

As it was not a flat section but part of the rather complex ribbing that was missing, I constructed an armature using perforated aluminium sheet This thin sheet can be cut easily with a pair of (old) scissors and this I did, making it slightly oversize. This was then pushed into a section of the existing loudspeaker rib moulding but from the inside of the cabinet. I used a softwood stick, carefully trimmed to fit, to simplify the task. I allowed a couple of flat overlap 'wings' on the mesh for bonding purposes and carefully trimmed the sound hole area to follow the cut-out shape of the existing ribs. The inner Bakelite surfaces were roughened with coarse abrasive paper before I bonded the armature in place with Araldite.

Once set, Plastic Padding chemical metal built up the outside surfaces to the level and shape of the remaining original rib. Several layers were needed. I finished the task with superfine Milliput. The whole of the cabinet surface was cut back with 1000 grit wet and dry paper, used wet with block soap lubricant. Once the surface had been flatted sufficiently, brisk polishing by hand with T-cut – two or three applications - and finishing with Brasso restored a very pleasing shine.

Disguising the replaced section was carried out as follows: I used a mixture of paints, the small or very small tins of gloss Humbrol modelling paint, available from do-it-yourself stores and model shops everywhere, also Plasti-Cote paint where no suitable Humbrol colour exists. This latter product comes in small jars with a screw-top lid. Beware – although convenient in use, any spillage over the threads in the glass means that the lid will never unscrew a second time.

The actual process was simpler to do than to describe. With this particular cabinet, first a smooth coat of Plasti-Cote 'nut brown' (B17) darkened slightly with Humbrol black (21) was applied to cover all the new area and overlapped slightly on the old. Then, not waiting for this coat to dry, careful mixtures of Humbrol Red (19), red (20) brown (10), yellow (69) and black (21 were applied, using two types of very fine artist's watercolour brushes, one pointed, the other flat – like a miniature housepainter's brush. Don't be tempted to use inferior brushes; they tend to splay their bristles in all directions when loaded with the heavy gloss paint. I pre-mixed the colours on a scrap of card, blending them so as to match as near as possible the existing colours in the Bakelite mottling. A small amount of the Georgian artist's oil colour 'indian red' was used to bring out the warm tones. These paint combinations were brushed and stippled into the wet nut brown base colour in a manner copying the existing mottle. The aim was to match both the colour and the appearance of the Bakelite and quite a lot of trial and error – plus patience – was needed before satisfactory results can be obtained. When the paint was hard dry it was rubbed down with 1000 grade wet-dry abrasive paper, wetted with turps substitute and wrapped around the end of a thin, flat stick. This left a smooth, flat finish to the painted area. Finally, very gently and carefully I buffed the paint surface back to a shine using Brasso and protected the entire cabinet with silicon spray polish. Bakelite varies in colour. Plain brown Bakelite can sometimes be spray painted with Vauxhall Brazil brown, a close colour match in *some* cases, though not all. Brazil brown is obtainable in aerosol can form from car accessory shops, though you may have to hunt around for it as it is many years since Vauxhall cars were finished in that colour. With mottled Bakelite (walnut effect), more artistry is needed, along the lines already described.

Ideally, rather than the oil-based paints mentioned above, use aerosol paint by spraying into containers – perhaps the lids of the aerosols – and mix as you go. Work quickly and clean the brush immediately after use or the rapid drying paint will destroy it. In theory, cellulose thinner is needed for this purpose but you may find that the old standby, WD-40, works pretty well as a brush cleaner. A big advantage of this method of painting is the ease of rubbing down and polishing that the harder finish of the aerosol paint provides.

CHAPTER 14
RESTORING AND REFINISHING WOODEN CABINETS

Most radio cabinets will have been spray lacquered when manufactured. Re-lacquering isn't too difficult a task but many cabinets will also have been 'toned' by the application of pigmented translucent lacquer. Fortunately this can be obtained in aerosol form.

Safety precautions

Where possible, work in the open air or in a garage or workshop with an open door. Paint stripper and aerosol fumes can be damaging to health especially if you are prone to asthma or other chest ailments. A face mask is advisable and this can and should be used when sanding, too.

Wear protective clothing or old clothes when using paint stripper as even the gel types are almost certain to splash a little. For the same reason eye protection is sensible. Never work with caustic solutions without protecting hands. Ordinary household rubber gloves are reasonably good for this, being thin enough to allow sensitivity when holding wire wool yet strong enough to give tear-free protection – for a while at least!

If you do get stripper on your hands, wash it off immediately, don't wait.

Philips 186a as found

White spirit kills the action of paint stripper pretty quickly but a good wash in warm soapy water works well. The heat of the water may cause the affected area to 'burn' but you must persevere and remove all trace of the solution. Its nasty stuff when in contact with skin as the effects are not immediate but once they develop it can prove painful.

Stripping

However you intend to finish a cabinet, the original finish must be removed. Power sanding is not advisable as it is fatally easy to cut through the very thin veneer to expose edges, ruining the cabinet. Use a paint stripper and follow the maker's instructions. Apply to only one surface at a time – do not try to strip a cabinet in one single sweep. Don't wait too long, however – no more than a couple of minutes should see the finish softened sufficiently to allow scraping off with a flat-bladed filler knife. Work quickly, using a paintbrush of perhaps 1" in size. Put plenty on and stipple the surface, agitating it with the brush. Some cabinet finishes are very resistant, others come away clean. With the former, scrape off the first layer and recoat with stripper. I recommend the use of a plastic paint scraper. Metal ones may scratch the cabinet and may dig in and cause damage. Wire wool, wetted with stripper, helps the removal of obstinate finish and also shaped mouldings that the knife cannot touch.

Grain filling

A characteristic of some hardwood timbers is 'open' grain, which shows itself as gaps between and parallel to the grain direction. These slight voids create an uneven surface and must be filled if a high surface smoothness is required, as is usually the case when French polishing or lacquering. One way to achieve this is to apply several layers of finish, rubbing each one down until you arrive at a point where the grain is level and no voids are apparent. This is labour intensive, however. Another and quicker way is to use a ready-made grain filling compound and these are readily available in a variety of timber shades. Rubbed across – not along –the grain, they fill the surface effectively and are easy to use. After sanding level with fine paper and a cork block, they will accept any finish.

There are points to watch, though: you should choose a colour as near as possible to the timber you are finishing, otherwise the grain filler will show. This can be covered easily if you are using toner spray but with light French polish any marked difference in shade will be difficult to hide completely. Do not use grain filler when finishing with Danish oil or the sheer transparency of the oil will show the slightly different colour of the filler.

Water-based grain fillers may raise the grain slightly but this is easily remedied by a light sanding when dry. French polish itself, applied by brush, will act as grain filler in cases where only a light filling seems required. Choose shellac-based sanding sealer as it has more body than the standard French polish.

The finished 186A

French polishing

This traditional finish does require patience and the development of a little skill in handling but, done well, cannot be beaten for appearance. It does not possess the hard glossiness of spray lacquer yet it has a glow of quality that is quite unique. The traditional process is, on the face of things, straightforward: a lint free rag is folded into a pad shape known as a 'shoe' or rubber, and filled with cotton waste. This waste is charged with French polish, the pad refolded and the application begins. Most books say that the polish should be applied in a figure-of-eight motion, working continuously without stopping or lifting the pad until the surface is covered. This is not easy and again I recommend that you practice on scrap material before committing yourself!

There are a few pointers that should help. **Wear disposable gloves**. Never to use the polish direct from the jar without first thinning with methylated spirits or you may find it is too thick, dries too quickly and creates a smeary ridged mess on your lovingly prepared cabinet.

With each successive coat, thin the polish more until you are using almost pure meths to provide a final buffing to the finish. Allow time between coats, especially toward the end of the process. Finish along the grain. If you make a mess, you have lost nothing but time. Meths will strip the polish back and you can start again. French polish – shellac – is available in quite a wide variety of qualities and in different forms. Ready-made in white, pale, golden brown and dark brown – among others – you should choose the colour to suit the job in hand, light timbers requiring a pale polish, of course. If you want to you can make your own polish by purchasing shellac in flake form and dissolving it in meths.

To speed the task, I suggest you apply first coats only slightly thinned, with a brush (along the grain) and reserve the applicator pad for the later, finishing coats. You must rub down with fine wire wool after brushing, however. This brushing method may be frowned upon by purists, but it is effective and a good time saver as well as a grain filler. French polish was never in general use for radio cabinets; the standard finish was spray lacquer.

Plastic coatings

To replicate the mirror-gloss cabinet finish of the type popular in the early sixties, use Rustin's Plastic Coating. This is a two-part cold-cure finish that is extremely hard when curing is complete. It can be applied by brush or, perhaps preferably, by roller. If rolling, I advise the use of a fine foam roller sleeve of the type using a thin layer of foam around a stout cardboard cylinder. Spongy rollers are extremely messy and wasteful in use. The finish may be burnished to a very high gloss using burnishing cream or T-cut. Not suitable for general use as it is just too bright and hard and cannot provide the look of the more traditional and softer lacquer finishes that were applied to the majority of receivers.

Spray lacquering and toning

Toning by tinted lacquer was used to darken and 'improve' low quality plywood. As usual, the first thing to do is to remove all fixtures from the cabinet: not just the chassis but speaker and baffle (where fitted), trim items, grille cloth, dial escutcheons and so on. Leave nothing that might be open to attack from paint stripper.

Suggested working method: clean off all sanding residue, first with a vacuum cleaner and a natural fibre hand brush of the sort that are used with dustpans, then with a tack-rag. These slightly sticky cleaning cloths may be purchased or you can, as I do, improvise and use a lint-free cloth (old cotton shirt is good) damped with cellulose thinners. Rub along the grain and turn the cloth occasionally. The volatility of the thinners means only a short wait for drying. Whenever possible, work from the back of the cabinet when spraying the top and sides and only spray the surface that is horizontal. This helps prevent sagging – 'curtaining' - and runs in the spray and importantly allows any overspray to land clear of the cabinet instead of pebble-dashing areas yet to be treated. A temporary support in the form of a flat board clamped to and overhanging the bench, onto which the cabinet may be hung, will allow the cabinet to be turned without having to rest an already sprayed side upon the bench.

Tips for success

Choose a warm, dry and windless day and work near an open door. Damp air will cause 'blooming' of the lacquer, which is a dull greyish haze on the gloss. If you are unfortunate enough to encounter bloom, perhaps as a result of a breeze blowing over the still-wet lacquer, a hair drier used to warm the area gently might rescue the surface by driving the moisture out. This must be done quickly before the surface hardens.

Always seal bare cabinets with clear lacquer first. Use several coats of toner to build up the density required and always finish with clear lacquer; this provides a protective coat for the toner which, understandably, does not have quite the gloss of clear lacquer.

Don't mix the types of lacquer or chemical reactions of an unwanted and crinkly nature may be the result.

Rub down with wet and dry paper, used wet with soap, perhaps after the first three or four light coats. Dry with warm air from a hair dryer. Don't leave all cutting back until the final coat.

If you must use T-Cut or other compounds between spray coats, ensure complete removal of any traces. This can be done with white spirit but it must be allowed to dry thoroughly or a reaction will cause trouble. I strongly advise against this, however.

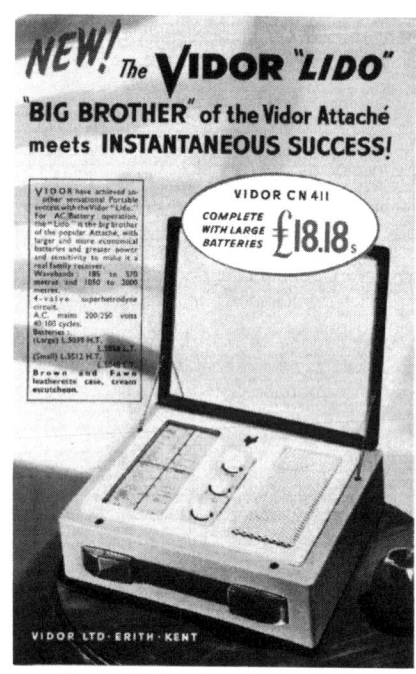

Danish oil

Not an original finish by any means but it does have its adherents. It is a very easy finish to apply and is guaranteed to give good results on cabinets that do not require toning and do not need a very high gloss surface. Strip the old surfaces as described then wash down thoroughly with white spirit and leave to dry. The Danish Oil can be applied by brush (my favoured method) or by rag. Either way, work along the grain, leave it to stand for a few minutes then gently rub off the excess with a clean lint-free rag such as old cotton shirt. Two or three applications may suffice but as many coats as you wish can be applied, though a light rub down with fine, wetted wet and dry paper might be beneficial after several layers. The oil will dry to an attractive eggshell-like gloss and the surface may be enhanced or maintained with wax polish.

Restoring Rexine and Vynide covered items

Portable valve radios of all years were mostly finished by covering with material designed to look like leather or crocodile skin. Rexine, a leather-effect fabric-based sheet material, was the covering of choice for most makers as well as the makers of portable gramophones and record players. It was supplanted by Vynide and Vynaire in the 1950s, the latter used for loudspeaker grilles where the placing of the loudspeaker was intended to be invisible (a styling tendency, perhaps with a band of the material running around an entire cabinet). The Vidor 'Lido' portable seen here was in a poor state – much worse than the photograph shows – mainly because it was rather unusually built into a steel case, which had corroded badly beneath the covering. This could be felt by an underlying roughness and detachment of the Vynide.

Vidor Lido as found

VINTAGE VALVE RADIOS 151

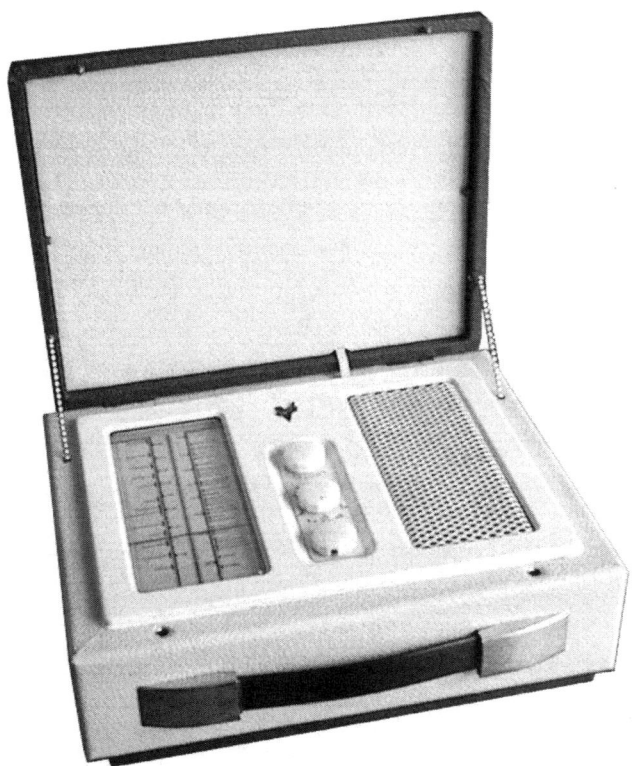

In one sense the corrosion proved useful in that the covering didn't take much persuasion to release what grip it had left, coming free in large enough pieces to use as patterns when cutting the new covering. The corrosion was so marked that a power drill fitted with an abrasive flap wheel had to be used to remove it, after which it was liberally dosed with rust killer.

The process was repeated several times, each time regrinding with the flap wheel and re-applying rust killer until at last all trace of rust had gone. Some filling of the pitted surface was needed and this was done with Plastic Padding car body filler. The new covering was glued into place with PVA wood glue, coating both the fabric and the metal and allowing time for the adhesive to become tacky. Only top-quality PVA woodworker's adhesive should be used; low-cost types are too thin in consistency and lack adhesive power.

Left: the finished Lido

Paint finishes
This Ever Ready model C/E dates from the late 1940s. The front and back of the cabinet is acrylic sheet.

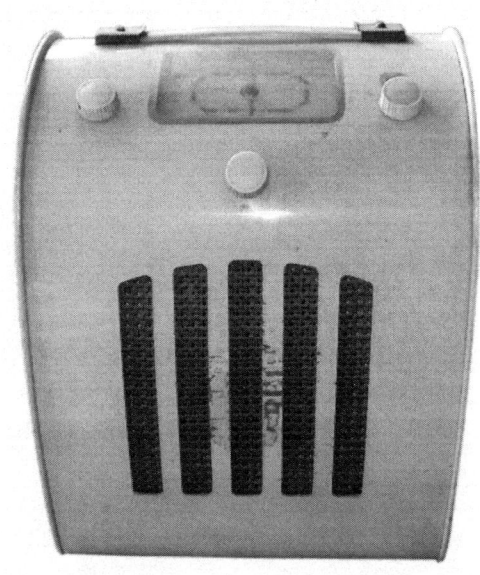

The substructure and the ends are of plywood. The end panels are finished in a crackle effect but with this example someone had decided to paint the entire cabinet, inside and out, a rather sickly shade of green. The paint was lavishly applied, too. Stripping the inside of the cabinet was not possible due to the unfinished nature of the wood surfaces, so it was sanded down and given a few coats of aerosol grey primer.

The end panels were spray-painted with a two-coat crackle finish, obtainable from DIY stores. The colour was chosen to match what would have been the original colour.

The flaking paint was rather laboriously scraped from the inside of the acrylic sheets (back and front) then the scale and control surrounds were masked and repainted in gold before the panels were sprayed cream.

Above: repainting the gold surrounds
Left: the completed receiver
Below: the resprayed front panel

Marconiphone record player

This record player is a typical example of the late 1950s-early 1960s reproducers. Semi-portable, with red leather-grained Vynide covering the plywood cabinet. Fitted with an autochanger for convenience it is otherwise quite basic with no pretensions to high fidelity.

Top left: player as found
Top right: stripping under way
Left: the finished player

The casing was recovered in grey and off-white and the autochanger was cleaned and polished with Bake-O-Brite. All fittings were removed, de-rusted and polished before replacing. The inner lid carried the Marconiphone logo so this was left intact but careful application of bleach restored the colour. New grille fabric completed the restoration.

Bush BA51 cabinet restoration

This 1938 battery receiver was looking very tired. After full chassis restoration, the cabinet was stripped then washed down with turps substitute and allowed to dry before sanding thoroughly with very fine paper on a cork block to remove any lingering trace of surface roughness. Surfaces were then wiped with a clean piece of towelling damped with cellulose thinner. This killed all trace of Nitromors from the grain as well as acting as a tack cloth to lift remaining dust from the cabinet surfaces.

It was now obvious that whilst the front panel was expensively veneered with Maple and Walnut, the sides and top were definitely not. Whatever had been used for veneer on these was inferior and its greyish, randomly grained appearance looked to me like standard birch ply. Worse still, one side was distinctly warmer in tint to the other and the top was darker than either. This kind of mismatch at least explained why such heavy toning had been used in the first place, to the extent that even the attractive Maple had been partly obscured. Consequently, the top and sides were re-toned with three or four lightly applied coats of dark Mahogany, after a couple of sealing coats of clear lacquer had been applied to all exterior surfaces. The front panel was masked during the toning operation.

7 or 8 coats of clear lacquer were then spray-applied to all cabinet surfaces. After leaving overnight for the lacquer to harden, the cabinet was flatted using 600 grade wet/dry paper, water-wetted and lubricated by rubbing on a block of household soap. Once completely dry, buffing with Brasso commenced. This was a long laborious process, only complete when all signs of flatting had been polished out and the surfaces showed a continuous soft gloss, with no evidence of voids or brighter grain. The purpose of this rather protracted exercise was to kill the sparkly, hard and overly-bright effect produced by spraying which in my opinion can spoil the vintage appearance of a cabinet. To complete the effect, dark wax furniture polish helped lose the inevitable pick-up of Brasso in the veneer edge joints and left the cabinet gleaming.

Before waxing, a coat of brown paint was applied to the edges of the two 'windows' in the cabinet front (the baffle opening and the scale aperture) and black paint revived the front foot strip and the two back footplates.

APPENDIX

CAPACITOR VALUE COMPARATOR

MicroFARAD (µF)	NanoFARAD (nF)	PicoFARAD (pF)
	0.01	10
	0.022	22
	0.047	47
0.0001	0.1	100
0.00022	0.22	220
0.00039	0.39	390
0.00047	0.47	470
0.00056	0.56	560
0.00068	0.68	680
0.00082	0.82	820
0.001	1	1000
0.0015	1.5	1500
0.0022	2.2	2200
0.0033	3.3	3300
0.0047	4.7	4700
0.0068	6.8	6800
0.01	10	
0.015	15	
0.022	22	
0.033	33	
0.047	47	
0.068	68	
0.1	100	
0.15	150	
0.22	220	
0.33	330	
0.47	470	
0.68	680	
1.0	1000	
1.5	1500	

Vintage radio capacitors (condensers) are usually marked in µF (MicroFarad) or pF (PicoFarad), where modern components tend to use nF (NanoFarad). This chart shows equivalence of values for replacement purposes. Example: 0.0001µF = 0.1 nF = 100pF. The physical size and shapes will vary, as will the construction of the capacitor. Those designed for use at RF tend to be silvered mica construction in the low values, and are likely to be marked in pF. Those designed for use at AF tend to be waxed paper or mixed dielectric types, generally marked in µF or nF values.

CAPACITOR COLOUR CODES
There are a number of methods of coding, depending upon the amount of information given. The coding is the same as for resistors. Colours are read from left to right, the first colour being nearest to one end. Some capacitors have an arrow denoting the direction the code is to be read.

ONE COLOUR: Tolerance only

TWO COLOURS: Tolerance and voltage rating

THREE COLOURS: Capacitance (in picoFarads)

FIVE COLOURS: The first three colours denote capacitance in picoFarads. The remaining two denote tolerance and voltage rating.

AMERICAN CAPACITORS
Slight variations on the above. The RMA three-dot code is used for capacitors having a voltage rating of 500V and a tolerance of 20%. The dots simply give the value in picoFarads.

The RMA six-dot code offers - top row: First, second and third significant figures. Bottom row: voltage rating, tolerance and DECIMAL MULTIPLIER.

American fixed ceramic capacitors have a broad band followed by four narrow bands or dots giving temperature coefficient, first significant figure, second significant figure, DECIMAL MULTIPLIER and tolerance.

RESISTOR COLOUR CODE CHART
Resistors used in vintage valve equipment tend to fall into three categories, only two of which are colour coded. The third category is the wire-wound type of resistor, where values are normally printed on the vitreous paint finish of the component.

Resistors are measured in OHMS. The symbol for resistance is the Greek letter OMEGA, which looks like a small upturned horseshoe. The OHM is the unit of resistance but is a very small unit for valve radio use and most resistors will be found to have high values i.e. thousands of ohms or even millions of ohms.

Rather than print out lots of zeros, the symbol 'k' -kilo - is used to denote thousands and the symbol 'M' - mega - is used to denote millions. Examples: 56000 ohms is printed 56kohms. 1,200,000 ohms is printed 1.2Mohms.

When buying modern resistors, the multiplier may be inserted in place of the decimal point, hence 1.2Mohms becomes 1M2 ohms. **Note that this code only refers to three or four banded resistors.**

Carbon resistors are colour coded either (1) as body-tip-spot or (2) triple bands of colour. A fourth band may be used on either type for tolerance, which is a measure of how close the actual value is to the coded indication. No band equals 20% tolerance.

Close tolerances only become important when the resistor value is quite low. Otherwise, valves will generally operate quite satisfactorily within the range of 20% above or below the code value.

For replacement purposes, fit similar tolerance replacements. Conversely, fitting a close-tolerance component when unnecessary will do no harm. **Replace with similar or higher-wattage components.**

On banded resistors, read from the end toward the centre. On body-tip-spot types, read in that order. If, on the latter type, a colour seems to be missing (either the spot or the tip) it is because the 'missing' value is the same as the body.

Example: Red body, red tip, brown spot = 220 ohms.

Colour	First figure — Body or first band	Second figure — Tip or second band	Third figure — Spot or third band	Tolerance
Black	0	0	x0	
Brown	1	1	x1	
Red	2	2	x2	
Orange	3	3	x3	
Yellow	4	4	x4	
Green	5	5	x5	
Blue	6	6	x6	
Violet	7	7	x7	
Grey	8	8	x8	
White	9	9	x9	
Gold				5%
Silver				10%

FURTHER EXAMPLES

Standard resistors

Band 1, red = 2. Band 2, yellow = 4. Band 3, orange = 3 (the number of zeros). Therefore the resistor is 24000 (24k)

Band 1, green. Band 2, blue. Band 3, red. Band 4, gold. Value (in ohms) 5600 (5.6k). Tolerance of 5%.

Vintage carbon stick resistors

Body, Orange = 3. Tip, White = 9. Spot, Green = 5 (the number of zeros). Therefore the resistor has a value of 3900000 (3.9M)

Body: red, tip: green, spot: orange. Value (in ohms): 25,000 (25K). No silver or gold band means a 20% tolerance.

VALVE BASE KEY (opposite)

Although the bases shown are stated as common, this is only partially true: in the case of 1930s British receivers, by far the most common holders used are the British 'B' series. Octal valves appear In late 1930s sets, especially American imported models and continued to be used during WWII and beyond. The most common octal base is the International Octal (I.O.) but quite a few sets will be found to use the Mazda range of octal valves, with a superficially similar base but with incompatibility due to differing pin spacing and locating spigot diameter compared to the International Octal.

Another 1930s base is the side-contact P5 and P7 base. Side-contact all-dry valves can be found in some immediately post-war receivers and occasionally these will be found inside a portable that might have been expected to hold B7G types. The all-dry side-contact types quickly gave way, first to octal-based equivalents and then to all-glass miniatures. The B7G valve base will be found in most all-dry post-war portable radios. Ever Ready used all three types in otherwise electrically and physically similar sets.

The later B8A base uses valves with a locating 'pip' on their metal base. This base type ran for a time concurrent with B9A. Some late 1940s sets used B8G based valves. These carry a metal base and have quite a large diameter yet use very thin pins. The UX types are also pre-WWII in origin.

Beginning in the early 1950s, B9A all-glass valves became the standard, used in TV, radio and Hi-Fi equipment until the demise of the valve caused by the development of power transistors. B9D bases, not shown in the diagram, were among those used for larger all-glass valves used in TV line timebase circuitry.

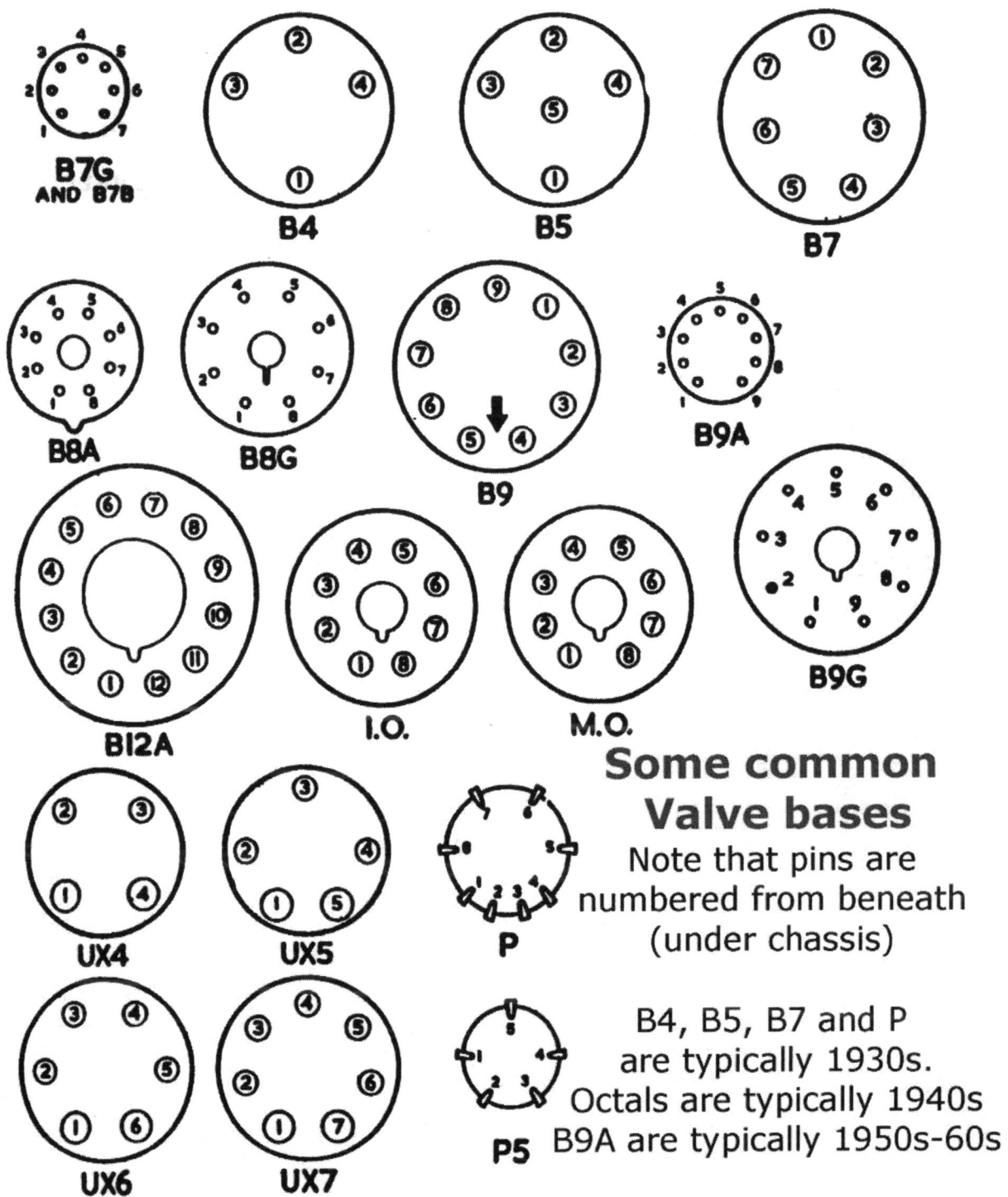

Some common Valve bases

Note that pins are numbered from beneath (under chassis)

B4, B5, B7 and P are typically 1930s. Octals are typically 1940s B9A are typically 1950s-60s

SUGGESTIONS FOR FURTHER READING

Books
There are few books published today on valve technology. The suggestions given below are therefore all books long out of print and must be searched for, the easiest way being via the internet's search engines. Another point to bear in mind is that due to the age of these publications, the presentation is not to modern standards either in the text or the illustrations. Most books published during the valve era would have been printed by the age-old letterpress system. The printed word itself will reflect the time period in its formality and nuance and may require a little adjusting on the part of the reader. Despite these points, the books mentioned are all extremely well thought of in radio circles and can be relied upon to provide accurate information.

A Beginner's Guide to Radio
Radio expert FJ Camm produced this book for the beginner and it is written, therefore, in very simple terms. Despite this, the book is of interest to anyone wishing to construct a simple series of all-dry battery powered 1, 2 and 3 valve TRF sets. Often nowadays there is difficulty obtaining coils for home-built valve sets. Here, you wind the coils yourself, with full guidance from the master! As always with FJ, the book is very readable. First published in 1955. My copy is dated 1962 and is the fifth edition, third impression, so there's quite a few of these out there somewhere. There is a page and a half devoted to the transistor, which was added by the staff of 'Practical Wireless' after Camm's death. Frankly, they shouldn't have bothered - the information is just not up to the standard of FJ's text. Perhaps later editions will be found to be better in this respect. Well worth looking for any edition of this useful book.

Practical Wireless Circuits
By FJ Camm. My copy is dated 1954 and is the 16th edition. I bought it new at the time. Earlier ones would not have the later all-dry octal and B7G valve circuits, though they are still worth reading.

Newne's Short-Wave Manual
By FJ Camm (first published 1940). A slim volume full of readable material but of course slanted toward short-wave reception, with coil winding data, constructional items and other useful information.

News Chronicle Wireless Constructor's Encyclopaedia
F.J. Camm was the brother of Sydney Camm, the aircraft designer. He was prolific as an author and all-encompassing as an editor, his name cropping up for many years on a number of 'practical' monthly titles by Newnes including Practical Wireless, Practical Television and Practical Mechanics. He also produced many books with a radio, television, technology, model-making and engineering bias over many years. As you might expect from such a voluminous source, much material presented as 'new' at the time was a revision of previously published content, hence a book published in the 1950s might be found to contain designs, diagrams and data from the 1930s, alongside more up-to-date items. Nevertheless, he wrote with a clear, engaging and authoritative style, so if you spot any titles by him, I recommend purchase.

Audel's Radioman's Guide
This is an American publication that holds masses of very comprehensive radio theory and practice. My copy dates from the WWII period but there are later year editions around.

Introduction to Valves
By Hallows and Millward. Good for basic valve operating principles and applications in domestic sets. Even though the first publication date is 1953, the text style can seem particularly archaic - very 1930s - at times.

Radio Servicing
A series of softback books by Patchett, Fozard et al (circa early sixties), all published by Norman Price. These little gems were considered by the trade at the time of their publication to be essential reading for the radio and television engineer. They are factual, concise, readable, reliable and well worth searching for. Highly recommended.

Radio and Television Servicing
Sometimes known as the 'red' books, this title represents a long series of books containing service data for radio and TV receivers, year-on-year from the post-war period onward. Originally published by Newnes but later volumes – possibly of lesser interest to the vintage restorer - were produced by other publishers. Useful when you need the information on a given receiver.

Foundations of Wireless
Originally written by A.L.M. Sowerby and published by Iliffe in 1936, M.G. Scroggie revised and enlarged the book in 1941 and it continued in several editions over many years. This is truly a masterful book containing all the essential knowledge for a first class grounding in valve radio. Not especially easy to read, but well worth making the effort.

Radio Laboratory Handbook
Scroggie again, and published by Iliffe, which covered the setting-up and running of a workshop. The book shows how to use test equipment and how to interpret the results. There are masses of formulae but it remains a quite readable and interesting book from the earlier valve era. My personal copy is not dated by the publishers but a handwritten inscription offers 'December 1940'

Wireless Servicing Manual
By W.T. Cocking. This is another Iliffe book from the late thirties/early forties. Lots of info on servicing, fault tracing and alignment. Written in the style of the time and can seem rather formal and dated today, but with a useful practical slant.

The Dictionary of Radio and Television Terms
This is by Ralph Stranger and is exactly what it says; it offers very clear and straightforward explanations of circuit action, components and principles. As might be expected in such a compact volume, some of the explanations lack depth. A Newnes publication, 1941.

Modern Practical Radio and Television
By C.A. Quarrington. This is a four-volume set published by Caxton from 1946 onward. It is exhaustively detailed, though written in a somewhat stiff and oddly, for the time of publication, rather heavy manner. It offers comprehensive coverage of the mid 20th century state of the art. My set of books was published in 1950. The value of the books perhaps lies more in their use as reference sources, rather than in any practical way. Sometimes offered for sale minus the fourth thinner 'circuits' volume.

The Radio Amateur's Handbook
This is (or was) published by the American Radio Relay League. I have a copy of the twentieth edition, dated 1943. It's full of information and constructional tips, plus lots of wartime radio component adverts. Fascinating to read.

Brimar Valve and Teletube Manual
Brimar valves published a series of these useful data books. The later ones show application circuits for their valves.

Magazines

Radio Bygones
A quality limited circulation (subscription) magazine. The coverage includes domestic and military radio equipment using both valve and vintage transistors.
Simply but excellently produced on quality paper, it is very much a technical journal but there are articles and content to suit every vintage enthusiast plus book reviews and book sales and the useful offer of free reader adverts. Content varies and can include construction projects, restoration of both military and domestic product, historical matters and biographies. There is somewhat of an emphasis on military equipment. Well worth obtaining a sample copy. Contact:

Radio Bygones, Wimborne Publishing Ltd., 113 Lynwood Drive, Merley, Wimborne, Dorset BH21 1UU. Telephone 01202 880299. Fax: 01202 843233

E-mail: radiobygones@wimborne.co.uk

Web sites: www.radiobygones.co.uk and www.radiobygones.com

The Radiophile
'The Radiophile' is a well-produced magazine mainly concerned with domestic valve radio and some vintage TV. The editor and major contributor is Chas E. Miller, well known as an authority on the subject to those of us who remember Practical Wireless and Practical Television from long years ago. Interesting articles, adverts, nostalgia and stories. In fact, there's altogether a very nostalgic and quirky 'old fashioned' feel and look to this popular magazine; ideal for those of us who yearn for the passing of the Practical Wireless of FJ Camm! As with all limited circulation magazines, this cannot be found on the newsagent's shelves so you must subscribe - but you can try one copy to see how you like it first. Write to:
The Radiophile (Administration Office), 'Larkhill', Newport Road, Woodseaves, Stafford ST20 0NP. United Kingdom. Telephone: 01785 284696 (office hours only). Fax: 01785 817744

BVWS Bulletin

This is the bulletin of the British Vintage Wireless Society, published quarterly. Membership of the society entitles you to the magazine. Crisply presented and printed, the content offered in its pages is very varied fare in the form of member's own articles; so it is for the members, by the members and restoration is a major feature of the member's submissions.
Visit the website: www.bvws.org.uk

Practical Wireless (PW)

This magazine is today a far cry from the Practical Wireless of FJ Camm. It is now aimed at the radio amateur rather than the constructor but it does usually carry a valve and vintage column.
The market for radio construction magazines has contracted out of recognition from the heady days of the 1930s - 1960s. This is the price of progress: building with transistors and microchips is fun and educational but of a different order to the construction skills needed to build valve radios and amplifiers.

Vintage magazines

Expect to find vintage magazines on internet auction sites and at vintage radio 'rallies' and auctions. Some of the very early material is now becoming scarce and therefore costly. The 1930s produced several good magazines, among which Amateur Wireless, Popular Wireless and Practical Wireless are examples. Only Practical Wireless survived into post-war years. For more on 1930s magazines, see 'Wireless World' below.

Practical Wireless

From its start in the early 1930s, F.J. Camm propelled this essentially practical magazine to the forefront. Weekly before WWII and monthly thereafter, there is no lack of sources for these very readable magazines. Very nostalgic and full of interesting articles and adverts. The supply limitations of the immediate post-war period saw a thin magazine but by the mid 1950s it was back to a good size, though it never regained the large format of the 1930s. Printed on paper little better than newsprint, check before buying that the magazine is still complete. Expect staples to have rusted and disappeared.

Radio Constructor

The title says it all. This publication, a post-war competitor for Practical Wireless, still has its devotees. Interesting content and adverts.

Wireless World

This magazine was always technical in its approach, often covering complex aspects of radio and television, though during the 1930s it showed a more amateur slant to its content. The post war offerings were aimed ever more at the professional and as such may not be ideal reading for the vintage enthusiast, though the production values were always high and the content reliable.
Amateur Wireless, Popular Wireless and other shorter-lived titles also date from the late 1920s and 1930s and are worth a look if you spot them. Amateur Wireless was absorbed into Practical Wireless. Popular Wireless carried the construction articles of John Scott Taggart and there are still some devotees of this designer's very individual approach. When Popular Wireless lost the battle with Practical Wireless, separate publication ceased in the late 1930s.

Harmsworth's Wireless Encyclopaedia

Not a magazine in format, yet not quite a book either... this weekly part-work was published in the early 1920s. As such it is of passing interest as an account of the approaches to the subject at the time. There is much mechanical detailing: how to use tools, for example, or how to fold metal, drill material etc. Also there are 'how to make' articles ranging from complete receiving sets to sub-units. Do not expect it to offer coverage of the later rapid developments in the technology as much happened well after this publication's date.

SOURCES FOR COMPONENTS AND MATERIALS

The author has no personal connection with these suppliers other than VRW Publications. All are in existence *at the time of publication.* The major component sources such as Farnells and RS are convenient sources – easiest via websites - of modern spares.

Grille cloth, Tygan, Rexine, handles and fittings

S.W. Chaplin,
43 Lime Avenue,
Leigh on Sea,
Essex SS9 3PA.
Tel: 01702 - 473740
Sid has a good range of quality materials including reproduction 'Tygan' grille materials, linen backed rexine, paper backed rexine, linen backed vynide. Also on offer are handles, both strap and drop types, suitable for suitcase portables and record players. Plus feet, cabinet hinges and catches, piping cord in gold and silver, loudspeaker mounting bolts, screws and nuts.
Just about all you need for recovering portable cases, replacing worn handles, hinges and catches and replacing sad-looking fabrics! Samples are available.
E-mail: sidney@tradradgrilles.freeserve.co.uk
This is a very useful service and Sid is extremely helpful. Highly recommended.

Components, valves and general vintage spares

Geoff Davies (Radio)
13 Bowen Road,
Rugby, CV22 5LF.
Tel: 01788 574774.
Geoff is a helpful and friendly supplier and has lists of reasonably priced spares including valves with a fast, reliable service by post. Phone for details or send stamp for lists.

Malcolm Bennett supplies valves and service data. For details, visit his website or E-mail your requirements.
http://www.valve.demon.co.uk

VINTAGE VALVE RADIOS

Websites

VRW Publications
Run by the author of this present work and offering a vast stock of reasonably priced service data. Enquiries are welcome by e-mail – tony@vintageradioworld.co.uk. The site has a great deal more of interest including new books and eBooks, restoration, personalities, history. Well worth a tour around.
Website: www.vintageradioworld.co.uk

Crowthorne tubes
Visit the Crowthorne tubes website for a host of parts, valves and equipment for the radio/television restorer or collector. The site is run by an enthusiast to help enthusiasts.
www.crowthornetubes.com

Savoy Hill Publications
Specialist suppliers of service manuals and period documents, adverts, literature and printed matter to do with the valve era generally. Service information is usually very thorough and often comes with other relevant material, therefore ideal if you are interested in the history of a set or a particular manufacturer. Because of the tremendous variety of material stocked it is probably quickest to contact by e-mail.
Very large collection of manuals for service equipment including valve testers, generators etc., plus original maker's valve data manuals
Contact: Savoy Hill Publications
Fir View, 7 Rabys Row, Scorrier, Redruth, Cornwall TR16 5AW
Phone/Fax: 01209 820771. Email: sales@savoy-hill.co.uk
Web site: www.savoy-hill.co.uk

If you are searching for replacement grille cloth, knobs, dial glass or back covers to suit your Philips radio you might just find what you need at this Dutch site:
http://www.radioverzameling.nl/shop

www.vintage-radio.com
This is the premier domestic vintage radio website and is a must to visit. There's a lot of information here, plus restorations, things to build and best of all, a superb and helpful on-line forum. Also available: Paul's CD-ROM/DVD collections of vintage radio service data. NOTE: the CD-ROMS and DVDs are also now available from Radio Bygones magazine.

American Radio data
If you are one of the many restorers working on USA products, try 'just radios' for your data. This site hails from Canada and has lots to offer beside circuit data. There's even a good range of condensers (capacitors) suitable for valve (tube) work.
http://www.justradios.com/

Here's a site from America that might be just what you are looking for if you renovate those great American radios. Schematics galore on a vast range of sets, all for free. Download or view directly. Also worth your while to take a look around the rest of the site. http://www.nostalgiaair.org/

A careful search on the internet will yield a host of other potentially useful sites, though the information provided varies in quality and there are a few sites that are distinctly poor in the content offered, so it is wise not to accept everything you read on face value.

Vintage radio forums can also be found on the internet and much can be learned by joining one or more of these. Again, treat all information as being well-meant but always verify whenever possible – do not accept guidance blindly.

Current magazines for the vintage radio enthusiast: see p.162 for details

GLOSSARY

A
AC: alternating current
Accumulator: a device for the storage of electricity (wet cell or battery)
Aerial: a device to concentrate either the magnetic lines of force or the electrical energy of a transmission (The former is a property of ferrite rods, the latter almost any metallic element but usually wire based)
AM: amplitude modulation. The radio-frequency carrier is modulated in strength by audio
Amp (ampere) Symbol A (or I): the unit of current
Amplifier: device using valves or transistors to magnify a signal
Anode: the electrode that attracts electrons
AVC: automatic volume control. Now called AGC, automatic gain control. *See delayed AVC*

B
Battery: a collection of single cells wired in series to increase voltage
Bias: *see grid bias*

C
Capacitor (vintage term: condenser): a device that stores electricity short-term and passes alternating signals, such as RF or AF
Capacitor, coupling: a capacitor that passes RF/AF signals, but not DC
Capacitor, decoupling: a capacitor that removes unwanted AC signals
Capacitor, dry type electrolytic: a capacitor that works by chemical means
Capacitor, reservoir: a DC storage capacitor, after rectification of AC
Capacitor, smoothing: part of a filter to remove AC ripple from a rectified DC supply
Capacitor, tuning: variable capacitor in parallel with a tuning coil
Capacitor, variable: any capacitor variable by manual means
Capacitor, wet type electrolytic: as 'dry' type, above
Cathode: emissive element in a valve. Also the positive electrode in any diode
Ceramic: pot
Choke: a coil wound to have high resistance to AC whilst passing DC
Choke, smoothing: an iron cored coil designed for high impedance at mains frequency
Choke, RF (vintage): a small usually air-cored coil with high impedance at radio frequency
Coil: a winding of wire on a former, for tuning
Coil, wave-wound: special way of machine winding to improve quality of a coil
Current: the flow of electrons around a circuit

D
DC: direct current: unidirectional flow
Delayed AVC: a system whereby the automatic gain control is delayed until a sufficiently strong signal is received. This prevents the loss of weak signals. *See AVC*
Demodulator: *see detector*
Detector: device to rectify radio-frequency signals to reveal superimposed audio

Dielectric: the insulating medium in a capacitor
Crystal diode: (vintage) a point contact rectifier, using a piece of crystal i.e. galena and a springy wire contact known as a cat's whisker (modern) a glass-enclosed semiconducting RF diode
Distortion: departure from accuracy of amplification or reproduction
Dry battery: *see battery*
Dry cell: source of chemically generated electric power. A single dry cell generates only 1.5V or less

E
Electrode: any element within a valve
Envelope: outer cover, e.g. glass bulb of a valve
ESR: Equivalent Series Resistance. All conductors possess some resistance. In effect the resistance present in an electrolytic capacitor can increase with age, perhaps to the point where the component malfunctions in practice even though tests indicate no fault. *See also Ripple rating*

F
Farad: unit of capacitance. A large unit, reduced to MicroFarad (µF) or PicoFarad (pF) for vintage radio
Ferrite: a mix of iron dust in a ceramic compound to form a magnetic medium
Field: current flowing through any conductor will create an electromagnetic field around it
Field coil, field winding: the source of magnetism of a mains energised loudspeaker
Filament: the electron-emissive element in a directly heated valve
FM: frequency modulation. The frequency of the RF carrier is modulated by audio
Fuse: device designed to fail at excess current levels

G
Grid: the control element of a valve
Grid bias: the means to set the working point of a valve

H
Heater: the heating element in an indirectly heated valve
Heterodyne: A frequency created by the interaction of two closely placed frequencies, an Intermediate Frequency. *See Superhet*
HF: high frequency. Modern term RF (radio frequency)
HT: high tension = high voltage

I
IF transformer: a finely wound transformer tuned to a given IF frequency, e.g. 470kHz
Indirectly heated valve: any valve with a cathode
Inductor: a coil in general
Insulator: any non-conducting material, e.g., most plastics, rubber

L
LF: low frequency. Modern term AF (audio frequency)
Loudspeaker, cone: a large-diameter paper cone with a metal rod at its apex. The rod is connected to a metal vane (or reed) which moves under the influence of the fluctuating field of an audio signal, causing the cone to move also, thereby reproducing sound

Loudspeaker, horn: an exponential horn, usually curved, driven by a modified telephone earpiece. The horn amplifies the weak sound in a similar manner to the horn of an acoustic gramophone
Loudspeaker, PM: superior permanent magnet loudspeaker, ubiquitous today
LT: low tension. Power for valve filaments

M
Magic Eye: see tuning indicator
Metal oxide rectifier: an alternative to a valve rectifier
MicroFarad (μF): one-millionth of a Farad. Unit commonly used in vintage radio

N
Non-linear resistor: a resistor that changes its value with heat, a thermistor

O
Ohm: Unit of resistance. Symbol: omega (Ω). One thousand ohms = 1 Kilohm. (kΩ). One million ohms = 1 Megohm (MΩ)

P
Parasitic oscillation: unwanted oscillation on an amplifier (RF or AF). Causes are poor layout, lack of screening. Stopper resistors mounted close to grid connections are used to prevent the problem.
Phase splitter: circuit to create twin opposed signals from one source
Plate: American term for anode
Potential: voltage
Potential difference: change in voltage, generally across a resistor
Potential divider: two or more fixed resistors in series. Voltage is taken from the junctions
Potentiometer: simply, an adjustable potential divider often connected so as to form a variable resistor

R
Reactance: inductive resistance
Reaction: positive RF feedback system used in TRF receivers to sharpen tuning and increase sensitivity
Rectifier: a device that converts alternating current into direct current
Resistance: the property possessed by resistors to impede current flow
Resistor, carbon: the standard resistor found in vintage radios
Resistor, wire-wound: usually resistance wire wrapped around a ceramic former, these resistors are often used for high current dissipation, such as power supplies
Resonance: in a tuned circuit, the point where rising impedance with rising frequency from an inductor meets falling impedance with rising frequency from a capacitor. This point is a peak at which the tuned circuit behaves resistively, magnifying any signal at that frequency
RF: radio frequency. (vintage term: HF)
RF amplifier: an amplifier with tuned circuits at RF
Ripple current: remaining AC fluctuations on rectified current.
Ripple rating: the ability of a capacitor to withstand AC ripple on a DC supply.

S

Screen grid: the second grid in a multi-electrode valve, there to decrease inter-electrode capacitance between the control grid and the anode

Sine wave: an AC waveform

Solid state: where electric current passes through solid medium as opposed to a vacuum tube (valve). A transistor is said to be solid state

Space charge: the cloud of electrons around the cathode or filament of a working valve

Superhet: Superheterodyne, a receiver using a local oscillator to create an intermediate frequency which is mixed with signals from an RF tuned circuit. The oscillator tuning is spaced apart from the RF tuning by the IF. The IF itself never changes, regardless of the frequency being tuned. This endows the superhet with high gain and stability. *See heterodyne*

Suppressor grid: a third grid in a multi-electrode valve, designed to limit secondary emission from the anode and minimise inter-electrode capacitance

T

Thermionic: where electrons are released through heat, as in the valve

Transformer: twin inductors coupled together, using the electric field to pass AC. Often air-cored at RF, laminated iron-cored at mains frequency

TRF: Tuned Radio Frequency, a receiver with one or more circuits amplifying at the tuned frequency

Tube: American term for valve. Alternatively an abbreviation of cathode-ray tube

Tuning Indicator: generally, a type of valve with a green fluorescent display consisting of leaves that expand when a station is being tuned, to act as a guide to precise tuning

V

Valve, diode: a two-electrode valve

Valve, heptode: a valve with seven grids

Valve, hexode: a valve with six electrodes

Valve, output: a valve capable of handling several watts of power

Valve, pentode: a valve with five electrodes

Valve, tetrode: a valve with four electrodes

Valve, triode: a three-electrode valve

Variable capacitor: a manually adjustable capacitor, generally tuning

Variable resistor: a manually adjustable resistor, i.e. a volume control. *See potentiometer*

Vari-mu (vari-μ): a valve with a varied spacing of grid wires, enabling bias voltage changes to affect gain

Volt: unit of electromotive force. Symbol V (or E)

Voltage: pressure of volts

W

Watt: unit of power, equal to 1amp X 1 volt (I X V)

Wattage: the rating of a power component, e.g. a resistor

...and finally...

The damage as found

Stripping the veneer

Veneer support below, wood filler above

Re-veneering

Case ready for finish

Toned and re-cellulosed

Repairing a severely damaged Goblin 'Time Spot' clock radio

Pye MM, early 1930s

On a personal note, the author feels rather sad for those who missed out on the halcyon days of 'build it yourself'. There was great pleasure and satisfaction gained when first a homebuilt receiver came to life or a valve amplifier filled the room with its warm sound. From the very start – a one-valve receiver based on an FJ Camm design – valve radio set me on a lifetime of fascination, personal goal-setting and skill development leading to a career in radio and television engineering and teaching. The days of home construction may have largely passed into history but there is still much enjoyment to be had restoring a fascinating piece of old but often astoundingly good technology: the valve radio.

If you have enjoyed this production, please visit
www.vintageradioworld.co.uk
for service data, books & information.

INDEX

A

AF amplification · 47
AF coupling · 48
AF output stages · 50
Alternating current · 11
Amplification · 40
Anode · 27, 31
Atomic theory · 9
Atom · 9
Auctions, internet · 84
Audio amplifier, basic · 29

B

Back covers, making · 119
Bakelite cabinet restoration · 138
Bakelite cabinets · 134
replacing missing sections · 146

C

Cabinet restoration · 134
Capacitor faults · 114
Capacitor function · 18
Capacitor measurement · 19
Capacitor types · 19
Capacitors · 17
Condensers · 17
Capacitors in parallel · 19
Capacitors, rebuilding · 121
Capacitors, replacing · 21
Chassis, cleaning of · 126
Choke · 22
Choke, RF · 43
Class 'A' output stage · 50
Class 'A-B' output stage · 50
Class 'B' output stage · *See* Push-pull
Cold checks · 93
Coil · 21
Common problems · 118
Components, suggested range of · 90
Conductors · 9
Current flow · 12

D

Demodulation · 28
Detection · *See* Demodulation
Detector, leaky-grid · 42
Diode · 25
Rectifier · *See* Metal rectifier
Direct current · 12

E

Edison lamp · 11
Ephemera · 79
Ethics of restoration · 109

F

Fault-finding
DC voltage checks · 100
dead set · 100
no reception · 100
visual checks · 99
under power · 100
Feedback, negative · 53
Frequency-changer · 45   *See* Local oscillator, mixer

G

Grid · 29

I

IF transformer problems · 105
Inductor · 21
Inductance · *See* Coil, transformer
Inductors, problems with · 117

L

LF choke · *See* Choke
Local oscillator · *Frequency-changer*
Local oscillator, basic circuit · *See* Mixer, frequency-changer
Loudness control · 53
Loudspeaker problems · 105
Loudspeaker, cone · *See* Loudspeakers
Loudspeaker, energised · 56
Loudspeaker, moving coil · 55
Loudspeaker, restoring · 56
Loudspeakers · 54

M

Mains transformer · 24
Materials, suggested range of · 90
Metal rectifier · 37
Microphony · 103
Miller effect · 30
Mixer · 45
More ephemera · *See* Ephemera
Motorboating · 102
Instability · 102
Moving coil loudspeaker · 55, 105

O

Ohms law · 16
Oscilloscope · 97
Output transformer · 24

P

Paint effects · 151
Passive components · *See* Components
Pentode AF amplifier · 30
Phase-splitter · *See* Push-pull
Photographic records · 109
Plate · *See* Anode
Potential Difference · 9
Power (watt) · 16
Power supplies, general · 38
Push-pull, R-C coupling · 50
Push-pull, transformer coupling · 51

Q

QPP output stage · 51
'Q' factor · 23

R

Receiver, choosing · 82
Receiver, superhet · 44
Receiver, TRF · 41 *See* Receiver, superhet
Receivers to avoid · 83
Receivers, representative · 63
Reception · 39
Rectifier, directly heated · 26
Rectifier, full-wave · 27, 37
Rectifier, half-wave · 36
Repairing a loudspeaker cone · 106
Resistance
Resistor · 11
Resistor types · 14
Resistor, non-linear · 17
Resistor, symbol · 13
Resistors in series · 16
Resistors, faults with · 102, 115
Rexine and Vynide cabinet repairs · 150

S

Safety lamp · 91. Using the safety lamp · 100
Safety, personal · 87
Short-circuit · 10
Current flow · 10
Signal diode · 25
Signal generator · 96
Signal tracer-injector · 97
Single-ended output stage · 32
Static electricity · 10

T

Test meter, analogue · 95
Test meter, digital · 95
Tools, suggested range of · 87
Transformer · 22
TRF, drawbacks in · 44
Tuned circuit · 40
Tuning indicators · 115
Typical chassis, above deck · 60
Typical chassis, below deck · 60

U

User safety · 118

V

Valve, beam tetrode · 34
Valve, diode · 26
Valve, directly heated · 31
Valve, indirectly heated · 31
Valve, tetrode · 31
Valve, triode · 28
Valves, substituting · 124
Vintage magazines · 108
Visual checks · *See* cold checks

W

Wood cabinets
   restoring · 147
   spray lacquering · 149
   woodworm · 134
   woodwork, internal · 128